Strategic Management in the Media

Strategic Management in the Media

From Theory to Practice

Lucy Küng

Los Angeles • London • New Delhi • Singapore

SAGE Publications Ltd
1 Oliver's Yard
55 City Road
London EC1Y 1SP

SAGE Publications Inc.
2455 Teller Road
Thousand Oaks, California 91320

SAGE Publications India Pvt Ltd
B 1/I 1 Mohan Cooperative Industrial Area
Mathura Road, New Delhi 110 044

SAGE Publications Asia-Pacific Pte Ltd
33 Pekin Street #02-01
Far East Square
Singapore 048763

Library of Congress Control Number available

British Library Cataloguing in Publication data

A catalogue record for this book is available
from the British Library

ISBN 978-1-4129-0312-7
ISBN 978-1-4129-0313-4 (pbk)

Typeset by C&M Digitals (P) Ltd., Chennai, India
Printed in Great Britain by The Cromwell Press Ltd, Trowbridge, Wiltshire
Printed on paper from sustainable resources

To Gebi and Hira Maya, of course.

Contents

Acknowledgements

This book seeks to build a bridge between academic theory and management practice in the media. The processes of research and writing have benefited immeasurably from discussions with both researchers and practitioners in the field.

I am therefore indebted to a number of executives who made time in their extraordinarily busy days to share their thoughts on the task of strategy in the media. These include James Cridland, Richard Deverell, Andy Duncan, Greg Dyke, Ilse Howling, Gill Hudson, Ian Locks, Jeremy Olivier, Richard Sambrook, Richard Stagg, Caroline van den Brul and Simon Waldman.

Insights concerning the rich and varied range of theoretical approaches with which the field of media can be investigated came from an always stimulating dialogue with colleagues, students and workshop participants at the Media Management and Transformation Centre at the University of Jönköping, particularly Robert Picard, and at the Institute for Media and Entertainment in New York, and with fellow board members of the European Media Management Association.

A book on an emerging discipline that straddles academic and practitioner perspectives will inevitably be a somewhat unknown quantity and I am therefore also grateful to Julia Hall and her successor Mila Steele, as well as the entire Sage team, for their expert support.

Lucy Küng
www.lucykeung.com
Zürich, August 2007

ONE

Introduction

> Between the economic determinations of the marketplace and the cultural discourses within media representations ... lies a terrain that has yet to be fully explored and adequately theorised. (Cottle, in Cottle, 2003: 13)

The media industry is changing fundamentally and fast. This represents a very real challenge to managers tasked with planning a strategy and implementing it successfully, to researchers studying the field, and to those designing and delivering academic courses focused on the media industry. This book seeks to provide assistance in several ways. First, it maps the contours of the media industry, detailing histories, business models, value drivers and current strategic issues in the various sectors that together constitute the industry. Second, it identifies the common themes surfacing in the strategic environment and the challenges these pose, as well as particular aspects of media organisations that influence the activities of strategic choice and implementation. Third, it explores the strategic models, concepts and approaches that are particularly relevant to this strategic context and these types of organisations, seeking to demonstrate their relevance through application to media industry cases and examples. Finally, it reviews the discipline of media management and the body of theory within it that addresses strategic management, and identifies a number of future research approaches and themes.

The goals therefore are clear. The complexity of the media industry – a mammoth and diverse set of sectors – and the sprawling and fragmented nature of strategic theory complicate the task. In order to cut through this complexity, the book has been written with three guiding principles in mind:

1. In terms of the media industry, it seeks to move beyond simply describing developments to interpreting them, and to providing insights that will aid strategy making in the media industry.
2. In terms of strategic theory, it attempts to move beyond simply outlining relevant concepts and tools to demonstrating their relevance through application (what good consultants

call demonstrating the 'so what'). In addition, it seeks to apply a broader set of strategic and management theories to the media field than is typically the case in works on media management.

3. In terms of language, the goal has been to strip out jargon as far as possible. This is partly to ensure relevance for practitioners as well as scientists, and partly because researchers and students in the field of media management, as this chapter discusses, have entered the field from many different areas of scholarship – liberal arts, social science, economics, political economics, to name just a few – and have therefore not been exposed to mainstream management theory and are likely to find some if its usages confusing.

Structure of the book

This book falls into two parts. At base, the field of strategy is concerned with how organisations respond to and align themselves with their external environment. At minimum they at least need to reconcile their operations with the vagaries of the external world. Ideally they should gain a degree of mastery over the context in which they find themselves. Thus the first section of this book analyses the media industry's external environment with a chapter by chapter breakdown of the various sectors that together make up the sector, discussion of the common themes in the strategic environment that are influencing strategic activity, and an overview of the concept and status of convergence.

The second part explores a number of strategic levers an organisation can employ to achieve mastery of its environment. These are drawn in the main from adaptive and interpretative areas of strategic theory (the rationale and implications for this are discussed in the Introduction to Part II); these include types of responses to technological change, options for organisation structure, increasing levels of creativity and innovation, interpretative elements such as cognition and culture, and leadership. Extensive use is made of case studies that draw on company examples from a range of sectors and geographic regions. Some cases feature in a number of different chapters, with each 'appearance' illustrating different aspects of strategic behaviour. This is intended to underline the complex and multi-facetted nature of strategic management, and provide overall a richer and more nuanced understanding of the examples presented.

What is media management?

The topic of strategy in the media industry is a subset of the field of media management. Since this is an embryonic field it is worth establishing at the outset of this book what this currently constitutes, which areas of scholarship it emerged from, and by extension its boundaries and internal dimensions.

The core task of media management is to build a bridge between the general theoretical disciplines of management and the specificities of the media industry. This goal seems relatively clear. However the field of media management in its present form is neither clearly defined nor cohesive. A review of the syllabi from the rash of media management courses that have sprung up over the last decade all over the world exhibit very few commonalities, and an enormously diverse range of theories, topics and core readings.

This is partly a function of newness. In contrast to media economics, which since its emergence in the 1970s has acquired an established set of theoretical approaches and an extensive body of literature, media management is still in its infancy; *The International Journal of Media Management* was established at St Gallen in 1998, the *Journal of Media Business Studies* in Jönköping 2004, the European Media Management Association (EMMA) in 2003 and the International Media Management Academic Forum in 2004. Media management therefore is both a new field and a rapidly growing one.

But, as mentioned in the quote at the start of this chapter, it is also an underexplored and under-theorised field (Cottle, 2003). To date mainstream management scholars have largely neglected the media industry, arguably because managerial practices and organisational patterns in the cultural industries are often at odds with established views of management (Lampel et al., 2000) This is regrettable, since the sector's expertise in harnessing knowledge and creativity, in confronting the challenge of rapidly changing technology, in reconciling the dilemmas of achieving both critical mass and flexibility, and of meeting business and public interest objectives, are highly relevant to other industry contexts.

Indeed the subject of media management has in the main been approached from media-related disciplines that are not grounded in the study of management and organisations. Chief among these are media economics, media studies, political economy, and mass communications and journalism. This reflects mainstream management's neglect of the field, as well as the fact that, as Albarran has observed, the field of media management 'crosses interdisciplinary lines, theoretical domains, and political systems' (Albarran et al., 2005: 3). The range of scientific backgrounds shared by researchers active in media management has given rise to a rich and varied literature applying an equally diverse range of theories from various disciplines including economics, econometrics, sociology, anthropology, technology management, political science, information science and political science.

To map out the current dimensions of the field's literature and the scope for the future development of the field, it is helpful to clarify the perspective and approach of the non-management academic disciplines that address, not always directly, the issue of management and strategy within media firms.

Media economics

Media management has grown up in the shadow of media economics. The latter applies economic principles and concepts to the media industries. To date it has dominated scholarly analysis of the media sector (Picard, 2002a).

Media economics tends to work at industry sector or market level. It looks at conditions and structures in the media industries and markets, and focuses on the deployment of resources, particularly financial ones, to meet the needs of audiences, advertisers and society (Picard, 2002a). Of particular concern are revenue and cost structures, pricing policy, the economics of the key processes of production, distribution and consumption and its effects on the behaviour of media firms, structural analysis of the sector, national market analysis, media ownership and concentration, competitive strategies of media firms, market structure and share, regulation, public policy and subsidy issues, consumer and advertiser demand, the impact of new technologies and consumer behaviours on the media and content industries, and the way these changes are impacting and influencing the development of media business models.

Audience economics is an extension of the media economics literature and addresses the implications of the media industry's dual product marketplace. It focuses on the economic dimensions and implications of audience behaviour and audience measurement, viewing media audiences as a product market with unique characteristics and significant points of interaction with media industries (Napoli, 2003).

In terms of strategy in the media field, media economists have looked at strategy formulation and implementation by large media organisations, in particular at the antecedents and/or consequences of change, with a focus on the environment, structure and performance, often applying rationalist models from the Industrial Organisation (IO) School. This has provided insights into media firms' diversification strategies (Chan-Olmsted and Chang, 2003; Dimmick and McDonald, 2003), structure, performance and strategic alignment (Albarran and Moellinger, 2002), transnational (Gershon, in Albarran et al., 2006) and competitive (Sjurts, 2005) strategies. A more pragmatic set of economically-influenced insights into the defining characteristics of the media industry come from analysts and consultants who have worked in the industries, these texts include Wolf's *Entertainment Economy* (1999) and Vogel's *Entertainment Industry Economics* (1999).

The media economics literature thus addresses the behaviour of media firms in aggregate, and provides valuable insights into the economic forces affecting the sector, the influence these have on strategic options, and the types of strategic choices media firms are making within these contexts and why. It therefore provides a valuable starting point for examining processes and phenomena inside media organisations, and for understanding the non-rational processes that also influence strategic behaviour.

Political economy approaches

When media management does not fall under the umbrella of media economics, it is often a subset of political economy scholarship. This field combines economics, politics and sociology perspectives to analyse the structure of the media industries and regulatory and policy issues, looking particularly at the economic determinants, ownership structures and political allegiances (Cottle, 2003).

Political economy approaches involve the 'study of social relations, particularly power relations, that mutually constitute the production, distribution, and consumption of resources' (Mosco, 1996: 25). In practice the application of such theories to the media field tends to involve (often but not exclusively neo-Marxian) critical studies of cultural production, looking also at the public policies that shape media systems and the political debates about media and communication policies (McChesney in Cottle, 2003). Typical examples would be Burns's seminal study of the BBC (1977), Tracey's study of how political, technological and economic forces have undermined public service broadcasting (1998), or Tunstall and Palmer's study of media moguls (1998).

Media studies

This cross-disciplinary field applies concepts from sociology, cultural studies, anthropology, psychology, art theory, information theory and economics to analyse the output of media organisations as a means of understanding society and its cultural discourses, and the effects of mass media upon individuals and society, as well as analysing actual media content and representations (Cottle, 2003). A typical study might analyse a film's aesthetic or narrative quality, but within the perspective of the filmmaking process and the movie industry's economic, technological and industrial context. There are separate strands looking at journalism, film, audience studies, television studies and radio studies, how corporate ownership of media production and distribution affects society, and the effects and techniques of advertising. Contemporary media studies include the analysis of new media, with an emphasis on the internet, video games, mobile devices, interactive television and other forms of mass media which developed from the 1990s.

Mass communications and journalism

The nature of media content and how it is processed and delivered to audiences forms the core focus of this discipline. It encompasses how the mass media have come to be organised in the way they are, how the mass media actually function – how content is produced and delivered – and the effect such content has on audiences, individually and collectively.

Media management – the state of play

These then are the major 'host' disciplines that have made the main incursions to date into the field of media management. The current state of the discipline reflects this development path. Viewed from a management perspective, media organisations have been largely addressed as businesses rather than organizations, at a macro rather than micro level, and much attention has been focused on the exogenous changes (technology, policy, regulation and consumption, for example) and their impact on media firms' output.

Viewed from an historical perspective, research into management in the media can been seen as reflecting changes in its strategic environment. The 1980s and 1990s were characterised by liberalisation, de-regulation and globalisation, and scholars responded by focusing particularly on issues of industry structure, the growth of the conglomerates and its implications, increases in alliances and joint ventures, and transnational management. Towards the end of the 1990s a first and second tier of global media conglomerates became established. These were multi-product divisional entities that presented a more complex management task, and media management scholars began to focus on the specific challenges they presented, particularly in terms of structures and processes. A focus on strategic resources emerged during this period applying approaches such as the resource-based view (RBV). The turn of the millennium saw dramatic developments in the media industry's underlying technologies. This gave rise to a flurry of research looking at the emerging distribution architecture and its ramifications for the established media industry, as well as at the concept of convergence and its rami-fications. The current fast pace of technological change, the development of new boundary-spanning categories of media products, and increasing competition for audience attention have led contemporary researchers to focus on business mod-els, organisational adaptation particularly in terms of structure, the branding of media products and emerging public policy issues. However, overall it can be argued that in comparison with the substantial amount of investigation into the media industry's strategic environment and the behaviour of its consumers and/or audiences, there is considerable scope for investigation into the processes and practices of strategy, into internal firm phenomena and dynamics and their rela-tionship with broader performance outcomes.

Defining the media industry

Having defined the theoretical boundaries of the field, it is time to establish the boundaries of the empirical context, the media industry. Defining the media industry is a surprisingly tricky proposition. Indeed, attempting to define it highlights both the ambiguity and vagueness surrounding the subject of media management, and the fundamental structural changes the sector is undergoing.

Even before convergence muddied the waters (as discussed in Chapter 4) there was no commonly accepted definition of the 'traditional' media industries nor agreement as to their constituent sectors. In view of the transformations taking place and range of motivations for those doing the defining, this is unlikely ever to emerge.

Europeans have, until the onset of convergence and the associated unifying impact of digital distribution, tended to view the media industries more narrowly than their US peers. They limit the sector to broadcasting (radio and

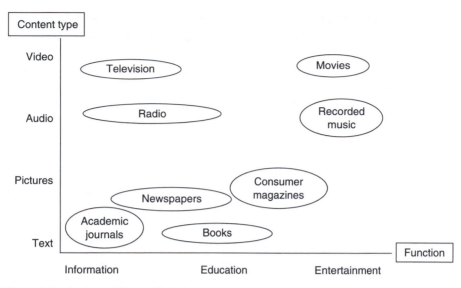

Figure 1.1 Sectors of the media industry

television), print (newspapers, magazines, journals and books), motion picture and recording industries. US analysts often include gaming, sports and theme parks (see, for example, Vogel, 1999; Wolf, 1999). When these are included the name can shift from the 'media' to the 'entertainment' industries. If the 'performing arts' are also induded the sector can sometimes become the 'cultural industries'. An additional variation is to include advertising, marketing and public relations, which can lead to the name altering to the 'creative industries'.

This book adopts Albarran's (1996) definition of the media industries as comprising the broadcasting industries (radio and television), the print industries (newspapers, magazines and books) and the film and recorded music industries. Figure 1.1. plots these sectors according to content type and function. (However, it should be noted that Garnham and Locksley's (in Blumler and Nossiter, 1991) classification of the 'cultural industries' exactly matches this definition.) Media firms according to this perspective are understood as entities that develop, produce and distribute messages (content) that inform, entertain and/or persuade. To sell the products that carry these messages they select an audience and develop the marketing, promotion and sales strategies to reach that audience (Lavine and Wackman, 1988).

Whether gaming belongs to the media sector is a moot point. Arguably it is a valid candidate, creating as it does mediated content to entertain consumers. That content is moving ever closer to the film sector, with photo realistic images, the involvement of leading actors, complex plot lines and an increasing emotional component more typical of the movie industry. Further, the sector has moved from minority activity to mass entertainment. However, this volume excludes the sector, partly from a pragmatic need to limit the scope of analysis, but also because it can be argued that this industry is more properly located in the consumer electronics or personal computing industries, since games consoles are powerful personal computers.

As the new media field develops and its products expand and become more mainstream we are seeing more variation in how the media industries are defined, and specifically ever closer links being drawn between the media and communications industries. This is, of course, a symptom of the convergence process that is discussed in subsequent chapters. The catalyst is digitalised content, which has long been central to the Internet and is of increasing strategic significance for mobile telephony businesses. Thus some researchers are starting to consider fixed and wireless communications, and adaptations of the Internet as part of the media sector. The inclusion of communications players in the sector is new for media scholars, but it should be noted that non-media industry classifications have long tended to bundle these sectors together. Thus, for example, US Bureau of Census data includes publishing, motion picture production, distribution and exhibition, music publishing and recording, radio and television broadcasting, cable networks and operators, wire and wireless telecommunications, satellite communications and advertising in the sector. This brand of definition views the media industries through the prism of technology rather than content and its various social and economic functions. According to this perspective the term media describes the technologies (printing, video recording, sound recording, etc.) which allow content to be created and packaged for consumers, and media organisations are defined as those that package the materials that are created through these technologies. According to this classification, television broadcasters, book publishers and radio stations qualify as media firms, but so too do Internet search engines and mobile telephony suppliers.

Characteristics of the mass media

The term media has long been synonymous with 'mass media'. Mass media products and firms share a number of common and defining characteristics which influence strategic activities on the part of the media firm.

First, media products are experiential goods. Their value derives from their immaterial attributes, from their originality, from the intellectual property, messages or stories they contain, from their use of symbols to engage and manipulate perception, experience and emotion (Garnham and Locksley in Blumler and Nossiter, 1991; Lampel et al., 2000).

Mass media products are based on technologies that allow the massive duplication of material – whether physical duplication via printing and record presses or electronic duplication via broadcast systems. The production process typically involves a single cycle of product development followed by mass production. Fixed costs are high. First copy costs are also high since the content investment is front-loaded in the initial development of the product.

Thereafter production costs are low and economies of scale effects mean these reduce rapidly with volume.

Because many media products can be re-versioned into different formats, media firms can sell and resell the same media product indefinitely with minimal additional production costs. This encourages them to maximise returns from sunk investments in content through expansion into as many product lines, outlets and geographic markets as possible. These factors influence decisions concerning levels of content investment, marketing, distribution and pricing (Owen and Wildman, 1992; Shapiro and Varian, 1999; Napoli, 2003) as well as the extent of vertical integration and scale of diversification (Chan-Olmsted, 2006).

However media products are also heterogeneous. Each one is unique – no two newspapers, magazines, news broadcasts, books are identical, although there are standard formats (often dictated by production technologies). A substantial proportion of media products are also perishable – newspapers, for example.

This, coupled with the fickle nature of public taste, means that that there is a high degree of product risk. (Which products will strike a chord with the market? Which content investments will pay off?) Constant product innovation is a fundamental requirement. Further, the value of media products derives from the knowledge and creative inspiration of those creating the content: the higher the level of novelty and creativity, the greater the potential for competitive advantage – thus the primacy of creativity as an organisational resource (these issues are discussed in Chapter 7).

Mass media products are also defined by the fact that they deliver an identical message to a potentially unlimited audience. Communication is one-way – the receiver of the message cannot communicate with the sender of the message using the same media, and the presentation or packaging of products is linear and fixed.

Broadcast mass media products are non-excludable and non-depleteable public goods, that is the cost of production is independent from the number of people who consume it – consumption by one individual does not limit the quantity available to other people. The cost of producing a television series or radio broadcast is independent of the number who will watch it. Other media products, such as books and films, have the characteristics of both private and public goods (Picard, 2002c). Their content can be classified as a public good in that the costs of its generation remain the same irrespective of how many consume it. But the form in which they are delivered to the consumer can be identified as a private good: if consumed by one person that product is not available to others (thus a shop may sell out of copies of a particular book, and a cinema may sell all of its seats for a particular showing).

Mass media business models

The business model for traditional media businesses (with the exception of public service broadcasters) is that they receive revenues from advertisers in return for 'delivering' audiences to them, those audiences having been attracted by the content media products offer. Characteristics of this model are that it has a significant component of indirect payment (a large proportion of costs being born by advertisers), is collective (payment models are based on aggregating the largest possible number of consumers) and based on standardised products.

Therefore, many media organisations producing advertising-supported media – newspapers, magazines, television and radio (non-PSB) – operate in a dual-product marketplace: in addition to producing content, they also 'produce' audiences – that is provide content to attract audiences, and these audiences are 'sold' to advertisers (Picard, 2002a; Napoli, 2003). This influences the content strategy. In general the goal will be to provide content which appeals to the largest number of consumers, however within this broad market those demographic groups that are most attractive to advertisers will receive a disproportionate amount of attention.

Even before the onset of convergence, this model was undergoing a process of restructuring, spurred by the introduction of cable and satellite transmission technologies which allowed direct payment for specific programming through subscription-based and pay-per-view systems. The indirect, collective business model which underpinned the mass media was beginning to be undermined. The new media however have undermined this model even further.

New media

Since the advent of the Internet the term 'mass media' has been synonymous with 'traditional media', which are seen as very different to new media. While there is substantial consensus concerning what the mass media constitute, new media is far more challenging to define. The term is vague and usage displays tremendous definitional variety. But there are common elements to these definitions. New media are based on computing technologies, use digital information, and usually involve connection to an open digital communication network. New media products combine different types of content, often involve communication, and can be products and/or services.

These characteristics mean the new media sector is profoundly different to the mass media one and those differences look set to grow. A decade ago this was confidently termed 'The New Economy'. The collapse of the dotcom sector put paid to such hyperbole, but there is still undisputedly a new segment of the media with a number of characteristics that make it very different to the 'old' one – notable amongst these are the close links between content, communication and community, and the active role of users.

Social responsibility requirements and regulation

One issue that distinguishes the media sector, and the task of management in the media, is the expectation that media organisations, irrespective of their commercial goals, act in a socially responsible way and promote specific social values. Indeed this factor may be one of the few points of commonality between say, the controller of children's programmes at a public service broadcaster in the UK and the manager of a free newspaper in Bolivia. It reflects an assumption that the media is a cultural force: it shapes society and its messages are fundamental to democracy. So the media must not only seek to maximise profits and returns to shareholders, but must also act in the public interest and promote social values such as social interaction, engagement, democratic participation, collective knowledge and cultural identities (Cottle, in Cottle, 2003; Picard, 2006). This requirement is enforced by law and as a result media firms contend with a slew of regulations affecting many aspects of strategic activity, for example the scope for growth, the types of products that can be made and the prices that can be charged.

There is no uniform understanding as to what constitutes social responsibility although a number of core societal functions have been identified:

- providing a forum for the exchange of opinions between different groups in a democratic society
- acting as an integrative influence – especially important in countries with high levels of immigration or linguistic differences
- protecting core values – the interests of children or a diversity of cultural expression for example
- furthering innovation in technological systems – for example to encourage citizens' uptake of new technologies. (Bertelsmann Foundation, 1995)

These core functions give rise to strictures designed to limit the potentially negative effectis of media products and promote potentially positive ones. Negatively-framed strictures limit and prevent socially undesirable elements such as the violation of human dignity, sexually explicit or violent content, content that could pose a threat to children, the violation of privacy, discrimination against minorities, the cooption of broadcasting into the service of powerful interests. Positive ones seek to ensure independence from political or commercial influences, plurality of opinion, promote the robust functioning of democracy through acting as a check on government, facilitate political discourse and ensure a diversity of opinions have a platform for expression, as well as ensure a plurality of opinions are expressed and that minority views have a platform. These requirements tend to affect generalist broadcasters more than thematic or niche ones, and the journalistic function, in particular.

The presence of regulation, and its influence on the operations of media organisations, is well known to scholars of political economics, mass communications and journalism theory, but can be a foreign notion to those approaching the media industry from purely business perspectives. What it means in practice for the media manager is that the regulatory framework exerts a strong influence on strategic options and by extension corporate strategies. These in turn guide programming and editorial decisions.

Overview of subsequent chapters

This book has 11 chapters and they address the following issues.

This first chapter, the Introduction to the book, describes its goals, structure and scope.

Chapters 2, 3 and 4 form Part I of the book. Together they explore the strategic context of the media industries. Chapter 2, 'Sectors of the Media Industry', provides a basis for the discussion of strategic management later in this book by exploring the context in which strategic activities take place, the strategic environment of the media. The media industry is not a monolithic entity, but rather a conglomeration of highly individualistic sectors. This chapter takes each of these in turn, analysing the elements such as history, industry segments, business models, the value chain, key players and emergent issues that are affecting strategy making.

Chapter 3, 'Trends in the Strategic Environment', draws on the previous chapter's analysis to identify a number of themes common to all sectors of the media industry that are shaping the strategic agenda in the field.

Chapter 4, 'Convergence and its Causes', explores another important aspect of the media industry's current strategic environment, convergence. It contrasts understanding of this term during the dotcom era with perceptions now, outlines the environmental and technological developments that have provoked it, and assesses its current status and implications for media organisations.

Chapter 5, 'Strategy in the Media Industries', is also the Introduction to Part II of this book. While Part I of this book provided an overview of the rich and variegated nature of the media industry's constituent sectors and strategic context, this chapter provides an overview of the rich and variegated nature of strategic theory. Strategic theory is an enormous, diverse and fragmented field. To reduce this complexity and variety this chapter applies a categorisation that 'organises' strategic theory into three core schools that are situated on a continuum moving from rationalist to symbolic approaches. It explores the relevance of each school or approach for the media field, situates existing work on strategy in the media industries within this categorisation and uses it to provide an overarching framework for the subsequent chapters in the book.

Chapter 6, 'Managing Technological Change', explores the often intricate relationship between technology, technological change, strategy and the media industries. It distinguishes between different types of change and identifies the requirements these place on firms and the factors that help or hinder effective responses.

Chapter 7, 'Creativity and Innovation', explores the role of creativity in the media, its strategic importance, and why this is increasing. It reviews theoretical understanding of the topic and explores the distinctions between creativity and innovation. Through discussion of one particular body of theory, theories of organisational creativity, it reviews how media organisations can raise levels of product creativity over the long term. It also examines how creativity and innovation can be applied to media organisations' wider strategy, structures, processes and business models.

Chapter 8, 'Cognition, Culture and Strategy', addresses core elements of the interpretative school of strategy, and their application to the media. In particular it looks at the role of cognitive structures and cultural beliefs, and their role in strategy processes in the media.

Chapter 9, 'Organisational Structure', reviews how the structures of organisations in the media are adapting in response to a changed strategic environment, and the implications of these developments for strategy and performance. It reviews the generic drivers of changes in structure in general and then looks more closely, from a chronological perspective, at the changes taking place in the media, particularly mergers, alliances, start-ups, networks and project-based organisations.

Chapter 10, 'Leadership', explores leadership in the media industries and its influence on strategy. It reviews theoretical understanding of leadership and the strands of this research that are most frequently applied to the sector. A number of cases are highlighted, including Michael Eisner, Rupert Murdoch and Greg Dyke, to both contextualise the theory and provide insights into the specific requirements and challenges surrounding strategic leadership in the media.

Chapter 11 provides the Conclusions to the book. Its main task is pattern recognition. Drawing on the analysis and discussion contained in this volume, this chapter draws conclusions on the contours of the emerging media industries, the implications of these for the strategic management task and for further research in the field, particularly concerning research themes and methodologies. The subtitle of the book is From Theory to Practice, and 'Conclusions' therefore close by departing from academic convention to offer a set of pragmatic recommendations for managers as they engage in the practice of strategy in a rapidly-changing media industry.

Part I

Strategic Context

TWO

Sectors of the Media Industry

Media companies worldwide are struggling to understand and adjust to wide-ranging external and internal changes that are altering modes of production, rapidly increasing competition, eroding their traditional audience and advertiser bases, altering established market dominance patterns, and changing the potential of firms. (Picard, 2004: 1)

The media industry is not monolithic but rather a conglomeration of different industries that have the creation of mediated content as a common activity. These sectors are constantly evolving. To an extent this has always been the case – as this chapter will show, change, particularly technological change, has been a constant ingredient in each sector's strategic context. However, the pace of these developments has typically been relatively measured. In recent decades, however, the pace of change has accelerated and it has also become more far-reaching, involving simultaneous developments in the fields of technology, regulation and consumer behaviour.

Strategy is situational and the appropriateness of any given approach will depend on the industry context (Hambrick, 1983). The rest of this chapter will explore the contexts of the constituent sectors that make up the media, and attempt to understand the forces of change at work in each and their implications for strategic management. It is therefore concerned with the macro environment, the technological, competitive and consumer context of media organisations. Porter, one of the most influential theorists in the field, views aligning an organisation with its strategic environment as the essence of competitive strategy (Porter, 1980). The starting point for analysis of a firm's environment is the dynamics of its industry sector.

The media industry comprises a collection of different sectors each of which, while sharing commonalities and experiencing common environmental changes, is also subject to competitive and change forces particular to that sector. In this chapter each of these sectors will be explored in turn and the strategic environment they present will be examined. Analysing seven different industrial sectors, each with different histories, production processes and business models, is not a straightforward task. Even within a single sector such as book publishing there are enormous differences between the large conglomerates focusing on all segments of the book market and smaller houses set up by one or two talented editors to cater for niche markets.

Despite these differences the sector analyses in this chapter follow a common approach, focusing for each one on those aspects that are critical for strategic management – historical development, the value chain, key players, business models and the emergent issues which will dominate strategic decisions in coming years.

The terrain covered by this chapter is extensive and could fill a book on its own. However, the analysis and discussion presented here is intended primarily to inform and provide a context for the strategic concepts that follow. In order to keep the length manageable and to retain focus the sector descriptions have been kept brief. And since the field is moving so fast there is a risk that detailed data will be out of date before the book leaves the printing presses. For that reason statistics have been avoided as far as possible.

A stated goal of this book is to move beyond description to analysis and interpretation. It might appear that this chapter is ignoring this aim, since much of its content is descriptive, but this is necessary to understand the strategic context and the forces driving strategic decisions. While a uniform approach has been adopted, the accounts of the various sectors vary. This results from surprising disparities in the research data available. For example, the film industry has been analysed extensively from a variety of perspectives – historical, economic and cultural – and by practitioners, scholars and journalists. This has generated an, at times, overwhelming volume of rich contextual data. At the other end of the spectrum stands the magazine industry, on which there is surprisingly little information available. Despite this, attempts have been made to ensure equivalent coverage of all sectors – although differences in data mean some sections are briefer than others.

The value chain

A company can outperform its rivals only if it can establish a difference that it can preserve. It must deliver greater value to customers or create comparable value at lower cost, or do both. The arithmetic of superior profitability then follows: delivering greater value allows a company to charge higher average unit prices; greater efficiency results in lower average unit costs. Ultimately, all differences between companies in cost or price derive from the hundreds of activities required to create, produce, sell, and deliver their products or services … Cost is generated by performing activities and cost advantage arises from performing particular activities more efficiently than competitors … activities, then, are the basic units of competitive advantage. Overall advantage or disadvantage results from all a company's activities, not only a few. (Porter, 1996: 62)

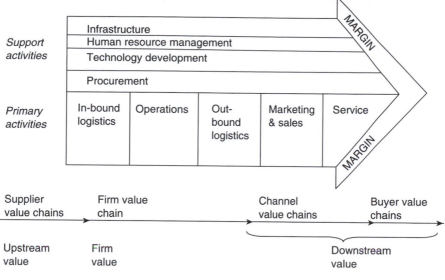

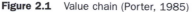

Figure 2.1 Value chain (Porter, 1985)

Each of the sections in this chapter includes an investigation of that sector's 'value chain' (Porter, 1985). This is an analytical construct with roots in industrial organisation theory and microeconomics. It uses the concept of 'value' from an economic perspective, and assumes that organisations employ a variety of resources to create products and services that are made available in the market. Successful companies manage to combine those resources in a way that creates products and services with more value than the combined value of the resources used. This surplus value represents profits or earnings.

The value chain disaggregates the activities of a firm into sequential stages stretching from the supply side to the demand side, from inputs to outputs, as shown in Figure 2.1. These stages represent the 'meta' tasks involved in the creation and distribution of a firm's goods and services. Value chain analysis in the original sense involves analysing each activity from the perspective of the 'value' it adds to the final product or service (known as 'margin'). The more competitive the value chain of an organisation, the more the overall product's value exceeds the sum of its parts, the more overall margin that can be realised as profits. Thus the model implicitly assumes that competitive advantage is created through scale, through vertically integrating as much of the value chain as possible.

Value chain analysis is an important piece of the analytic puzzle when taking many types of strategic decision, for example concerning the extent of vertical integration (which confusingly means the extent of horizontal control along the value chain), or concerning economies of scale and scope (whether to leverage resources across many segments, or focus on one narrow field). Thus, for example, when Steve Case, then CEO of AOL, decided to acquire Time Warner he was pursuing a strategy of vertical integration which should theoretically have led to greater economies of scale and scope. These would be achieved through an increase in the number of media platforms under control and in the amount of content to put on those platforms (although as discussed later in this book, this strategy did not succeed).

A firm's value chain is embedded in the value chains of the upstream and downstream businesses in the sector. Thus a newspaper company's value chain is linked to those of, amongst others, the newswire companies (content supply), newsprint and ink suppliers (production), and organisations delivering newspapers to homes and retail outlets. An industry's 'value system' links the individual value chains of different players within a sector into a system or 'chain' of activities stretching from originator to the consumer.

Porter (1996) viewed the failure of many firm's strategies as resulting from difficulties in translating a strategy that has been designed to align an organisation with its environment into specific action steps. He developed the value chain as a bridge between the activities of strategy formulation and implementation. Breaking down an organisation's value creating activities into strategically relevant stages allows each one to be analysed and the behaviour of costs and potential sources of differentiation to be uncovered. This analysis indicates how core processes and activities might be altered to increase value for customers and advantage relative to competitors, or modified to create new types of businesses.

The value chain has been a tool of preference for analysing convergence in the media industry for practitioners, consultants and academics (see, for example, Tapscott, 1996; Yoffie, 1997; Downes and Mui, 1998). However, in the majority of these examples it is not used in the 'pure' form described above – where individual firm activities are disaggregated and analysed – but rather at industry level as a shorthand means of depicting graphically the various stages by which media products are created and delivered to the end consumer. It is applied in this sense in the following pages. This chapter includes value chain analyses for each of the sectors of the media it discusses. However, it should be noted that because of the current pace and scope of technological development, particularly concerning distribution, this type of analysis is increasingly hard to apply.

Deconstruction of the value chain

A recurrent theme in the discourse surrounding the changes in the media industry over the last decade is that developments such as digitalisation and the Internet are rendering the concept of the value chain redundant (see, for example, Rayport and Svioka, 1995; Yoffie, 1997; Downes and Mui, 1998). These arguments are captured in the following quote.

Convergence is causing value chains to deconstruct, fragmenting into multiple businesses with separate sources of competitive advantage. Porter's model bundles all
the functions in a value chain together, averaging out the advantage provided
at each constituent stage. What matters is competitive advantage over the whole
chain – as long as the sum shows competitive advantage, it doesn't matter specifically where the advantage comes from. However, when value chains are
deconstructed, advantage on average no longer matters. Organizations can't sub-
sidize poor performance in one activity by combining it with others in which they
are advantaged, since competitors will emerge who focus on maximising performance at just one specific step. Thus to survive, a competitor has to be advantaged
in each and every activity. (Evans and Wurster, 2000: 58)

As this chapter shows, before the advent of the Internet and digitalisation the
mass media industries had relatively straightforward value chains and in many
sectors players had high levels of control over the entire sequence of stages.
Normally these were some variant of the following sequence: developing content, packaging content, distributing content and organising for the reception
of content. Since then, significant changes have taken place in the value chains
of the various sectors that comprise the mass media industries. These collectively go under the title of deconstruction – the dismantling and reformulation
of traditional business structures (Evans and Wurster, 2000: 39) – but this collective term covers a number of distinct changes:

Disintermediation/unbundling

Disintermediation and/or unbundling occurs because technological advances,
particularly those concerning new means to distribute and receive content,
coupled with the deregulation of markets, make it feasible to de-couple specific stages from hitherto tightly enmeshed value chains.

This reduces entry barriers encouraging new types of businesses that
concentrate on specific stages of the value chain (Bradley and Nolan, 1998;
Henzler, 1998). The example of MTV, discussed below, is one of a business
that started life by adding a new stage to the value chain: aggregation, or sourcing external content (music videos) and bundling this into channels. For
incumbents, unbundling allows them to split up vertically integrated value
chains into multiple businesses each of which can function as a separate business with its own sources of competitive advantage (Evans and Wurster, 1997).
This challenges the concept of averaging value across an entire chain, suggesting that if significant competitive advantage cannot be created at a particular
stage it should be outsourced (Evans and Wurster, 2000). This alters firms'
strategic perspective, which becomes at once narrower and broader: narrower
in that they are forced to concentrate on core competencies; broader in that
non-core activities are outsourced and relations need to be maintained with
outsourcing partners.

MTV   MTV[1] is a classic example of an organisation created from 'unbundling' a stage of the value chain that was hitherto part of integrated players' value chains – packaging – into a discrete stand-alone business. As such it also represented the emergence of a new stage in the value chain – aggregation, or the sourcing of external content and packaging this into channels. This was to become standard practice for new cable and satellite channels in Europe.

In 1981 MTV was founded by the Warner Amex Satellite Entertainment Company (WASEC), a joint venture between Warner Communications and American Express. The partners saw a business in packaging promotional videos, a marketing tool for pop music, into a music television channel that would appeal to youth audiences and to artists seeking to promote themselves.

MTV is a good example of the way mindset (in this case on the part of the music industry) can create a self-inflicted limitation on strategic growth. Although record stores were clear that the new channel had struck a chord with young audiences, so to speak, and was having a positive impact on sales, the music majors and advertisers persisted in doubting the appeal of music videos. Attitudes changed only in 1985 with the worldwide broadcast of the Live Aid charity concerts on both sides of the Atlantic. These demonstrated the size of the market for pop music and MTV's ability to promote record sales.

The original MTV product was an idiosyncratic combination of videos and video jockey commentaries about bands and performers. It sought to create a counter-culture image, typified by its graffiti-style logo. As music videos became more expensive the channel gradually abandoned its alternative, low budget roots. In 1984 MTV Networks went public, and in 1985 American Express sold its interest to Warner, who later sold MTV to Viacom.

As the popularity of MTV grew a virtuous circle was created whereby as record companies recognised the potential of the network as a marketing medium, they invested more in the quality of their videos. As content improved, viewers increased and MTV grew into a major force in cable television and in the music industry. However by 1987 interest in continuous music videos was waning and the channel moved towards more standard programming, such as documentaries, including reality television shows such as *The Osbournes*, live broadcasts and series such as *Beavis and Butthead*.

In 1987 MTV Europe was launched and thereafter the company gradually expanded internationally, eventually reaching 90 countries on five continents. In recent years its policy has been to localise content as far as possible. Channels are locally run and free to interpret the MTV brand as they see fit. Presenters use native language and show local artists as well as international ones. Digital television allows MTV to target even smaller niches, allowing it to attract both international and local advertising.

The strength of MTV's business model has brought rival music channels into the field on every continent. Internet and mobile platforms are also potentially serious competitors and the company is investing heavily in developing wireless and broadband businesses, as well as developing its own music download service. In the future growth may be more challenging, but from a strategic perspective these pressures may well be beneficial in that they are forcing the channel to shift its reliance away from traditional mass media formats and develop businesses on new platforms.

Fragmentation, extension and contraction

A related concept is fragmentation (although the terms unbundling and fragmentation are very similar and often used interchangeably). Value chains fragment when stand-alone single stages are unbundled into a number of discrete activities. Thus the content stage can fragment from producing content in-house to be distributed by the company's own distribution network into different content-related activities: buying-in content from third parties and enhancing external content, as well as producing its own content.

Fragmentation inevitably leads to value chain extension whereby more stages are added, elongating chains. This is particularly apparent at distribution stages. So, fragmentation in newspaper value chains means newspapers can distribute their content in paper, online, mobile and podcast formats. Similarly, television series are screened 'conventionally' on broadcast networks, but also distributed as episodes in the Internet, or for replay on a video iPod.

It should be noted that there are also examples of value chains contracting. An example is record companies that use the Internet to discover new artists and then distribute their work over the Internet, bypassing conventional production, marketing and distribution activities.

Endemol   Endemol is an example of a new breed of media organisation (a television format supplier working on a global basis) that emerged as a result of fragmentation in television value chains, specifically the trend towards the outsourcing of programming that occurred partly in response to an increase in channels needing content. Endemol is the creator of a series of highly successful television formats, including *Big Brother*, and the largest player in its sector worldwide (Moran with Malbon, 2006). It has developed a business model that focuses on a specialist aspect of the content stage of the value chain – reality soaps, gaming, dating and infotainment. These should be capable of development into multi-episodic, locally replicable content formats with strong brands that can be exploited simultaneously across multiple media platforms in many different national markets and are attractive to advertisers and sponsors.

A diagram of Endemol's central value creation processes would resemble not a chain but a vertically integrated transnational hub focused on the content stage of the value chain group, with spokes radiating out across different delivery platforms and linking with the value chains of joint venture and outsourcing partners. This constellation is based on the opportunities created by convergence, fragmentation and globalisation and would have been unimaginable 20 years ago. In 2002 it owned around 500 formats, sought to create around 100 new ones each year, and employed around 3,300 full-time employees (Moran with Malbon, 2006).

The many innovations companies such as Endemol have introduced have forced traditional players to rethink their activities and the sources of value they focus on. For example, the Internet and mobile platforms are integral to Endemol's content formulae, thus websites linked to television programmes run live video streams to attract Internet audiences, and mobile messaging is used to build interest in broadcast and online programming. In addition to the sale of licences to produce the programmes, a long-standing revenue stream for television, Endemol places equivalent emphasis on revenue streams that have hitherto been seen as ancillary – advertising, sponsorship and transaction fees from Internet and mobile services. An additional revenue source are the deals made to produce Endemol formats. To this end the organisation has invested heavily in international expansion, creating a worldwide network of production companies through acquisition (which brings the additional benefit of acquiring new formats) and joint ventures.

Non-linear chains

So far all terms assume that value chains continue to be chains – that is sequential strings of activities. Some argue that the changes under way in the media sector mean that value chains are ceasing to be linear constructs and that non-sequential, interactive alignments, such as fluid cross-sectoral business networks represent the way forward (Kelly, 1997).

While many of these assertions were the product of new-economy enthusiasm, it is nonetheless clear that non-linear chains are emerging – Endemol's business model, for example, combines vertical integration with high levels of alliance activity and distribution over many different platforms. A further example is when musicians post tracks online, garner a fan base – perhaps through the use of blogs – and as a result of their success are signed up by a record label to market and distribute their products.

Business model

Another term that features in the sector analyses in this chapter is 'business model'. Like 'value chain' this is ubiquitous, but unlike the term 'value chain' there is no single definition. Usage varies widely by sector and professional specialisation. In standard business usage it denotes how the combination of costs will be covered, the value proposition for customers and the means by which income will be generated. Thus MTV's launch business model offered low risk and high returns. It was based on exploiting content that was attractive to a segment cherished by advertisers (teenagers) but very inexpensive (videos were a promotional tool that were financed by musicians and their music companies). So, MTV's advertising rates could undercut competitors and still generate healthy cash flows, even if audiences were modest.

Academics tend to use the term in two ways. Information technologists use it to map the product, service or process architectures. Strategists use it to describe the configuration of resources in response to a particular strategic orientation. For example, Prahalad and Venkaktraman (2000) suggest that Internet-business strategies require continuous experimentation with new business models through different permutations of reducing costs (cost leadership strategy) and enhancing services, often through personalisation (differentiation strategy).

This book uses the term 'business model' to denote the relationship between the processes by which products are produced and distributed to consumers, and the way in which financial returns are generated and distributed between participants in the sector. Thus it captures the essence of the business – providing a basic description of the product (the needs it serves, the ways it is produced), and the source of revenues for the provider (Magretta, 2002). This information, when combined with the sector's value chain, provides insights into the underlying characteristics of a sector that influence strategic behaviour within it.

Having explained the analysis tools this chapter will apply, it now moves on to explore the various sectors that comprise the media industries and their respective strategic contexts.

Book publishing – 'books are different'

Book publishing sees itself as somewhat removed from the vagaries of the more aggressively commercial parts of the media. While no longer run by bibliophiles, aspects of the bibliophile culture – a deep respect for literature and the art of book production, a distain for commercial pressures – can still be found in remoter outposts of the industry, although as this section will show, these characteristics are disappearing fast. Certainly many players in the sector have traditionally been motivated by a love of books and literature, rather than the search for profits. This extends to authors, with a substantial proportion of books written not because a publishing house wants to publish them, but because authors want to write them. Coser (cited in Hesmondhalgh, 2002: 166) found that only three to four of every 10,000 unsolicited books submitted to a publishing house are accepted and that 50 per cent of all published books with an ISBN sell fewer than 250 copies.

The central task of a publisher is straightforward: to find books that people want to read, to ensure that potential readers know about them, to make them available in distribution outlets and to avoid carrying too much stock. However, falling consumer demand and structural problems in the industry complicate this process. Reading frequency is declining. A 2004 report on US reading habits by the National Endowment for the Arts found that the percentage of adults reading fiction dropped by 10 per cent between 1982 and 2002, and that fewer than half of Americans read novels, short stories, plays or poetry. The greatest drop was in 18–24-year-olds, where the number reading literature fell by 28 per cent – perhaps not surprising in view of this market segment's heavy use of digital media. The industry's response has been to increase the number and variety of books published, hoping to spark public interest. This means that at the same time as reading frequency is declining, the number of new titles published is rising – in the US this grew from 39,000 in 1975 to 122,000 in 2000.

Book publishing is not an attractive segment from an economic perspective (Picard, 2002a) and performs poorly in comparison with other sectors of the media. Growth is low – an average of 1–3 per cent per annum over the last 10 years (Greco, 2004) – operating margins are falling and marketing costs are increasing (Vogel, 1999). Overheads, manufacturing costs and returns (unsold books sent back by retailers) account for nearly 50 per cent of total costs (*Standard and Poor's Publishing Industry Survey*, 2002). It is unlikely that these trends will reverse and substantial questions exist about the long-term future of books and the publishers that produce them.

History

The history of the book in the twentieth and twenty-first centuries has been influenced by changes in retailing to a surprising degree. The book as a consumer product first emerged after the Second World War when Allen Lane of Penguin launched the low-priced paperback. The industry was then a cottage one in the hands of many small, often family-owned, publishers. During the 1970s and 1980s independent bookstores emerged and publishers developed more sophisticated approaches to book marketing including sales forces. Bookselling became progressively sophisticated, with bookstore chains developing in the 1980s and superstores in the 1990s. Consolidation in retailing changed the balance of power between publishers and booksellers. The new chains demanded higher discounts and sought more influence over publishers' decisions. Publishers began to adopt standard consumer marketing techniques, particularly for the handful of titles viewed as potential bestsellers.

Segments

The publishing industry divides its output into a number of categories.

Trade or consumer books   This segment comprises books aimed at the general market to be consumed during leisure time. It is one of the most volatile areas of publishing since the field is crowded and consumer tastes are fickle, and it is also enormously diverse. Key subdivisions are fiction and non-fiction, and mass market versus trade (mass market titles have smaller formats, lower prices and higher print runs than trade titles), but there are many sub-categories, ranging from romance, chick-lit, and crime and thrillers, to travel guides and children's books. Some of these niches display growth rates far in excess of the modest rates observed in the segment in general. Religious books, which includes Bibles and inspirational books, has been one of the fastest-growing segments in the US in recent years.

Professional books Professional books offer information and education content for adults but are not designed specifically for use within an academic or educational setting. They fall into four categories: business, law, medical, and technical and scientific titles.

Business books are for people seeking to improve their skills and knowledge and one of the most profitable segments of the industry. Price sensitivity is low (many books are bought on expenses) but sales are linked to corporate profitability and sensitive to economic fluctuations. Thus the sector was buoyant in the 1990s, dipped during the dotcom boom and regained its strength as economies strengthened again.

Digital delivery and the Internet have become integral to legal, medical, and technical and scientific publishing, a response to growing competition from electronic information sources which offer advantages in terms of storage, search and retrieval. The associated investments in hardware and software have added to cost bases, but have also created a powerful barrier to entry for new players.

Educational books This segment includes textbooks for universities and schools. Its dynamics are very different to those of trade publishing: comparatively few titles are published, investment in concept development, content and presentation is significant, and each title is extensively researched and heavily marketed. However, the returns can also be substantial: the definitive textbook for an entry-level degree course with international appeal will generate high returns for decades if properly managed. It is also a competitive segment with concentrated buyers and increasing price sensitivity, which has been exacerbated by the availability of second-hand textbooks online.

Digital technologies are changing both communication between publishers, authors, faculty and students, and the nature of the products themselves. Publishers support their texts with an array of resources for lecturers that includes lecture plans, supporting reading and even assessment tools. Educational books are fast becoming a hybrid of service and product, and publishers are increasingly becoming course publishers.

School textbooks are a sizeable sector of the book market. While sensitive to short-term changes in school funding it is relatively stable, since demographic changes affecting school enrolments can be predicted far in advance and textbook purchases are linked to school curricula, which tend to be set for many years. Changes occur relatively slowly and are well communicated to publishers.

As classroom teaching shifts onto digital platforms, demand for digital content and online learning is increasing. Thus, school textbook publishers are also developing a raft of related online services such as assessment services and lesson planning. In this context, the growing emphasis on educational testing and standards coupled with a worldwide emphasis on the importance of literacy present growth opportunities.

Academic books   Scholars and books have always had a close interrelationship and a segment of the publishing industry, the academic and university presses, has grown up around this relationship. These publishers publish academic monographs – specialist non-fiction titles on a wide variety of academic subjects for small market niches. This segment faces an uncertain future. It has been damaged by cuts in library budgets, the increasing price of academic journals and the growth in digital printing which allows academics to self-publish. Increasingly, authors are required to contribute substantially to the costs of publishing by traditional monograph publishing houses, with the fees they are charged often more than covering the direct costs incurred by the publishers for handling their book.

Key players

Publishing conglomerates   For centuries book publishing was a fragmented industry with a large number of small privately owned publishing houses. From the 1960s onwards the industry consolidated, with this trend gathering pace towards the close of the century. Thus, for example, in the 1990s HarperCollins was bought by News International, and Random House and Transworld by Bertelsmann. Pearson bought Putnam, and in 2004 Hachette bought Orion and Hodder Headline.

The acceleration in consolidation was a response to consolidation in book retailing, falling demand and the worsening economics of the sector. Publishers hoped for economies of scale in core processes (paper buying, marketing, information systems, warehousing, etc.), reductions in operating costs and overheads, and therefore higher margins. Rationalisation did improve the cost base of the handful of large publishers who emerged from the consolidation phase. However, the economics of the sector remain problematic and further rounds of internal rationalisation – merging imprints, reducing lists, outsourcing editorial functions – are under way.

Independent publishers   Although publishing is dominated by the activities of the conglomerates, because entry barriers to the industry are low, and because of advances in digital printing services falling, the emergence of small new publishers is an ongoing phenomenon. However, independents can find it difficult to gain access to rapidly consolidating distribution systems and retail outlets, although online booksellers have provided a partial solution to these problems and digital on-demand book manufacturers increasingly offer distribution to wholesalers and retailers.

Book-publishing value chain

The normal cycle for publishing a book from finished manuscript to presence in-store takes twelve months and involves the following stages.

Writing   It is commonly assumed that authors write manuscripts, submit these to publishers and the best are selected for publication. In reality, the number of unsolicited projects that are accepted directly by publishers is minuscule. The majority of books that are published reach publishing houses via an agent or have been initiated by editors.

As discussed earlier it is extraordinarily difficult for a first-time author to have a book accepted by a major house. This does not, however, stem the stream of new projects flowing onto editors' desks. These tend to be reviewed very quickly if at all, and as a result some quality submissions are overlooked, creating an opportunity for smaller publishers and the frequent phenomenon of bestsellers that have been rejected by the major houses, only to be success-fully published by smaller independents.

Agent   Agents play an important function in the industry, filtering out promising projects from the prodigious number circulating at any given time and presenting these to publishers. In the main they represent established authors and it is not easy for new authors to persuade an agent to take them on. Should they manage this the agent will generally charge 15 per cent of an author's advance and other earnings, with advances calculated as a percentage of anticipated sales.

Packager   Packagers are a little known part of the book publishing industry. They develop projects on behalf of publishers (either side can take the initiative) and carry out all the tasks involved in the production of a book, sometimes, but not always, including the printing. They focus on two types of books – complex, highly designed and therefore labour-intensive books such as reference titles, textbooks or coffee-table books, and series books such as teen or children's fiction. Their role is growing because they allow publishers to increase their lists and turnover without adding to their fixed cost base or editorial workload.

Publishing   This stage includes all the editorial processes involved in trans-forming a manuscript into print-ready form–editing, design and layout proof reading and production. Digital technologies have simplified and reduced the cost of many of these, but the constituent tasks remain unchanged.

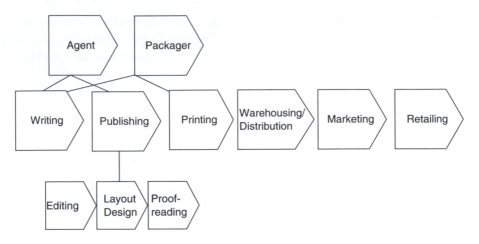

Figure 2.2 Value chain – book publishing

The element of publishing that receives the most attention is editing. The editor is often viewed as a romantic figure who lovingly crafts an author's words and helps authors to find their true voice. The reality is that in-house line editors are increasingly rare. Today line editing is generally done by free-lancers who are paid by the hour at relatively modest rates. In-house editors, especially commissioning editors, remain one of the chief creative forces in the sector, but their role is increasingly one of directing and coordinating the publishing process: selecting titles, recruiting freelancers, working with designers and briefing marketing teams. The influence of an editor with a track record of bestselling titles is significant since his or her titles will receive more attention from sales and marketing staff, book clubs, retailers and reviewers. Once it is edited and designed the manuscript is turned into proofs by the typesetter.

Printing   When the proofs have been proofread, corrected and checked, print-ready files are produced for the printer. Until the advent of digital technology offset presses were mostly used. These made most economic sense at print runs of 5,000 copies and above which dissuaded publishers from taking on books with limited market appeal, and meant that a book that sold out its initial print run slowly would generally only be reprinted once a substantial volume of orders had built up – thus books for which there was a market might nonetheless go out of print.

Digital presses offer a solution to these problems. Not only do they make self-publishing a viable option for authors who are not accepted by publishing houses, but they also make short runs economically viable. This, in turn, allows publishers to keep backlist titles in print, experiment more and reprint faster. They also reduce returns, remainders and stock-keeping costs.

Warehousing and distribution These unglamorous back-end processes are closely intertwined activities and have a significant influence on publishers' financial performance. Distribution is expensive – according to the UK Booksellers Association it typically costs 13 per cent of sales (the standard for consumer goods is 6 per cent), and taken together warehousing and distribution can account for up to half of a publisher's annual cash flow.

The industry's sales and distribution systems are outdated and complex which reduces publishers' ability to gauge accurately sales, stock levels or demand (Greco, 2004). These industry-wide problems are surprisingly intransigent. In 2004 Penguin UK's unsuccessful attempt to modernise its distribution left shops without books, caused significant losses and ultimately the departure of the CEO.

Marketing Trade and mass market titles are 'subscribed' in advance by retail outlets, and publishers base final print-run decisions on advance subscription figures. The major book retailing chains buy for all their outlets through one central office. These sales are handled by publishers' marketing managers who visit the chains well ahead of publication to discuss upcoming titles and get the retailers' input on cover design, title, price, etc. Smaller chains and independent bookstores are visited by sales representatives who subscribe individual titles.

The level of orders received for new books is often a function of the marketing support the publisher promises to provide (paid in-store promotions, advertisements, etc.) and the amount of publicity the publisher plans to generate for a title (author appearances, reviews, serialisations, etc.). Publishers focus marketing attention and activity on the period immediately before and around publication. Thereafter attention shifts to the next crop of books coming off the presses. Books that fail to sell well within 90 days are usually withdrawn from the shops, returned to publishers and their places given to newer titles.

This system is very inefficient since word of mouth recommendations are one of the most powerful marketing tools for books. Word of mouth publicity however moves slowly and consequently at the point when books are beginning to 'lift' in the marketplace they tend to be withdrawn from sale.

The system also works against backlist titles. As with the music industry, these titles carry higher profit margins than frontlist ones, since publishing expenses have been written off (in any given year about 40 per cent of revenue comes from the backlist). However, the press of new titles means that shops carry only limited backlist titles. Online bookselling provides a solution to these structural problems, perhaps explaining why it has become such an important medium for book sales, since it provides permanent access to older, specialist titles and out of print books.

Prizes are an important focus of marketing activities but less important than might be expected in driving book sales. A survey made in October 2004 of total UK sales over the previous twelve months of books that had won the Booker Prize found that while the 2002 Booker Prize winner, *The Life of Pi*, sold 258,000 copies, the 2001 winner, *Ned Kelly*, sold only 7,000 copies. They do, however, guarantee library sales and mean that books tend to stay on bookshop shelves longer.

Retailing   The health of the book publishing sector is strongly influenced by the activities of retailers. In the main, book publishers sell to bookshops who then sell on to consumers. This distance between producer and end user – if readers can be called that – means publishers are far less well informed about buyer behaviour than just about any other sector of the media.

Like other aspects of the book industry, bookselling was long regarded not as a commercial activity but as a specialist activity, a vocation for those who cared about literature. Consolidation in book retailing in the 1980s drove out many smaller retailers and created a small number of large retail chains. These introduced retailing techniques that had long been standard for other sectors: exploiting economies of scale to buy in volume at high discounts, improving stock control systems, using buyer intelligence to inform purchasing decisions, ordering fewer titles but backing those titles more strongly (for the UK chain Waterstones, 50 per cent of sales are generated by just three per cent of titles), and introducing in-store promotions (notably the 'three for two' paperback offers).

The spread of retail chains, coupled with online retailing, has damaged independent booksellers who cannot compete in terms of price or range. Many have closed. In 1990 independent bookstores accounted for nearly a third of all book purchases in the US, but by 1998 this figure had fallen by half (Croteau and Hoynes, 2001).

For publishers the chains have been a mixed blessing. Their sophisticated marketing techniques (instore cafes, longer opening hours, signing sessions and readings, etc.) have increased book sales, but the higher discounts they demand have eroded publishers' margins. They have also increased publishers' costs (publishers must subsidise instore promotions) and accelerated the focus on blockbusters at the expense of diversity. In recent years supermarkets have started to carry books at very high discounts – again a mixed blessing. They sell to customers who might not visit bookshops but also to customers who might otherwise patronise independent bookshops.

While the majority of books are sold through retailers (around 70 per cent) the Internet has become a permanent retail channel. Books are one of the successful online products: low-risk, low-cost and can be described well online, with the help of reviews and customer ratings. While publishers have benefited overall from higher backlist sales and reduced returns (these are negligible from online retailers), book retailers are divided about how important this new channel is, whether or not it has expanded the overall market or taken sales away from traditional retailers.

Strategic issues facing book publishing

Declining demand   The publishing industry is suffering from long-term changes in reading habits: fewer people read daily and an increasing number of people never read books at all. The majority of those who are book buyers have high levels of education and belong to professional households, and these individuals are busier with less time to read, plus they have more alternative ways of spending what free time they have. Younger consumers in particular, who are the heaviest consumers of electronic media, are less and less likely to turn to books to fill their (decreasing) leisure time. The result is that sales revenue in most geographic markets is stagnating or even declining, while the number of books sold and the percentage of the population buying books has decreased significantly.

Overpublishing   This is an endemic problem for the industry. It has two facets – the first concerns the number of new titles published. The industry's response to weakening demand and uncertainty about public taste has been to publish an increasingly broad range of titles, hoping some of these will spark interest (the 'mud against the wall' strategy discussed in the following chapter). As a result the sector now produces more unique products than any other branch of the media (Croyteau and Hoynes, 2001). Behind this approach lies the fact that it is seductively inexpensive to produce a book: there is an over-supply of manuscripts, the majority of authors will accept small advances, and the cost of printing is falling as digital technologies improve. However, the hidden costs are high. Each title involves a host of unique decisions on format, price, paper stock, cover design, title, publication date, publicity and marketing support. Each of these decisions must be internally communicated and coordinated. Since a major publishing house will have hundreds of projects under development, plus a backlist, resources are spread thinly, meaning the majority of titles receive minimal support. Thus, increasing the volume of new products might increase the odds of finding a surprise hit, but it also undermines this goal in that each new book is competing internally for resources with many others. The result is that the majority of titles deliver low returns, certainly less than other sectors of the media would tolerate for unique products, which in turn reduces the resources available to invest in new titles.

The second aspect to overpublishing is that publishers over-print. This results from the current economics of printing which encourage publishers to be optimistic when setting print runs. However, according to a long-established arrangement retailers may return unsold books to publishers for a full refund. This not only complicates publishers' sales data since many books that have been ordered by retailers eventually dribble back to the publishers' warehouses, but it also affects profitability. The Association of American Publishers found in 2003 that 41 per cent of paperbacks and 31 per cent of adult hardbacks were returned. The UK's Booksellers Association calculated that in 2005 returns cost the industry £100 million in total, and that every returned book represented a direct cost of £1 per copy for publishers and 50p for booksellers.

The rise of the blockbuster   In publishing, as with other sectors of the media, the 'mud against the wall' strategy is being joined by a new one, the 'blockbuster' or hit model. This involves identifying a very few titles with mass market potential and focusing the bulk of available resources on these. This approach has been reinforced by industry consolidation which has created larger publishers who can afford larger advances and more substantial marketing budgets, as well as intense competition between these players which are locked in a declining sector and prepared to pay exceptional amounts for the scant number of authors they feel have guaranteed mass market potential.

The result is a roster of superstar authors – Stephen King, Dan Brown, John Grisham, Daniel Steele, J. K. Rowling and so on – who are managed as brands supported by merchandising, multi-format publishing and repurposing across different media platforms. Brand principles influence creative processes too: authors develop a recognisable format that directs reader expectations in terms of plot, characters and writing style.

This strategy is attractive to publishers because it bypasses the uncertainty endemic to the sector. One of the hardest things about selling 'experience goods' like books and movies is persuading the public to try something they don't know. Brand-name authors, especially those who write books with continuing characters, appeal to the public because their books are a known quantity. The problem is that these books command the majority of their publishers' resources at the expense of more diverse and unusual titles and they are often sold at massive discounts as loss leaders, effectively making other titles appear more expensive.

In focusing on bestsellers and neglecting the mid-list book and backlist titles the publishing and bookselling industries are missing out on a valuable revenue source. Online retailing has demonstrated that mid-list, niche and specialist titles do have a market: it has been estimated that over half of Amazon.com's book sales come from titles outside its top 130,000 titles (Anderson, 2006).

E-books   Despite optimistic prognoses during the dotcom era, the e-book market has yet to take off. Standards concerning file formats, reader software, hardware platforms and digital rights management and protection have not yet emerged, and as a result there are relatively few products and a dearth of compelling content. In turn consumer interest is muted and there is not enough market potential to justify the effort and expense of e-publishing. However, advances in portable e-paper may cause a growth in downloaded books – perhaps in specific segments (male-dominated science fiction is a frequently cited candidate).

To date e-books have not exploited the potential of the medium – particularly in incorporating images, print and sound. It might be that this industry will really take off when e-books cease to be viewed as an alternative to paper ones, but an entirely new category of creative media product.

Most growth in the digital delivery of books is in scientific, technical and medical publishing. Companies such as Elsevier, John Wiley and McGraw-Hill are delivering an increasing amount of content via the Internet. E-books also offer promise for the educational market although piracy is a substantial threat – a pirated version of a major global textbook on a peer-to-peer network could wipe out many years' investment in that title.

Newspapers

> In the newspaper industry, it often feels like a thousand cuts inflicted by a thousand enemies. The game is changing before our eyes, and new competitors are scoring successes even before we see them coming. (*Blueprint for Transformation*, American Press Institute, 2006: 6)

Newspapers are an influential medium and their political and social impact has been analysed extensively. Current difficulties (shrinking profit margins, declining circulation, increased competition from online media) have led to increased scrutiny from the investment community, but analysis from a strategic perspective is limited (Albarran et al., 2006).

In 2002, consumers spent 176 hours per person per year reading newspapers,[2] making them the fourth most popular media product after television (1,701 hours), radio (994 hours), and recorded music (201 hours). Over the past five years, newspaper sales worldwide increased by 4.75 per cent, and well over one billion people read a newspaper every day.[3] However the long-term outlook is bleak. The Internet is diverting both readers and advertisers. Free newspapers have reduced both single copy sales and advertising revenues. The increase in sales is concentrated in emerging economies. Asia currently leads the world in newspaper readership, the highest readership found in China, India and Japan (World Association of Newspapers, 2004), and most new titles are published in Asia and Africa. Mature markets have been in decline for decades and strategies such as changes to format, redesigns and promotional offers have served to slow rather than reverse this.

History

The newspaper sector is a mature industry with a history that is closely linked to advances in printing technology.[4] The first steps towards mass printing were made in fifteenth-century China with the invention of moveable type using clay moulds. In 1477 Gutenberg combined precision-cast moveable type with a wine press rebuilt as a printing machine to print a bible using hand-set characters (200 copies were produced in five years). By the late fifteenth century manuscript newssheets were being circulated in German cities. In the first half of the seventeenth century there were regular newspapers in Germany, France, Belgium and England. These concentrated on news from Europe and occasionally America or Asia. Newspapers began to cover local issues in the second half of the seventeenth century. In 1798 lithography was invented which was to become the industry's standard process for printing. The page size of newspapers increased during the eighteenth century to reduce the taxes levied on the number of pages. The invention of the telegraph in 1844 sped up reporting and transformed the industry, allowing information to be transferred in minutes. In 1851 the news agency Reuters was established.

The industrial revolution of the nineteenth century brought with it urbanisation, improved literacy and a mass market for newspapers. At the same time, presses capable of printing thousands of newspapers per hour and linotype were invented. These advances combined to turn newspapers from a minority habit for around 15 per cent of the population into a mass market product that became the primary means of disseminating and receiving information about local and world events (Baistow, 1985). In 1880 photographs were added to newspapers and by the 1890s circulations of popular titles were approaching a million copies per issue. During this period many of the features of today's newspapers appeared: banner headlines, illustrations, cartoons and expanded sports coverage. These features coalesced in the *Daily Mail*, the first 'tabloid' newspaper published by Lord Northcliffe in London in 1903.

The period from 1890 to 1920 is known as the 'golden age' of newspapers. It was dominated by the 'press barons' – larger than life characters such as Northcliffe, Beaverbrook and Hearst, who ran huge publishing empires and wielded enormous political and social influence. The use and abuse they made of their publications to influence political developments and gain personal publicity affected public perceptions of the press and were ultimately to lead to restrictions on the power of the proprietors and the size of their media holdings (Greenslade, 2003).

Until the arrival of radio, newspapers had a monopoly on the supply of information to the public. As the frequency of radio news bulletins increased, along with the size of their audiences, newspapers shifted their coverage to provide longer articles with more context and analysis (Fidler, 1997). Sales grew steadily until the next major boost during World War II, although page extents were severely reduced in wartime due to paper rationing. By 1946 London's daily newspapers were together selling over 13 million copies, with Sunday paper sales reaching 25 million. These were the highest-selling papers in the world, mainly because Britain's geography and well-developed communications network meant they could be distributed efficiently throughout the country.

This was the apogee of newspaper sales. Subsequent years brought developments which were to profoundly affect the industry (Baistow, 1985). The first was the arrival of market research. Hitherto, a paper's advertising income depended on the skill of the sales team. Market research, by analysing readership and categorising it in terms of potential purchasing power, allowed a particular newspaper's reach among specific audience groups to be measured and evaluated against other publications. The second was television. When television emerged readers embraced the new medium and advertisers followed them. For example, when commercial television was launched in the UK in 1956 the press in total took 90 per cent of all advertising revenues. By the mid-1960s, although advertising expenditure had trebled, print media's share of advertising expenditures had fallen to 65 per cent.

Newspaper readership went into a decline in the US also, a process that accelerated in the 1980s as the television network programming improved, and cable television, particularly all-news cable channels, emerged (Shaver and Shaver, 2006). This decline was however masked by a population growth that kept circulations relatively intact (Picard, 2002a).

In response, newspapers shifted the focus of coverage, with an increasing emphasis on local news – today US local newspapers are the prime source of news on community events. Some local papers closed and others were acquired by regional or national newspaper chains, allowing them to pool resources and achieve certain economies of scale and scope (Croteau and Hoynes, 2001). Newspapers also began to target more up-market readers with special sections on subjects such as 'living', 'home', 'technology', 'entertainment'. Technological advances allowed publishers to extend this strategy by 'zoning', whereby different versions are produced for different audience segments – urban and suburban audiences for example. This allows papers to hook readers by covering issues close to them and to provide advertisers with access to specific groups (Croteau and Hoynes, 2001).

These measures may have mitigated the impact of television, but between 1940 and 1990 newspaper circulation in the US dropped from one newspaper per two adults to one per three, and whereas four out of five Americans in 1964 read a paper every day, by 2005 only half did.

Segments

Newspapers can be classified according to:

1. *Frequency of publication.* The options are, daily (morning or evening), weekly and Sunday/weekend. Frequency of publication influences editorial content: daily papers focus on news and practical current information; weekly or weekend publications are larger, providing analysis of news events, lifestyle articles, more specialised sections and advertising inserts.
2. *Pitch of content.* Mass market titles cover news in a simple and compressed style and focus on personalities, scandal, celebrity gossip and sport. They also tend to occupy a clear political position – right or left. The quality papers provide more 'hard' news and give space to politics, economics, society and international affairs. In general, mass market papers outsell quality ones by a factor of up to 10.
3. *Geographic area.* A newspaper's scope can be local, regional, national or international. In the US, the majority of papers are local ones, while in Europe the majority of publications are national. The number of truly international newspapers is small; examples include *Christian Science Monitor*, *The International Herald Tribune*, the *Wall Street Journal* and the *Financial Times*. This reflects the considerable costs involved in international newsgathering, printing and distribution: the *Financial Times* is printed in 18 cities, available in 140 countries and has an international network of over 500 journalists.

Business model

Of the three sectors of the publishing industry (newspapers, magazines and books) newspaper publishing is the largest by total value, followed by magazines and books. Like all print media products the newspaper traditionally has high fixed costs (typesetting and layout, printing, paper, storage and distribution) so volume sales are necessary to bring unit prices down to mass market levels. This gave rise to the traditional national newspaper content model which is similar to the portmanteau broadcast model: carrying a broad range of different types of content to ensure appeal to an equally broad range of readers.

Despite the high capital requirements, for most of the second half of the twentieth century newspaper publishing has been one of the most profitable industries with healthy returns, strong cash flows, high margins and the largest share of advertising expenditures of all media (Picard, 2003; Boczkowski, 2004). The high fixed costs of printing and distribution have been an important barrier to entry (Meyer, 2004).

The majority of the world's newspapers are privately owned, reflecting the fact that they bring steady profits and returns on investments as well as community profile and status. For that reason publicly traded newspaper companies have traditionally been viewed as sound investments and are attractive to large institutional investors (Picard, 2003).

Newspapers have not always been a mass media product. For their first 100 years US newspapers were read by an elite 15–25 per cent of the population who were educated, politically and socially active and willing to pay the high cover prices. During the nineteenth century processes of industrialisation created a mass market and newspapers dropped their prices to appeal to this. At this point the contemporary business model began to emerge where newspapers make the bulk of their revenues from selling advertising space. By 1880 advertising provided one-half of US newspaper revenues, by 1910 two-thirds, and by 2000 nearly 80 per cent, although proportionately retail advertising has been declining, balanced out by a corresponding growth in classified advertising (Picard, 2002a). In most advanced economies advertising accounts for over 60 per cent of total revenues for regional and local papers and over 50 per cent of national ones. The quality press tend to depend more heavily on advertising revenue than the tabloid press, which garners most revenues from sales.

Newspapers (apart from the free dailies discussed later in this chapter) therefore have two interlinked markets, readers and advertisers. A newspaper's appeal to advertisers depends on its circulation (the average number of copies distributed), the number of readers (readership may be higher than circulation because copies can be read by more than one person) and those readers' socio-economic profile. The higher the advertising income, the more is available to invest in content, and the more flexibility there is in setting the cover price.

Newspaper publishing value chain

The value chain of the newspaper industry is set out in Figure 2.3 and comprises the following stages.

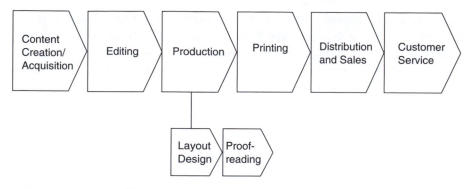

Figure 2.3 Newspaper value chain

Content creation, acquisition and editing   Content can be generated internally or externally. In-house content is more expensive than bought-in material, and editorial overheads are one of a newspaper's largest fixed costs (Doyle, 2002b). This is especially so if the newspaper engages in serious foreign affairs coverage which requires an expensive international network of correspondents and bureaux. External content comes from a variety of sources of which the press agencies or wire services are the most important. The ratio of internal to external content reflects the paper's editorial voice and positioning and brand values. Newspaper readership is characterised by strong brand loyalty which provides a basis for customer lock-in and a barrier to entry for new players.

A quality paper will source over half its content in-house and have a large permanent journalistic staff as a result. Mass market papers tend to have fewer in-house journalists, and free newspapers yet fewer, with those they do have primarily engaged on reworking copy from news wires and other external sources.

In addition to editorial content, there is advertising content. While there are clear internal distinctions between the two types of content (described as 'church' and 'state'), editorial and advertising activities are closely interlinked. Advertising income subsidises a newspaper's cover price, and the volume of adverts determines the number of pages a newspaper will have, and by extension the amount of space for editorial content. It is therefore critical that the two areas work closely together, with journalists including some copy that will provide editorial 'hooks' for advertising sales. Fewer advertisements mean that a paper will have fewer pages and therefore appear to offer less value for money, and be less attractive to readers. A strong advertising sales force is therefore central to the success of a newspaper.

The processes of generating and editing content are strategically significant. Picard (2006) points out that as the amount of original content falls and the amount of news agency copy increases, editing gains in strategic significance and becomes central to the process of creating value for readers.

Production   This stage involves turning content in the form of text, graphics and adverts into a coherent product. Production activities (layout, design, proofreading) were historically the province of non-journalists but computer-based production processes have blurred the boundary between editing and production and journalists are increasingly engaged in proofreading and layout.[5]

Printing   At this stage the digital prototype is converted to a physical product. It can either be done in-house, or contracted out, using excess capacity in other publishers' printing plants. Printing is labour and equipment intensive and publishers seek to maximise capacity utilisation: the more editions printed (daily, weekly, special, etc.) the higher the utilisation and the lower the per copy costs.

Distribution and sales   The logistics of newspaper distribution are complex and vary according to geographic region: it can be done by wholesalers or retailers, or directly by the publisher. Access to distribution systems is a significant barrier to entry, and is, for example, cited as having long prevented the introduction of Sunday newspapers in Germany. Subscription sales bring the advantage of stable revenues and direct contact with readers, but the disadvantage of requiring doorstep delivery which is expensive. Sales via newsstands and kiosks are simpler and less expensive – papers are simply delivered to independent wholesalers – but publishers lose direct sales contact with readers. Distribution of newspapers sold on newsstands is normally done by a combination of wholesalers or retailers. Distribution of newspapers sold on subscription basis can be done by the publishers themselves, or contracted out to specialist firms.

Customer service   This involves selling and managing subscriptions, as well as handling enquiries and complaints from readers. It can either be handled in-house, or subcontracted to call centres. In an era of competition for customer attention, this stage of the value chain is becoming increasingly important: better customer knowledge allows a newspaper to focus its content more closely on the needs of its readers.

Strategic issues facing the newspaper sector

Downward metrics   Newspapers are battling a gradual marginalisation in the face of digital media products. In countries where levels of penetration are already high, circulation, readership and penetration are all deteriorating (Picard, 2003; van der Wurff, 2005; Price, 2006). The circulation of paid newspapers has declined by 2–4 per cent annually in most markets for over a decade (Bughin and Poppe, 2005), with declines most marked in the mature markets of Europe, North American and Australia. While the World Association of

Newspapers reported a worldwide increase in sales for 2005, this growth was concentrated in developing countries such as China, India, Pakistan, Africa and South America.

In Europe the average newspaper reader gets older by the year and free daily newspapers, which have proved disproportionately popular with younger audiences are exacerbating this problem. It is not clear whether young people's current habits will persist as they age – the industry hopes they will gradually acquire the newspaper reading routines of their parents, but there is no clear evidence to suggest that they will.

Newspapers have applied a broad range of tactical responses: content upgrades, special supplements and magazines, promotional offers of books, DVDs, CDs and wallcharts, free subscription trials, and improved home and newsstand distribution. These appear to have slowed rather than reversed the decline.

Tabloid formats A strategic response observable in a surprisingly broad range of geographic markets is to switch to a smaller format (Bughin and Poppe, 2005). The logic is that compact editions will attract readers who are not interested by traditional newspapers – particularly teenagers and women. Smaller formats can also, depending on printing arrangements, reduce newsprint costs and printing costs if printing is outsourced. This strategy has increased circulation for some papers, although it is not clear if these improvements will be long term. Plus, hoped-for improvements in advertising revenue may fail to materialise because the page size is smaller and fewer adverts can be placed near to the front of publications.

The Internet The Internet has undermined the newspaper business in many ways. It is a substitute source of news and information, especially for younger readers. It offers the possibility of unbundling content and targeting smaller audience niches. Most critically, it has siphoned off a substantial proportion of classified advertising. Classified advertising is perfectly suited to an online environment – interactivity, frequent updates and archive features mean buyers can search systematically according to specific criteria from a wider range of offers. Employment and real estate adverts have been particularly affected. Since classified advertising accounts for 30 per cent of all revenues, this development is a serious one (Evans and Wurster, 2000).

As a result, newspapers have devoted enormous amounts of strategic attention to the Internet – the majority have an online edition, and increasingly websites feature most of the content of the print edition. Many of them require registration to access (without payment, but necessary for newspapers to track online usage). A minority charge subscription fees.

Yet, as with other sectors of the media industry, the Internet's effects are not entirely negative. From an editorial perspective, early strategies that involved the repurposing of content from the mother publication have largely been replaced by more sophisticated ones that build on the potential of the Internet. Increasing amounts of text are created specifically for the Internet, new narrative forms are developing, and the potential of the community is being exploited. Newspapers have also realised that online versions can expand readership and attract new demographic groups – particularly specialist readers, or readers from overseas. Relationships with existing readers can be deepened by offering new services or content about local communities. However, while online visits and advertising volumes are increasing, online revenues have yet to compensate for lost classified revenues.[6]

Free newspapers   The first free daily, *Metro*, was launched in 1995 in Sweden by the Modern Times Group and over 20 editions in other countries followed. Since then, over 80 papers have been launched worldwide with almost 10 million copies distributed in 2002 (Bakker, 2002).

Free daily newspapers are distributed in major cities and survive on advertising income alone. They are designed to be read quickly and are particularly attractive to younger readers. Initially they were not taken seriously by journalists or by advertisers; now they are an established segment and a considerable threat to established players since they challenge circulation sales at a time when the Internet is putting pressure on advertising income.

Magazines

Until recently the magazine industry considered the Internet little more than a gimmick, and magazine websites were a place for second-rate journalists and off-cuts of content considered too weak for the print version. By the time publishers woke up to their spectacularly poor judgement, the Internet had made a move on its audience. (*FHM* Editor Ed Needham, June 2006)[7]

The newspaper and magazine sectors have similar business models (they sell a physical product to readers and, simultaneously, access to those readers to advertisers) and production processes. The magazine is however a more recent phenomenon. It is published less frequently, on higher quality stock, and in general addresses far more specific reader interests.

As Daly et al. (1997)[8] note, the beginnings of magazine publishing were characterised by fierce competition and high levels of entrepreneurial risk, conditions that have characterised the sector ever since. Two rival publishers started magazines in Philadelphia in 1741. Both provided information about the British colonies and both closed six months later due to lack of reader interest. The development of magazines also reflects advances in printing technology, as for the newspaper industry. The first mass market magazines began to appear around 150 years later when advances in printing made the publication and distribution of large numbers of copies economically viable. By the middle of the twentieth century printing technologies had evolved to a point where it was possible to combine articles, graphics and colour illustrations into publications for sale at mass market prices (Fidler, 1997). In the US this gave rise to some iconic publications (including *Life*, *Look* and the *Saturday Evening Post*) which had high circulations and strong advertising incomes.

Like newspapers, magazines were badly hit when television emerged and captured substantial proportions of advertising budgets, and they continued to suffer from competition from other media products as well as from international competition. The advent of desk-top publishing systems and cheaper offset printing in the late 1980s alleviated the situation somewhat by allowing improvements in quality, efficiency and design but they also reduced entry costs and led to a surge in smaller niche publications (Hesmondhalgh, 2002).

The favoured response by established magazine publishers was to step up the rate of new launches, most of which were aimed at niche markets. But a successful launch often brings only temporary respite only since they tend to be copied quickly (Aris and Bughin, 2005). The majority, however, do not survive more than three years (Fidler, 1997). Further, this strategy can exacerbate structural problems in that more new products from existing publishers, coupled with lower barriers to entry mean more competition for readers and for advertising, increasing specialisation, and declining circulations; over two-thirds of US magazines now have a circulation of less than 500,000.[9]

Internationalisation is another strategy: *Vogue*, *Elle* and *Maxim* are just a few of the magazines that have launched a raft of foreign-language editions for foreign markets. Another response by publishers in mature markets such as Western Europe and America is expansion into emerging markets such as Eastern Europe (Aris and Bughin, 2005).

But while magazines are not a growth segment they have weathered recent changes in the media industry better than some. In 2004 84 per cent of US adults read magazines (MRI, Spring 2005) with the average reader spending about 45 minutes per issue.[10] The sector has benefited overall from increased brand advertising in consumer magazines and growth in business-to-business advertising in the trade and professional sector.

This resilience could be because readers tend to have an intimate relationship with magazines – this is especially the case with women's magazines. Magazine content is closely tailored to specific interests, has a unique voice and seeks to engage with readers in a personal way, thus it is at less risk of commoditisation than, say, news and current affairs coverage. Further the tactile attributes of a magazine – the glossy paper, the weight and so on – contribute to the reading experience and some publications are as much a home accessory as a media product.

Magazines are well positioned to expand onto a wide range of new delivery systems. They have established skills in creating loyalty, addressing niche segments and building specific communities of interest. However, increased competition for advertising and reader attention has made growth harder and led to an unrelenting pressure on costs. Most magazines have reduced headcounts, and many jobs within the industry have become more complex as print and online operations are combined.

Segments

The magazine industry has three core categories: consumer (women's titles, general interest and special interest), business and professional (business-to-business, industry-related and trade magazines) and academic (journals).

Consumer magazines   The consumer magazine segment is highly concentrated. For example, in the US six corporations publish the majority of all titles. Consumer magazines target specific groups of readers, are highly dependent on advertising income, and are widely available – in contrast to, say, trade magazines, that are available only by subscription. In 2004 in the US the top three subject categories were celebrity, fashion and home decoration.

The news weeklies such as *Time* and *Newsweek* have long been one of the most stable branches of consumer magazines but are experiencing the greatest difficulties in the digital environment (Picard, 2006). Along with the consumer business magazines (such as *Business Week*, *Forbes* and *Fortune*) they are experiencing readership declines similar to that of major newspapers and for many of the same reasons – the availability of other sources of news and news analysis, much of it free. Their responses include cost cutting, increasing subscription prices, selling online access to archives and articles, changing their editorial approach to focus less on hard news and more on lifestyle and entertainment, upgrading the quality of their paper to convince upmarket brands they are a suitable environment for expensive advertising, and integrating web and print operations more closely.

Sales of special interest consumer magazines (focusing on particular hobbies, for example) have fallen in recent years because consumers are increasingly 'time poor' and much of the expert information they contain is now easily available online. The various segments of the industry display varied fortunes. Men's magazines have experienced steep declines in sales, probably due to young male readers turning to the Internet and mobile phones for information and entertainment, although some attribute this to a failure to innovate.

The weekly magazine segment is growing, partly due to an explosion of celebrity magazines (in 2002 there were more magazine pages devoted to celebrities than any other category),[11] partly due to an increase in supermarket sales, where low-cost weekly magazines sell better than high-price monthly ones, and partly due to the fact that they appear to suit female readers whose lives have speeded up and who welcome more frequent publications. Weekly magazines have higher editorial costs, are more stressful to produce and have lower cover prices, but these disadvantages are outweighed by the increase in sales volume that results. Increasingly they compete with newspapers, rather than other magazines.

Business and professional magazines   Specialised business or trade magazines are aimed at specific industries or professions. These are predominately sold via subscription and have high cover prices. Financially this is the biggest sector of the industry but its size is becoming hard to gauge accurately since publishers have moved into new areas of information provision, including exhibitions, conferences, research, recruitment, and so on. This segment has weathered the digital revolution relatively well. Magazines that provide focused editorial content to a niche that is not served by other magazines or websites are thriving although those publications that were essentially product catalogues have disappeared (the Internet can perform this service far better).

In addition to the Internet, magazine publishers are experimenting with delivering content to other platforms such as mobile phones, PDAs, iPods, etc. A further new strategic direction involves what the industry terms 'people media'. This involves bringing consumers with interests in specialist subjects together at functions including seminars, conferences, breakfast briefings and the like. This is popular with sponsors since it offers direct access to specific audiences.

Academic journals   These are a unique segment of magazine publishing that operate outside the mainstream sector. Academic journals focus on particular scientific and academic disciplines and publish articles by scholars and scientists which either disseminate research findings or review the current state of knowledge in a field. Their articles contain highly specific information and are intended for a specialist audience. They are selected for publication by a stringent process known as peer review – independent assessment by peers in the field. Authors are frequently required to rewrite and submit articles several times before they are accepted.

These journals play an irreplaceable role in the scientific and academic communities, something that the sector's business model exploits. Establishing an academic career and progressing within it is normally contingent on achieving publication in leading journals and academics are expected to be, if not research active, at least research informed. Thus, university libraries must carry specific journals and academics must read them. The bulk of the editorial work is done voluntarily by leading academics (such activities are important for career progression) and authors are not paid for their articles, nor for reviewing other authors'.

Academic journals are sold by subscription and represent a multi-million dollar global business that has become very concentrated in recent decades. The segment has been at the forefront of adopting digital technologies. Journals are now supplied and accessed online in addition to in print form, and many universities have ceased to carry paper versions. This is preferable for academics because electronic journals are easier to search and articles can be downloaded. But digital versions are priced no lower than print ones, even though they cost substantially less to produce and distribute, and journal prices have increased substantially as has the number of journals published. As a result, even though most university libraries have increased their spending on journals, they carry fewer publications.

There are high levels of dissatisfaction within the academic community about this situation. University administrations are encouraging academics to consider the price of the journals they submit to as well as reputation. Scholars, unhappy with the stranglehold journals exert on the dissemination of new research and the slowness of the publication process, are experimenting with open access models that exploit the Internet as a means of improving the accessibility and the speed by which new findings can be communicated within their communities.

Business model

The revenue streams for magazines are advertising, subscriptions and newsstand sales, with advertising providing broadly half of all revenues (Fidler, 1997). In the US subscriptions dominate, in Europe, newsstand sales are stronger. For example, in 2004 over 85 per cent of US sales were from subscriptions, and between 1994 and 2004 subscriptions in the US grew by five per cent, with single copy sales accounting for the remaining 14 per cent[12] (the industry estimates that around 60 per cent of newsstand magazines are not sold). The US Postal Service calculated that magazines represent 3.4 per cent of the total mail stream.[13] Supermarket, mass merchandisers and drugstores combined represent 60 per cent of single copy sales.

In 2004 the ratio for consumer magazines in the US was 48 per cent advertising and 52 per cent editorial pages.[14] In 2003, 54 per cent of US magazine revenue came from advertising and 46 per cent from circulation, with automotive as the leading advertising category.[15]

Magazine publishing value chain

While formats and publishing frequency differ, there are similarities between the newspaper and magazine industries' value chains. Both carry editorial and advertising content. Both have four 'meta' stages: information gathering, information processing and layout, production and delivery, and for both magazines and newspapers at each stage there has been a gradual shift towards electronic alternatives. The magazine industry value chain is shown in Figure 2.4.

Content creation/acquisition   As with newspapers, a magazine's content reflects its editorial vision, and this in turn both reflects its market positioning and is a key source of intangible value. The task of developing an over-arching vision that resonates with readers and fits with the market falls to the Editor (or Editor-in-Chief) and demands both creative flair and a deep knowledge of the market and readers' interests.

An editor's vision drives the content acquisition process and needs to be communicated to all those working on the magazine – writers, editors, photographers,

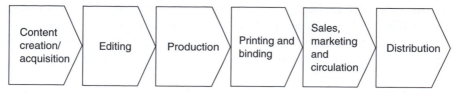

Figure 2.4 Value chain magazines

designers, typographers, layout artists, illustrators. Content can be generated internally or externally. High levels of freelance material have historically been standard for magazine publishing as a means of ensuring content diversity, and cost pressures are exacerbating this trend, with fewer permanent staff and more contributions from freelancers, who are in the main receiving the same or less remuneration than a decade ago. Amongst internal staff, fewer individuals are involved on single stories, and journalists are increasingly expected to deliver both print and online versions of their articles. Advertising pages are generated externally in advertising agencies or design studios and sent to the magazine.

Editing and production   These two stages are closely interlinked. They involve merging editorial and advertising content into a coherent product that matches the editorial vision and interests of the target reader. The core tasks are editing text, selecting graphics and laying out the pages. A rough pagination for the magazine will have been prepared while the issue was at planning stage but final layouts are designed once it is known how many advertising pages have been sold. A critical aspect at this stage is cover design – including cover lines and promotional offers – since this is one of the key factors driving newsstand sales.

Printing and binding   Printing is normally outsourced and can account for 60 per cent of a magazine's cost base, thus decisions about choice of printer, size (the trim), paper (stock) and so on have significant repercussions for overall profitability. Advances in printing technology in recent years have created an ever broader range of printing options. Printing is followed by binding – transforming printed pages into folded, trimmed and bound magazines.

Sales, marketing and circulation   This stage involves two distinct processes: selling space in the magazine to advertisers and promoting the magazine to readers. Like distribution (below) this stage of the value chain is complex and has significant implications: the number of advertising pages dictates the number of editorial pages in the magazine and the budgets for editorial content and consumer marketing, plus the sector's high fixed costs mean that a small change in advertising sales can have a significant effect on profits.

Marketing to advertisers involves persuading them that a publication provides a cost-effective means of reaching appropriate readers. Circulation and readership data are central to this process: potential advertisers need information on the number of readers and the time spent reading the publication. Much work is also done building awareness of a magazine to both advertisers and consumers through direct mail and advertising campaigns. Market research and testing underpin these activities.

Adverts inside the magazine are generated by sales representatives who cover specific geographic regions or categories of advertisers and seek to build long-term relationships with clients and their advertising agencies. It is a fiercely competitive activity, and a sales staff must be well informed of potential advertisers' expectations and brand values. Advertising sales conform to Pareto's Law; 80 per cent of sales are generated by 20 per cent of advertisers. Editors are often heavily engaged in marketing activities. Their involvement can range from appearing in the media as a commentator on certain issues to supporting advertisers' product launches.

Magazines can be acquired via subscription, single copy purchase, or free distribution to particular reader groups (controlled circulation). Managing these processes breaks down into a number of basic tasks: identifying potential magazine readers, managing single copy sales, maintaining subscriber lists, and providing printers with subscriber names.

Distribution   Single-copy sales reach their sales outlets via national distributors (usually independent organisations such as National Magazine Distributors or W. H. Smith) and wholesalers who deliver publications to the sales outlets and also take back unsold copies. Single-copy sales are complex, chiefly because physical distribution to newsstands is costly and requires carefully gauged decisions: a magazine should be available to as many potential readers as possible, but providing copies to all potentially relevant outlets is prohibitively expensive. Publishers receive around half of a magazine's cover price with the distributor, wholesaler and retailer receiving the rest.

Subscription magazines are distributed in the main by post (although alternative delivery systems that are offshoots of newspaper delivery services do exist). Postal charges are another significant element of the industry's cost structure: in 2006 the US post estimated that the value of magazines in the mail was around 3.4 per cent of the total mail stream.[16]

The circulation of a magazine is verified by independent organisations which publish information on a magazine's average paid circulation and rate base – the number of buyers as well as the numbers on which the magazine bases the rates charged to advertisers.

Strategic issues facing the magazine sector

The Internet   Historically viewed, the Internet is one of the most significant changes in decades to the magazine industry (an equivalent non-Internet related one being the introduction of computer-based printing systems). It has contributed to a wholesale alteration to business models, although this needs to be viewed against other developments that are not directly attributable to the Internet, notably the increase in niche titles and the simultaneous decline in the appeal of generalist titles, in particular magazines devoted to news and current events. These developments have been painful – a number of titles have disappeared and revenues have declined as advertising has migrated to the Internet, although some insiders argue a 'clean up' of weaker titles was long overdue.

On average, consumers spend about as much time on print media today as they do on the Internet, however the time they spend on the Internet is growing disproportionately and this looks set to continue. Further, magazine advertising spending is stagnant, while the Internet shows growth at a compound annual rate of 22 per cent.[17] Thus, the Internet has diverted consumers' and advertisers' attention and spending.

To date, many predictions concerning the impact of the Internet on the magazine sector have not held true. Magazines have not shifted wholesale from paper to online versions, and the spate of online-only magazines has largely subsided, with only a few notable examples such as *Salon* and *Slate* surviving. Rather, the Internet has been responsible for subtler changes that represent a more gradual evolution of the magazine industry.

While the Internet is a threat to advertising and circulation income, it is also a path to growth where the Internet is one element of a multi-platform strategy that extends magazine brands from traditional print activities onto the Internet, and in many cases mobile media and even live events.

Virtually all magazines now have an online presence. Online and print editions have become more closely integrated, with writers required to work on both platforms. In such cases the Internet is no longer a venue for republishing print copy, but an opportunity to fulfil a range of services: recruiting new subscribers for print editions, continually updating content, providing layered content that allows readers to access back issues and has links to relevant sites, allowing readers to search back issues, deepening the reader relationship by building an interactive community, engaging them in interactive experiences (games, polls, contests, etc.), and conducting research.

Television

The truth is, the more television there is, the less any of it matters. (Jeremy Paxman, McTaggart Lecture, MediaGuardian International Film Festival, 2007)

Despite the challenges posed by newer media products, television is still a surprisingly pervasive part of daily life. In the US people spend more time with television than with any other media product,[18] with women watching four and a half hours a day, men around four, and children around three hours.[19] In the UK the vast majority of people watch television every day, and 82 per cent of adults live in homes with more than one set.[20]

Although it was invented in 1929 and introduced to the US public in 1939 television did not develop into a mass medium until the 1950s. In 1950, only 9 per cent of US households owned a television (Television Bureau of Advertising, 2001), but by 1955 the figure had risen to 64.5 per cent of US households (Television Bureau of Advertising, 2001) and by 1965 at least one TV was in 92.6 per cent of US households. This was an era when society was more cohesive and consumers had fewer choices; as a result they tended to watch the same programmes, see the same advertisements, and buy the same products. Reinforcing this was the fact that broadcasting spectrum was scarce and broadcasters needed to ensure that their schedules appealed to broad swathes of the population at once – mass audiences. Since there were then far fewer equivalent leisure alternatives, mass audiences did in the main watch television and a broadcast licence was in the words of William Paley 'a licence to print money'.

But from the 1970s onwards this mass market paradigm began to weaken. In the 1970s VCRs and cable television were introduced in the US. After modest beginnings, both were to become staples in US homes. Europe in the 1980s saw the introduction of cable and satellite transmission. These developments provoked an explosive growth in the number of domestic commercial broadcasters, dramatically altering patterns of competition (Picard, 2003). Upheaval was to continue with the introduction of digital television from the mid-1990s which further increased the number of broadcast channels and further fragmented audiences. By 2000 it was standard for viewers with cable or satellite to have access to an average of 202.6 available channels (Television Bureau of Advertising, 2001).

Television used to be a group activity. Families would watch together and organise their schedules around broadcasting times. The US network audiences still constitute one of the biggest mass audiences, but that audience has been fragmented by competition from cable television, the Internet and other sources of entertainment, as well as personal video recorders.

Currently, the television sector is in a state of flux, with national and international television ecologies changing fundamentally as technological advances in distribution and production increase the number of channels available, regulatory regimes become more market orientated, the battle for consumer attention becomes fiercer and the cost of popular content rises dramatically. Life for organisations in the sector is becoming more complex and more uncertain.

Segments and their business models

Today, the television industry can be grouped into four sectors, primarily according to business model. These are described below.

Advertising-funded television   The first US television station licence was issued in 1941. This, like those that followed, was for commercial broadcasting (educational stations, later known as Public Broadcasting, began in the US in the 1960s). From the late 1940s to the mid-1950s three main broadcasting networks emerged: CBS, NBC and ABC.

The emergence of television and radio coincided with the rise of multinational consumer product companies, and a symbiotic relationship between the two developed that still underpins commercial free-to-air broadcasting: broadcasters transmit programming to audiences; advertisers pay those broadcasters for an opportunity to expose those audiences to their marketing messages. Thus, like newspapers and magazines, advertising-financed broadcasters have a dual market, viewers and advertisers.

Advertising funding has inbuilt disadvantages. It is sensitive to the state of the economy and corporate health – advertising budgets are among the first to be cut when economies worsen. It also influences programming options in that for the business model to function the television company must be confident it can deliver large audiences that include the consumer groups audiences most want to address. This militates for programming that will please as many as possible and not offend, and against experimental or niche concepts.

This advertising funding model came under strain in the late 1990s when a proliferation in channels – cable, satellite and digital – increased consumer choice. Audience volumes fell and broadcasters found it harder to achieve the viewer levels required by advertisers, while advertisers found they needed to buy more airtime in order to reach the number of viewers they sought.

US Networks   Advertising funding has been a standard business model for commercial free-to-air broadcasters all over the world, and the US networks are leading exponents. Limitations in channel capacity and the high capital investments required to set up television stations meant that the radio networks were best positioned to exploit television when it was developed, and the first three networks (ABC, NBC and CBS) that dominated the sector until the 1970s all had roots in radio (Croteau and Hoynes, 2001). They were joined in the 1990s by Fox, an ambitious venture by Murdoch's News Corporation.

Described as 'programme and audience delivery wholesalers' (Vogel, 1999: 139) the networks offer portmanteau channels covering the full span of programming: entertainment, news, special events and sports, both to the television stations they own themselves and to their network affiliates, whose advertising time and signal distribution they lease. For the most part these broadcasters are integrated factory producers, spanning the whole range of broadcasting activities: production, news bureaux, technical and administrative services, advertising sales offices and owning their own distribution.

Resolutely part of the commercial sector, and in comparison with their European counterparts relatively lightly regulated, the networks are commercial organisations that have profit maximisation as their major goal. The sale of advertising time has always been their principal source of revenues, and during the 1960s and 1970s the television networks were highly successful, attracting mass audiences of tens of millions viewers each evening, with Thursday night's three hours of primetime regularly attracting the largest number of viewers and the highest advertising spend. However, by the 1980s criticism of their 'least objectionable programming' formula was increasing. The head programmer of NBC, Paul Klein, coined this term, and explained it as resting on the belief that on any given night, viewers tuned in at 8.00pm (for a specific show) and kept watching whatever NBC happened to show until bedtime. There was a belief that viewers would flow from one show to a similar one in the next period, and the only way viewers would stop watching a network show was if they were startled out of it. At the time the networks were attracting around 90 per cent of primetime viewers.[21] Now, however, all the networks are in decline and are experiencing difficulties attracting the level of audience figures they have reached in recent years. One response has been to turn to types of programming it hopes will guarantee audiences – National Football League games, reality TV formats and the edgier programming that has until recently been only aired by cable broadcasters.

Cable   The introduction of cable in the US in the 1980s brought a major new competitor for the US networks that was to undermine fatally their domestic strength. Within 10 years their audiences dropped by 25 per cent, with teen viewers dropping by 30 per cent and children by 80 per cent. Their failure to respond to these developments was instrumental in the changes in ownership that took place during the 1980s, when ABC, NBC and CBS were all acquired.

While the networks have traditionally sought to provide generalist high budget content for large mainstream audiences, cable offers a different programming proposition. 'Narrowcasters' rather than 'broadcasters', they offer special interest programming. Channels are devoted to a particular genre – sports, movies, cartoons, natural history, shopping, weather, etc., with successful ones delivering precisely targeted viewers to advertisers. In the US at least cable broadcasters are regulated more loosely than the networks, bringing greater creative freedom and allowing them more latitude in terms of what they broadcast. This allows them to offer programming that strays into risqué areas – mainstream fare with a tinge of explicit content – for example, Home Box Office's *Sex in the City* or *The Sopranos*.

Cable television is also based on a different, and, for successful cable channels more robust, business model. It is subscription-financed which means broadcasters enjoy a dual revenue stream: advertising income and subscription fees. Thus even small audiences can be financially viable. However, even though production costs are generally lower than with networks it is estimated that only one-third of cable channels break even financially and to mitigate this most cable operators offer a range of different cable channels.

Public service broadcasting   Public service broadcasting is a dominant element of European broadcasting and has played a leading role both in the development of broadcasting technologies and broadcasting content. Currently the model is declining in importance in many countries, the result of an increasing number of niche channels, looser regulation and more competition for consumers' attention.

The core differentiating factor in the PSB concept is to address audiences as citizens. In addition to providing engaging and entertaining programming PSB broadcasters also seek to promote social values such as furthering an informed democracy, promoting knowledge and learning, and enabling a cultural identity to flourish (Ofcom, 2004: 47). Further than that, PSB has always been a hard concept to define. It is far more than simply a financing arrangement. The UK's Peacock Committee (1986) found that there were as many interpretations of the concept as contributors to the debate. It is sometimes defined in terms of requirements concerning the range of genres broadcast: for example, the UK's regulator, Ofcom, requires commercial terrestrial broadcasters to include news, current affairs, regional news, religion, children's, arts, education and multicultural programming. But PSB can also be understood as a set of principles governing the overall broadcasting system (Kuhn, 1985). A number of characteristics common to PSB broadcasters can, however, be identified:[22]

- National in scope, providing a universal service to all irrespective of income or location
- Omnibus service provision – that is providing a balanced output and balanced scheduling across all programme genres. Particularly important is political output, and this must be politically neutral and non-partisan
- Semi-autonomous. Public service broadcasters operate under broadly worded mandates with much flexibility of interpretation and a degree of financial independence from government and commercial bodies
- Commitment to fulfil an overt social and cultural mission concerning issues such as catering for minorities and fostering national and community identities
- Public accountability, publicly financed, with commercial elements closely regulated.

Television industry value chain

From the mid-1980s onwards a series of developments restructured the television industry and with it the sector's value chain. Exceptionally this section of the chapter features two chains, the first predating these changes and the second showing their effects. This is possible because television was one of the first sectors to undergo a fundamental restructuring and it is therefore possible to capture a before and after picture. Two value chains are included for a number of reasons: they underline the utility of the value chain as a

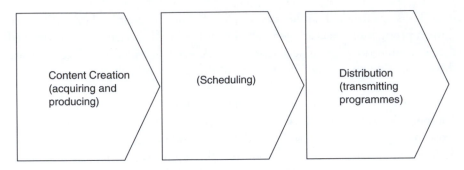

Figure 2.5 Traditional value chain for the television industry

means of capturing systemic changes in media industry sectors; they are a textbook example of value chain disintermediation; and they provide graphic evidence of the growing complexity confronting all media industries.

Traditional value chain   Until the 1980s a strong regulatory framework combined with dominant national players and a relatively stable technological base gave rise to a straightforward value chain for broadcasters that survived for decades. This is shown in Figure 2.5. This comprised three stages and had high degrees of vertical integration (as a rule broadcasting organizations had control over each stage). The first was acquiring or developing content. This involved either creating content in-house or commissioning it from external suppliers – production companies, news agencies, etc. For in-house production this stage involved concept development, budgeting, and pre-production, production and post-production stages. The second stage was scheduling. This was far more than simply planning what to broadcast when, but an important basis for competitive advantage whereby programmes were scheduled against those of rival channels to attract audiences away from competing broadcasters. The transmission stage involved the broadcasting of the channels.

Emerging value chain   For the television industry, gradual market liberalisation coupled with technological developments yielded a host of changes: spectrum scarcity was relieved, the number of channels increased, demand for content rose, subscription-financed services were introduced, subscription management infrastructures created a more sophisticated consumer 'interface', and the electronic programme guide changed viewer selection behaviour. Overall this has led to a fragmentation in channels, audiences and funding options which has been reflected in the industry's value chain whereby the various stages which once represented bundles of fully integrated processes have been 'unbundled' creating a longer chain. This is shown in Figure 2.6.

Content creation/acquisition   Content comprises a broad range of genres – news channels, sporting events, films, drama, and so on – and can be sourced

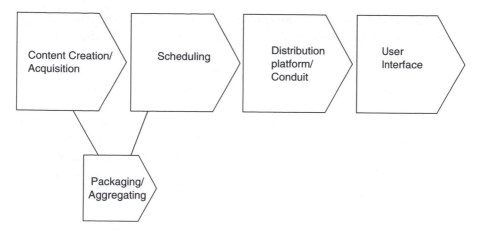

Figure 2.6   Emerging value chain for the television Industry

from a wide range of suppliers ranging from small independent producers to global format creators and Hollywood studios.

The content segment has acquired tremendous economic leverage in recent years, reflecting its disproportionate importance in attracting consumers in an era when they are increasingly bombarded with different media offerings. However, as a sector it is fragmented, with content producers remaining specialised according to content type. Newsgathering, documentary film-making and developing talk show formats involve fundamentally different activities and present limited opportunities for consolidation. Recent years have seen an increase in formatted shows – mainly reality and quiz programmes – that are broadcast around the world, for example *Who Wants to Be a Millionaire?*, *Big Brother* and *Pop Idol*. These are produced by new players in the value chain, global format producers.

Packaging/aggregating   This stage involves packaging content from external sources and structuring it into coherent channels and for many broadcasters represents a new stage between content acquisition and scheduling, depending on whether content is aggregated at programme or schedule level. This is effectively a new stage in the value chain and has in the past provided a point of entry for new players such as MTV, who initially simply bundled together a source of content that had until that point been neglected by television, music videos. The UK's Channel Four represents a different breed of content aggregator. It pioneered the 'publisher' broadcaster model whereby broadcasters develop no programming themselves but create channels, and collections of channels ('bouquets') from independent suppliers.

This has given rise to a new media competence, media aggregation. This involves securing and bundling content into channels to suit particular audiences. Packagers are essentially intermediaries and their world is one of alliances. A packager's success depends on the ability to build three sets of relationships: with content providers to secure access to quality content; with the organisations providing the distribution for the content they package; and with viewers. This is a marketing challenge and involves creating a strong brand identity.

Distribution platform and conduit   Although distinct stages in the value chain, distribution platform and conduit can be analysed together since both are experiencing similar types of change.

Distribution is done by the network operators, who build and manage distribution networks. These networks had, until the development of digital television, operated on the basis of one-to-many transmission and high capacity channels. The digital revolution in media technologies has led to a profusion of options. The digital signal can be received by aerial, satellite, cable or broadband. Digital television offers more channels, and also allows new services, such as high definition, wireless broadcast, and local television. It also means distinctions between transmissions systems are becoming less relevant and distribution is becoming commoditised, eliminating any competitive advantages that might arise as a result of exclusive distribution arrangements.

User interface   This segment of the value chain is essentially domestic distribution. It includes all the equipment and services that are needed to access the television services – set-top box manufacturers, component manufacturers and software component providers (software that controls the functions of the hardware and user accessibility). This is an important stage in the value chain since it allows a direct relationship with the consumers of content. It has seen rapid technological development and is subject to the same forces of fragmentation that are evident elsewhere in the value chain. New types of interface that slot in between the stages of user conduit and the end user are constantly developing, such as the conditional access system which was developed initially as a means to enforce payment of subscription fees, and plays an important role in enabling the delivery of interactive services. One of the most significant changes to the television value chain concerns the EPG (electronic programme guide). This represents the first major shift in power from the broadcasters to consumers, in that it allows viewers to select what they want to watch from a broad array of potential television, radio and film options.

Strategic issues facing the television industry

Competition   Along with newspaper publishers, television broadcasters are seeing their dominance erode as customers and advertisers shift to new sources of entertainment and information. The number of channels has increased dramatically as has the number of alternative media products and services. Television is now just one option amongst hundreds. Like newspapers, television is also facing a profound demographic problem: their consumers are aging and they are failing to attract younger audiences. There are no easy solutions to these kinds of intractable problems. A perhaps inevitable response is to try to make programming more compelling and accessible. This can mean over-simplification, selecting controversial subject matter, pushing the boundaries of taste and decency, perhaps even misleading the public by staging reality show events or editing them to give a false impression. Recent scandals in the UK suggest this approach is backfiring and damaging audience trust in the medium, but alternative strategic responses have yet to appear.

Shift from analogue to digital   A significant development in television concerns digital technologies' impact on production and distribution. Most advanced countries are planning to replace their analogue systems with digital ones over the next decade or so. Roll-out has begun in much of Europe, a number of countries have well-established digital systems and many have firm dates for 'analogue switch-off'. This process is politically driven: by switching off analogue transmission governments can free up the spectrum for other uses.

Digital broadcasting represents the first improvement in television transmission systems since the introduction of colour television in the 1960s. Digitalisation allows video and audio signals to be stored and broadcast in a 'bitstream' of digits ('0's and '1's rather than as a continuously varying wave – which is how traditional analogue television signals are broadcast. This offers a number of benefits. It increases the quality of the broadcast signal, improving picture and sound quality. It decreases the amount of broadcasting spectrum used, meaning more channels can be broadcast, and allows the broadcasting of computer data and the development of interactive services.

In terms of transmission, digital television takes three main forms; digital cable, digital satellite and digital terrestrial. Its mainstream launch can be viewed as 1998, when two services were launched in the UK, BSkyB (digital satellite) and OnDigital (digital terrestrial). In 1999 Sweden also launched a digital terrestrial service. Most digital television is broadcast on a pay-TV basis, with the UK's Freeview service a rare example of a free-to-air digital television service.

Digital broadcasting brings two main changes to content. It provides more space for traditional channels and it allows new broadcast services. These range from subscription services, pay-TV and pay-per-view, as well as the basic ones, being the control and data services required for the decoder to de-multiplex and decode the services, and also the advanced ones, providing services to end consumers such as interactive TV, T-commerce and access to the Internet.

The introduction of digital television has many implications for the television industry. First, it represents a shift in the underlying business models. Under analogue systems, once a television set had been purchased, television reception was either free (since it was advertising financed) or licence-fee funded. New sets were purchased on average every 7–10 years, and cost €25–50 on an annualised basis (Picard, 2002a). Digital television systems operate on an entirely different model. Consumers must buy a set-top box (although these are often subsidised by the television companies or by the government), or a new television set with special features built-in, and then 'buy' programming on a subscription basis. Indeed, until the mid-1990s in Europe the terms digital-TV and pay-TV were synonymous, since digital television had primarily been used to provide access to premium channels of movies and key sporting events. This is a significant shift: in the UK over half of homes now have digital television, and, as a result, subscription revenues now outweigh income from advertisers.

An equally important development is that digitalisation accelerates the fragmentation of viewing that was already observable in the television arena. As the number of channels increase, individual behaviour diverges and the mass audience fragments. This process was already well established as a result of the emergence of cable and satellite television, but digitalisation has accelerated it by increasing significantly the number of television channels broadcast and introducing specialised channels into the channel mix. Digital homes spread their viewing more widely, reducing the market shares of leading channels.

For broadcasters digital television means an increase in partnerships – with organisations providing the distribution architecture, call centres, equipment manufacturers, content suppliers, and so on. This increases the complexity of the value chain.

The nature and evolution of market demand is also increasingly uncertain. Before the advent of digital technologies scarcity of transmission frequency meant that only a limited number of channels were technologically possible. This, as we have seen, created a momentum towards the creation of mass audiences. Digital technology is creating an abundance of new channels, and new platforms allow new actors to enter the market. But while the number of channels has increased dramatically, the amount of time spent viewing television has not risen proportionately: demand for content is growing more slowly than the supply of programming. The resulting increase in choice means broadcasters will need to develop a more sophisticated understanding of consumer preferences and adjust their business models to accommodate smaller audiences.

In addition to providing improved broadcast quality and a plethora of new channels, digital television introduces interactivity into the relationship between broadcaster and viewer. By merging the functions of broadcasting, computing and telecommunications it creates the potential for a range of new services which can take the form of related supplementary information to accompany the video stream (enhanced television), or interactive services that are independent of television programmes (e-commerce, home banking, etc.).

At this point it is difficult to see what impact this functionality will have – so far customer reaction to interactive features has been muted. In general, digital homes tend to watch a slightly enlarged range of channels, but make little use of interactive features, although betting services are popular.

The Internet and interactivity The impact of the Internet on television is strong but indirect. Just as the e-book is stuck in infancy in terms of product development and market uptake, so too has the Internet as yet failed to develop into a mainstream delivery medium for television content. The biggest impact of the Internet on television so far has been its diversionary properties: its ability to divert audience attention and advertising away from television programming.

As with other sectors, if the causal net is broadened to include digital developments, then a slightly more complex picture emerges. Digital distribution allows programming to be broadcast on a number of different devices, notably mobile phones and iPods. As time-shifting and place-shifting become more widespread, as mass audiences for network programmes fragment, these emerging platforms may provide a means of gaining additional revenues from sunk investments in content, of compensating for falls in advertising income, and potentially of building audiences for traditional advertising-supported programming.

Call-TV formats, where viewers interact with TV shows by calling premium rate telephone numbers or sending text messages to 'vote' or answer quiz questions are expanding into an important revenue stream, one that is growing far faster than advertising revenues. Viewers who use these functions are more likely to tune in again, tell friends about the programme and to buy related merchandise. This added interest can generate higher ratings and advertising revenues, although recent scandals in the UK show that such systems are open to abuse by broadcasters.

HDTV A parallel development in broadcasting systems concerns the introduction of high definition television (HDTV). High definition significantly improves image and sound quality. The evidence so far is that once consumers are exposed to this they are dissatisfied with non-HD programming. However, consumers need a television screen that is capable of showing images at the higher resolution that HD demands.

The US and Japan have taken the lead in HDTV with many stations already equipped with HD broadcast capability, and many European broadcasters have also committed to the technology. High definition production is also increasing – the BBC will have all programmes produced in HD by 2010 – not least because most major markets will only accept programmes in HD formats.

Radio

It's not true I had nothing on, I had the radio on. (Marilyn Monroe)

Despite being the oldest electronic medium, a century after its invention radio is still deeply entrenched in daily life, and, surprisingly perhaps, thriving in the current technological climate. In the US radio reaches over 95 per cent of consumers each week and car radio reaches four out of five adults each week.[23] Penetration in mainland Europe is around 80 per cent and matches that of television. In 2000 UNESCO reported that for a world population of 5.9 billion there were 2.45 billion radio devices.

This resilience reflects radio's many intrinsic advantages. It is portable, can be consumed just about anywhere and while performing other tasks, and the costs of entry and operation are low. It is based on stable technologies, is easy and inexpensive to consume (programming has traditionally been 'free' and radio sets cheap to buy), and is perceived as personal and trustworthy.

History

When radio was originally created in the 1910s it was envisaged as a form of one-to-one communication, similar to a telephone or telegram (Hesmondhalgh, 2002). It was initially adopted by the military and amateurs for personal communication purposes but in the early 1920s companies in a number of countries began to experiment with broadcasting music and other forms of entertainment. This gave rise to an explosive unregulated growth period similar to the recent dotcom era (Spar, 2003) with radio stations, 'pouring onto the airwaves in raucous gangs, jumping across frequencies and "stealing" spaces that had already been allocated' (Spar, 2003: 126).

In response, the larger operators in the US pressured regulators to abandon the open markets – 'a rare example of a roughshod industry beseeching the government to impose order' (Spar; 2003: 126). Regulation, the industry saw, was necessary given the limited amount of spectrum available, the need to allocate access fairly, and to maintain standards. The resulting Radio Act of 1927 established the Federal Radio Commission which was tasked with overseeing the administration of these licences (Spar, 2003). Thus the government had control over granting licences but not ownership. The state's role was extended via the 1934 Communications Act, which set up the Federal Communications Commission to monitor the fledgling radio industry (Hesmondhalgh, 2002).

In the intervening years the industry continued to develop on both sides of the Atlantic. Frequency-modulated (FM) radio was invented by Edwin Armstrong at RCA in 1933. This offered higher fidelity sound with less static and required less transmittal power. However, RCA feared this would threaten its dominance of the AM market and crippled the new development (ultimately causing Armstrong to commit suicide). By the time World War II broke out the industry was well established as was listening to the radio as a family activity. Broadcasting in the US had evolved into a commercial industry with two key players, NBC and CBS, and a clear regulatory regime.

A parallel consolidation process also established the radio sector in Europe, but here it was primarily publicly financed. By the outbreak of World War II radio was a powerful social force. Roosevelt, Churchill and Hitler all made extensive use of radio as a public information channel. In the 1970s European radio started to change with the launch of 'pirate radio stations'. From the 1980s onward the sector was gradually liberalised resulting in a rapid increase in commercial stations. The highpoint was 1994 when there were 7,600 stations. Thereafter, a further period of consolidation set in which led this figure to decline to 5,500 by 2000, of which 5,100 were private and 400 public.[24]

In the 1990s the US radio industry lobbied Congress to relieve station ownership restrictions. In 1996 the limit of 40 stations was removed leading to thousands of radio stations changing hands. It also triggered further consolidation and a number of radio conglomerates emerged (see below) This in turn reduced diversity in programming with the introduction of national playlists for certain broadcast formats.

Key players

In the US private networks such as Chancellor Media, CBS and Clear Channel dominate the sector. In Europe PSB stations have traditionally been the largest players, but the commercial sector has grown strongly in recent years and the two groups are fast approaching parity in revenues.

Europe's commercial sector is fragmented with few pan-European companies. An exception is Bertelsmann's RTL Group which broadcasts in Germany, France, Belgium, Luxembourg and the Netherlands. Another is Group Europe 1 (part of the Lagardere Group) which has stations in France, Spain, the former USSR, the Czech Republic, Poland and Germany.

A radio station's format is specified in its licence – it is generally not possible for an established station to switch formats without agreement from regulators (although public service broadcasters enjoy more latitude in terms of reformatting their channels). In recent years programming formats have proliferated – by 2000 there were approximately 24 core formats in the US. In 2003 the most popular were country (2,088 stations), news and talk (1,224 stations).[25]

Business model

Radio broadcasters fall into two categories – public service and commercial. Public service radio is financed via licence fee income (although in many countries PSB radio stations can receive advertising revenues). Commercial radio is supported by revenues from the sale of airtime to advertisers.

The licence fee funding model that supports public service broadcasters in Europe provides them with guaranteed funding irrespective of audience size and the health of the economy. They also tend to enjoy the best analogue frequencies. However they also usually must conform to content requirements, often involving quotas concerning the amount of cultural and factual content broadcast. Public service radio in the US (National Public Radio) receives an element of state subsidy but in the main is financed through tax-deductible donations and voluntary subscriptions.

Commercial stations do not have content quotas and generally concentrate on the most attractive audience segments. Success with audiences translates into higher revenues and profits. This is because radio broadcasting has high fixed costs and low variable ones, meaning economies of scale are significant.

Figure 2.7   Value chain – radio

Radio represents approximately one-third of an average consumer's media exposure yet its share of advertising revenue is far behind that of television and newspapers.[26] Consumer goods companies traditionally favour television or print media, with the exception of the music industry, where radio is one of the most important promotion channels. This is despite the fact that radio advertising is relatively cheap and allows advertisers to connect with their local communities. It has been suggested this prejudice on the part of advertisers stems from the fact that radio is not a visual medium, and less attractive because local and regional advertising tend to mean lower budgets.

Radio broadcasting value chain

The value chain for the radio industry has five stages (as shown in Figure 2.7) – although this is currently undergoing significant change and may not be true for long. It is still commonplace for public service broadcasters to control all stages while some commercial players concentrate on specific portions of the chain, collaborating with business partners to complete the chain.

Content creation/acquisition   This includes all activities connected with the acquisition of content. Depending on the station's or network's programme format, content can range from news, weather and information, to music, original drama, phone-ins and live concerts. New delivery platforms such as the Internet and MP3 players have complicated the rights aspects of this stage (see under Podcasting, below). The acquisition of advertising also falls into this stage.

Production   This involves the planning, execution, coordination and management of the content production process. New platforms for receiving radio mean that production also includes making the content ready for use on different types of platform.

Packaging/scheduling   This concerns combining the various types of content together into broadcast schedules. This stage is undergoing significant change. Specifically, content increasingly needs to be able to be broken down into its constituent parts to allow it to be packaged in different ways for different platforms and accessed in different ways by listeners.

Advertising sales   Commercial radio stations typically sell airtime to local advertisers through in-house sales forces, and to national and regional advertisers through sales representative firms. Media planners buy according to the target demographic and time of day required. Research services are an important supporting aspect of this activity.

Distribution   The final stage of the value chain used to involve the transmission of scheduled broadcasts for consumers to listen to on their radios. In recent years it has become considerably more complex with new devices for transmitting programming and new ways of accessing programmes. (For discussion, see under 'Technological developments', below.)

Strategic issues facing the radio industry

Radio is also being transformed as a result of de-regulation and technological developments, particularly digital delivery and delivery over non-traditional platforms. Radio will not disappear, indeed these developments seem to be reinvigorating the sector, but like all sectors of the media it must contend with ongoing change, particularly in the nature of competition and of audiences. Radio has strategic advantages – its low cost, the scope of its penetration and its close relationship with consumers. But is also has strategic limitations, particularly that it cannot deliver graphic, personalised or interactive content.

Deregulation   National radio systems are being gradually deregulated the world over. In Europe ownership restrictions are being relaxed, more commercial licences have been made available, and the number of minutes per hour allowed for advertising has been increased, causing the commercial sector to grow. In the US the 1996 Telecoms Act allowed a wave of consolidation; this, coupled with increased automation, led to reductions in the cost base, and increased earnings and advertising revenues. The sector however is still fragmented, and more consolidation is expected to take place.

Technological developments   Radio is a robust medium. While the print, music and movie industries have responded awkwardly to technological discontinuities, radio has crested such challenges more gracefully. This may be because radio is less threatened by substitution – radio listening has always been an activity that can be carried out while performing other tasks.

However, radio must contend with the facts that there are now many more platforms by which to reach audiences, and consumers now have far more ways of getting hold of the music they once heard on the radio, as well as new ways of listening to the radio: digital radio has proved a popular aspect of digital television offerings, mobile phone handsets and PDAs are increasingly radio-enabled, and the consumption of Internet radio broadcasting (streaming) is fast approaching mainstream status. In addition, satellite radio and digital broadcasting (DAB) are growing in popularity. These simultaneously increase competition for radio stations, but also increase the overall number of listeners.

Internet radio   As of July 2003, four in 10 Americans had listened to Internet radio, and that figure had grown fivefold in five years, with listening split between radio programming available only on the Internet and radio station programming rebroadcast on the Internet. This growth looks set to continue with improvements in wireless Internet. Over two-thirds of these radio listeners saw the Internet as simply another form of radio – rather than a different and new medium.[27] For the industry, however, this is a considerable change, first, because Internet radio follows an on-demand rather than broadcast model, meaning listeners can choose when and what they want to hear, and second, because it allows listeners to hear programming from all over the world.

Podcasting   This term is an amalgam of 'pod' and 'broadcasting'. Podcast programmes are delivered directly to audiences as MP3 files over the Internet using the RSS infrastructure. Podcasts can be created with minimal equipment: a microphone, straightforward software and Internet access. Many podcasts are analogous to blogs in that they are essentially amateur radio shows on the net, although 'established' radio stations and increasingly newspapers offer podcasts of particular shows and iTunes, the online music store, has thousands of podcasts to download. A radio station seeking to rebroadcast programmes by podcast requires copyright clearance – and this explains why the majority of podcasts from established radio stations involve speech radio (for which stations own broadcast rights). However, the platform is also attractive for independent musicians who do not have contracts with music companies since it allows them to release tracks worldwide without needing backing from a music company.

Satellite radio   To date this is primarily a US development. It operates much like satellite television whereby consumers purchase a special radio, an adaptor for a conventional radio, or car equipped with satellite radio, and then pay a monthly fee to receive broadcast channels. Two US firms launched services in the US – Sirius and XM – although at the time of writing these look set to merge. Both aim at commuters and involve small antennae placed in car windows which receive the signals and retransmit these to receivers plugged into car stereos.

Satellite radio involves content from digital studios being uplinked to satellites and downlinked to receivers and repeater stations. Capital costs are high and services are expensive in comparison to traditional radio. However, it offers more channels, including niche channels, has no adverts, and the sound quality is high. In the US, where many local stations have a radius of only 40 miles meaning in-car radios need to be continually re-tuned, satellite radio offers the significant advantage of continuous national coverage. Further, because it operates on a subscription basis it operates under far less stringent regulation.

Thus, Howard Stern, whose morning chat show was deemed too strong for conventional radio can broadcast with impunity on satellite platforms.

Digital radio   Digital audio broadcasting (DAB) started in the 1990s and many large European radio stations now produce, store and broadcast in digital format. Despite the fact that a shift to digital involves large-scale projects and collaboration by government, broadcasters and equipment manufacturers, it is viewed as a step forward by all parties since it represents a more efficient use of the spectrum: 10 channels of digital broadcasting can be compressed into the spectrum occupied by one analogue channel. This allows broadcasters to provide a wider range of programming simultaneously on the same frequency, and lowers transmission costs. Listeners benefit from higher quality sound, better reception, easier programme selection, the ability to 'pause' and 'rewind' programmes while they are being broadcast, and the provision of programme-associated data such as text labelling of channels or music.

Uptake of DAB on the part of consumers was initially slow, chiefly due to the price of domestic receivers, but this is now increasing as lower priced digital radios become available. That said, international patterns differ, and while several million sets have been sold in Europe and Asia a world market is unlikely in the near future because Europe, the US and Japan have settled on different digital radio standards.

Digital audio broadcasting also poses challenges for broadcasters in that it broadens massively the number of channels available at a point where penetration of radio devices is almost total. This creates two strategic imperatives. The first is to segment audiences, identify attractive niches, and develop creative formats to serve these and thereby increase both audience share and advertising revenues – interactivity and consumer-generated content can be used to reinforce these processes. The second involves brand development. A strong brand can secure long-term viability and provide a platform for future growth.

A further challenge is that rights acquisition and the management of archive assets become complex. Traditionally, broadcast rights were acquired on a limited use basis. In a digital environment broadcasters need to be able to make content permanently available, or at least for a longer period. Talent and collecting societies do not always accept the automatic extension of use, and even if they do, it is unfeasible for all but the largest broadcasters to renegotiate all of their contracts with the rights holders. There are similar difficulties concerning the use of archive material, which not only needs converting from analogue formats, but the associated rights and contractual information may not be easy to find.

Film

This film cost $31 million. With that kind of money I could have invaded some country. (Clint Eastwood)

The film industry emerged in the 1920s and its historical development falls into three phases. The first, which ran from the 1930s to the 1950s, is known as the 'classical era'. Television had not yet become widespread, demand was strong and box office revenues were healthy. The industry was run by a cartel of eight studios which had a virtually guaranteed market for even the most unpromising films (Bart and Guber, 2003).

The industry ran according to the 'studio system' whereby studios had control of the entire value chain from actors to projectionists and produced a steady flow of standardised movies that generated predictable revenues, plus a few prestige pictures. Stars were signed up for exclusive, long-term contracts. Production processes were systematised in that stable crews worked together under a single production head or a few key producers. Directors were often freelancers who would contribute ideas on casting and editing, but did not have overall control (Bart and Guber, 2002). Four studios also owned or leased cinemas, including the majority of first-run cinemas in big cities that accounted for 75 per cent of box office receipts in the US (Bart and Guber, 2002).

The high point of cinema attendances was the decade after the Second World War. By the 1940s a round of mergers had left the industry dominated by five companies. The US Justice Department decided this represented inordinate control and in 1948 forced the majors to sell off their cinema chains and abandon various practices used to thwart independent producers. The studios lost both guaranteed outlets and guaranteed cash flow. The Justice Department's decision coincided with a movement of the population to the suburbs that reduced attendance at city centre cinemas. These changes marked the end of the studio system (Croteau and Hoynes, 2001). A further blow came with the development of television. By 1952 television sets were in half of American homes and television replaced movie going as the primary leisure activity.

The second industry phase is known as the 'New Hollywood' and lasted from 1951 to 1975. This involved a changing role for studios, a growth in independent production and changes in patterns of media consumption (Schatz in Collins et al., 1993). The studios were suffering from falling revenues, increasing competition from television, and less control over distribution. They needed to be more selective and focus on films that would have the best chance of being distributed, and also to find new ways to differentiate their products from those on television.

Their strategy was threefold. First they reduced the number of films made by changing from continuous production to a film-by-film basis. This meant their fixed cost base had to be reduced, so studios began to cut the numbers of permanent employees and lease production facilities. The second strategy was to make their films more glamorous and extravagant than those made for television. Third, they experimented with new technologies such as colour film, wider screens and stereophonic sound to further differentiate their products.

The shift to more lavish productions marked the beginnings of the 'blockbuster': expensive, high profile movies that if successful would cover losses from many other smaller films (Croteau and Hoynes, 2001). Typical subjects at this point were historical and biblical epics, literary adaptations and transplanted stage musicals – films such as *The Ten Commandments* (1956) and *The Sound of Music* (1965). The rise of the blockbuster made Hollywood increasingly hit driven from the 1950s onwards (Schatz in Collins et al., 1993). It also affected power relations in Hollywood: stars acquired more influence over production, and they consolidated this by employing agents and lawyers.

Concentration on fewer but more complex and expensive products made the success of each production more important. In response, studios began to search for the key stars, directors or producers that might reduce the risks associated with big budget films. They were reluctant to offer permanent, exclusive contracts since fewer films meant the stars would be under-used, and fickle consumer tastes meant that popularity could wane fast so that stars had shorter productive lives. But this increased leading actors' opportunities to negotiate contracts, and competition between studios for their services. As a result the cost of leading talent escalated, studios' costs rose and they lost control over a key production factor (Schatz in Collins et al., 1993).

The mid-1950s saw the beginnings of content repurposing – re-using the same content on additional distribution platforms, earning additional revenue streams each time. The Hollywood majors began to sell or lease pre-1948 features to television syndicators. In the late 1950s they started to embrace their competitors and diversify into television series production to keep their facilities in operation (increasing numbers of films were being shot on location) (Schatz in Collins et al., 1993).

The third industry phase dates from the mid-1970s onward. At this point the movie industry became caught up in a media-industry-wide consolidation process. From the 1950s onward there had been a trend for major studios to become part of diversified media conglomerates that were active in a wide range of activities ranging from books to theme parks. This reflected an intensified interest in acquiring studios arising from a range of factors – de-regulation, privatisation, the opening of international markets (Wasko, 2003). But while film production consolidated, its delivery systems and markets fragmented. Cable television, home video recorders, and changes to lifestyle as a result of suburban migration meant that by the start of the 1970s annual cinema admissions in the US had fallen to 1.7 billion from more than 4 billion in the mid 1950s. Over the next three decades the industry responded by enforcing the blockbuster model even more aggressively, cutting back on quantity but boosting quality, at least in the technical dimension, by increasing special effects. The top grossing films from 1968 to 2003 all featured extraordinary special effects. Three films in particular mark the changes that took place in Hollywood at this time (Schatz in Collins et al., 1993).

The first is *Jaws* (1975). In addition to being one of the first high-tech, high-cost thrillers, this film heralded a new style of making movies, one that consolidated a number of emerging industry practices (Schatz in Collins et al.,

1993). First, it demonstrated the power of content synergies: the film was based on a novel, the movie rights of which had been pre-sold before publication and publicity from the deal and from the movie spurred book sales, and vice versa. Second, it presaged the dominant role agents were to acquire: the entire deal was packaged by International Creative Management (ICM) who represented the book's author, Peter Benchley, sold the movie rights and represented the production team. (Both ICM and its main rival, Creative Artists Agency (CAA) were founded in 1974.) Third, it launched a raft of marketing techniques that were to become common practice. Most noticeable was 'front loading', that is nationwide release supported by saturation advertising to maximise box-office performance in the opening weekend. This was designed to ensure a strong early showing and provide a platform for early publicity before any damage could be done by negative reviews or poor word of mouth. These techniques represented a step change in marketing strategy and investment for the industry. This strategy worked because the release of *Jaws* coincided with the growth of the multiplex cinema in the shopping centre: by 1975 such cinemas were commonplace in shopping centres, creating an overall increase in the number of cinemas.

Just as *Jaws* can be viewed as demonstrating the emergence of agents, new marketing techniques and the rise of the shopping mall multiplex, another hit of this period, *Saturday Night Fever* (1978), illustrates the erosion of barriers between sectors of the media industry and the cross-media exploitation strategies that emerged as a result (Schatz in Collins et al., 1993). This movie starred a television sitcom star, John Travolta (one of the first stars to 'cross over' from TV to film). The soundtrack by the Bee Gees dominated the pop music charts, and helped trigger a disco craze in clubs and the music industry.

The third example, *Star Wars* (1977), represented a new type of movie – the super blockbuster. These were movies that could develop into franchises, with huge potential for sequels and prequels, and for commercial tie-ins and merchandising arrangements of all types. They targeted younger audiences and followed a basic formula designed to appeal to viewers with shorter attention spans: plot-driven (although neither plot nor characters are complex), a powerful score and musical theme, a fast-paced shooting style and a reliance on special effects.

The mid-1970s also saw a new relationship develop between television and cinema: the emergence of cable television and with it the US Federal Communications Commission's 'Must Carry' and 'Prime Access' rules increased demand for syndicated series and movies. The quality of television programming improved and in response movies became yet more sophisticated and costs yet more bloated. During the 1980s the price of producing an average film increased by 200 per cent, and the cost of a new film's first two week's promotion rose to $12 million (Shawcross, 1992). However, these responses did not guarantee success. High special effects budgets did not translate always into strong box office performance, and audiences became increasingly unpredictable and appeared to tire more quickly of particular genres or stars.

The introduction of home video recorders was another significant development. Hollywood was hostile to the invention and in 1984 asked the US Supreme Court to outlaw the video cassette recorder on piracy grounds. This request was refused since the technology could also be used for 'substantial non-infringing uses'. That decision was ultimately fortuitous for the industry in that it led to the video-rentals industry. This became a profitable new income stream, one that greatly increased earnings from blockbusters, since these proved to be the most popular home video commodity.

The manufacturers of VCRs, however, became embroiled in a costly battle over standards that was to become a textbook case of how not to introduce a new consumer technology. The VCR was launched by two companies offering competing systems: Sony introduced Betamax in 1975 and Matsushita introduced VHS in 1977. These two were incompatible systems, meaning material recorded for one system could not be played on the other. Customers were either confused or unwilling to purchase until a market leader had emerged. Eventually after an expensive battle the VHS format won out – although it was less sophisticated it was more flexible, efficient and, critically, Matsushita had acquired a far larger library of exclusive content that could be used on its systems.

Key players

Studios   Bart and Guber (2003) observe that since the 1930s the film industry has followed a pattern whereby an oligopoly forms which splinters in response to industry challenges followed by the creation of a new group of key players. Today's key players take the form of sprawling multinationals with tentacles spreading into every sector of the media industry. (With the exception of Bertelsmann, all of the global media majors have film divisions.) At the time of writing the key players are Sony Pictures/Columbia Pictures (Sony), Fox Filmed Entertainment/20th Century Fox (News Corporation), Buena Vista Motion Pictures Group/Walt Disney Pictures/Touchstone (The Walt Disney Company), Warner Brothers Entertainment/New Line Cinema/HBO (Time Warner), Paramount Motion Pictures Group (Viacom) and NBC Universal (General Electric/Vivendi).

Fierce competition between these studios coupled with an adherence to the hit model has increased the cost of producing and marketing motion pictures to the point where in 2000 the average major studio film cost $55 million to produce and $27 million to advertise and market.[28] The result is that only one in 10 films retrieves its investment from domestic exhibition and four out of 10 never recoup their original investment.

Given this failure rate and the scale of financial losses, it is curious that the major studios continue to invest at this level. One reason is the strategic importance of repurposing. These conglomerates have businesses in many different sectors of the media and need a constant stream of products to feed their global distribution architecture. Ancillary revenue streams from businesses such as theme parks, music divisions and television networks can offset losses from cinema distribution.

Indies The 'indie' or independent sector makes lower budget movies (often in the $2–5 million range) of a type that Hollywood increasingly shuns – character-based films, films that reflect a filmmaker's idiosyncratic vision, those which take artistic risks, and/or are rooted in specific cultural environments. The golden period for indies was the mid-1980s to the 1990s. By the late 1990s the major studios had seen the potential of this category of film and the majority had created indies of their own, increasing competition for projects and making finance harder to find.

Today the independent sector operates in an increasingly tough environment. Funding is particularly difficult with producers stitching together complex combinations of equity, tax-based finance, pre-sales and distribution deals in foreign territories which unravel easily, especially if production is delayed. Pre-sales are difficult to achieve when competing against commercial products from Hollywood and there are challenges in securing cinematic release and ensuring that films open long enough for word of mouth to build.

Business model

Originally the movie industry had just one source of revenues: receipts from seats sold in movie theatres. Successive advances in media technology have brought additional revenue streams, although the industry tends to be slow in recognising new technologies' potential and has in general greeted such developments with hostility. Thus, after initially refusing to provide programmes for television fearing a further contraction of cinema audiences, the studios eventually became key suppliers of programming. Similarly they tried to block the VCR, yet video and DVD sales and rentals were to become a major revenue stream for the film majors, overshadowing box-office revenues.[29]

Nowadays 'first cycle' revenues (normally covering a seven-year period) include cinema receipts, video and DVD, pay per view, pay-TV, free television, non-theatrical receipts (airlines, schools, etc.), merchandise and music. These are known as 'windows of exhibition', and are designed to ensure that revenues flow in for many years after a film is released in the cinema.

Film industry value chain

The core stages of the movie industry value chain are set out in Figure 2.8 and described below.

Acquisition/development The basic idea for a new film can take many forms: an original idea, an actual event, a play, a novel, a script, an article, even a poem.

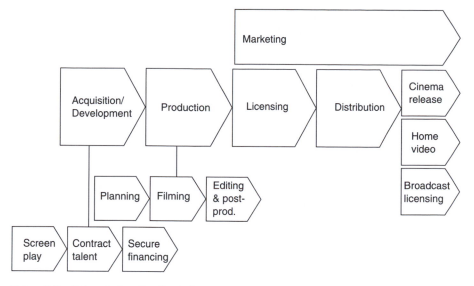

Figure 2.8   Value chain – the film industry

Around 50 per cent of ideas are adaptations of concepts from other sources (books, television, plays, etc.) or sequels or remakes of other films. This reflects the fact that films based on previous works are among the highest grossing productions (Wasko, 2003), and that uncertainties about public taste mean executives often feel safer framing new ideas in the context of past successes (Bart and Guber, 2003).

Development refers to the initial preparatory stage when a concept is turned into a screenplay or script which is used as a basis for funding decisions and to attract talent. Development involves acquiring rights, preparing an outline, synopsis and treatment, and writing, polishing and revising drafts. Scripts can be revised endlessly and development costs can rise to many millions for key projects requiring several drafts by leading screenwriters, partly because multiple drafts are viewed as evidence of meticulous preparation and creativity (Bart and Guber, 2003). At any one point a major studio will have around 1,000 scripts and plots under consideration, over 80 per cent of which will never become films but languish in what is known as 'development hell'. The most promising scripts can command asking prices of over $1 million and to ensure access to these producers employ 'trackers' to locate the best new ideas while they are still with agents and publishers and before they are formally offered to studios. Agents are central to the development stage. Not only do they match ideas to studios, but they also assemble entire packages of writers, actors and directors.[30]

Production   The decision to go ahead with a new movie is called 'greenlighting'. Once this has happened production starts, and this has three sub-stages. Pre-production begins when a movie is approved for production. It takes between two and six months and normally involves a small group of individuals in consultation with the director. The basic task is the initial planning, including organising the production, scouting locations, casting, hiring production personnel, and preparing the final budget, shooting script and shooting schedule.

Principal production (the shooting of the film) is the core production process and the most costly. The number of people involved increases dramatically: film-making is a very collaborative art form, and the shooting stage represents the high point of this with the creation of project teams of directors, actors, crews and sub-contractors. The director coordinates these various work streams and has the ultimate say in all decisions. This period is tense since time pressure is intense (it normally takes 6–12 weeks), financial risks are high, star egos are at play and there is often conflict between studio executives and directors (Bart and Guber, 2003).

Under the studio system directors would make four to five films a year. Currently a director can go four years between films, but will earn a great deal more for each one: top directors command up to $10 million per film, and new-comers around $3 million. On top of this fee they receive percentages of gross receipts, expense allowances and a wide range of perks.

During post-production the film is prepared for screening. This is a less pressurised stage that takes from four to 12 months, involving a smaller team of technical creative experts who edit the film, add special effects, dialogue, sound effects and score. A mid-stage milestone is the delivery of the director's cut to the studio. This triggers a further round of editing, screenings to focus groups, and, critically, the submission to the ratings board.

Marketing   The marketing and promotion process begins during production, continues during shooting, and gets most active on release. Marketing costs have risen dramatically over the last few years and can now be higher than production, with much of this spend concentrated on the films' opening. Market research is used to pre-test concepts and titles, to identify target audiences and develop a marketing strategy. The marketing plan involves advertising, the development of trailers and publicity. Publicity includes reviews, articles about the film in the press, interviews with the stars, and so on.

Licensing   This stage involves establishing the distribution agreements. Such deals are complex but critical since they give the distributor the right to decide how, where and when a film is distributed and how it is advertised and promoted. They also govern how money flows as well as power relationships in the industry (Wasko, 2003). Since the 1970s distribution strategies have become more complex and more significant. Blockbuster movies will be pre-booked in 3,000–4,000 screens, requiring distributors to commit themselves to significant campaigns heavily dependent on significant television purchases.

Distribution   Films are licensed to distributors for a specific period of time and the distributor arranges the cinema release, storage and transport of prints, accounting and collecting receipts from cinemas. The distributor also conducts market research and is responsible for the marketing strategy. The major distributors, part of the larger industry conglomerates, have tremendous influence over script, title, casting and final edits.

In 2003 there were around 6,000 cinemas in the US with around 35,000 screens. Movies are typically shown for a minimum of four weeks and big budget movies by major studios tend to be shown on 3,000–3,500 screens during opening weekend. If a movie is successful, theatres have an option to show the movie for further weeks – perhaps an additional four or eight. Less successful movies virtually disappear from the cinemas after four weeks.

Digital projection promises to alter distribution fundamentally. It allows movies to be delivered as digitally scanned versions of the master film print that can be uploaded to a server and projected digitally. This means better picture quality, significant costs savings for the studios and better copyright protection, since movies can be encrypted before distribution and unlocked by the cinema. Cinemas can vary exhibition methods, perhaps show one film more often, or a selection of movies in rotation.

Digital distribution to consumers – allowing customers to purchase and download films from the Internet at the same time that they are released on DVD – is also gathering pace. While the studios are concerned about piracy theft, they recognise they must provide a legitimate response to illegal downloading, and that this could be a response to falling cinema attendances and DVD sales. Should such systems succeed they will benefit from lower shipping and inventory costs, but could damage relationships with retail chains.

Strategic issues facing the film industry

Stars　The economics of the movie industry are negatively affected by the industry's dependence on a small number of stars which it believes are central to its success. Star-driven movies get bookings in prime cinemas at the best times of year, are shown on the biggest screens at multiplexes and distributors spend more promoting them.

This dependence dates back to the studio system. Under the studio system leading actors were under contract for a number of films over a number of years to studios who crafted their images and built their following. Salaries were affordable and overall costs were under control. But in the late 1950s stars such as James Stewart and Charlton Heston began to demand reduced payment upfront but a share of the total revenues. This risk-sharing approach appealed to studios who were then suffering from falling attendances. Eventually, however, these agreements evolved into no-risk deals for the stars. Today a top star will receive up to $25m in upfront payments against 20 per cent of gross receipts, plus a share of income from the home video and DVD sales, merchandising, music and other ancillary revenues. In addition there is a weekly expense allowance, cars and staff such as bodyguards, trainers and chefs. In addition, stars often make demands about the nature of the film itself,

requiring a minimum overall budget (often around $15m), a top-rank direc-
tor, a major distributor, a good script and an intriguing character.

The stars also exert indirect influence on the content of films. In order to
finance star casting a film must be geared to the largest possible audience –
often teenagers and young adults. To appeal to this span the story must be
accessible to the global market, which means in turn simple plots and minimal
dialogue.

Piracy   Studios have always been plagued by piracy but in recent years new
distribution platforms have given the problem several new dimensions. The
most significant are the sale of illegal copies and Internet piracy. Sales of
pirated DVDs offer high returns and relatively low risks and have proved
attractive to organised crime groups. Police seizures of these products are
growing year on year. So far the industry has been shielded from the full force
of Internet piracy by the long download times involved, although faster
Internet connections will reduce this protection.

Music

> The whole music business in the United States is based on numbers, based on unit sales and
> not on quality. It's not based on beauty, it's based on hype and it's based on cocaine. It's based
> on giving presents of large packages of dollars to play records on the air. (Frank Zappa)

The music industry is a vibrant sector rife with contradictions. It has high levels
of independent small-scale niche activity – as evidenced by the constant
stream of indie labels and new genres, but also one of the highest levels of
concentration with over 80 per cent of new releases coming from just four global
conglomerates.

As with other branches of the media, technological advance has shaped the
development of the sector (see below) but societal developments are an equally
important influence. For example, in the US after the Second World War growing
numbers of middle-class teens, coupled with the growth of advertising and of the
retail industry, led to the emergence of the music industry as we now know it
(Vogel, 1999). In recent decades growth in the developed markets, the Americas,
Western Europe and Japan, has slowed due to competition from other digital
media products (PCs, the Internet, mobile phones, games consoles, etc.), with the
music industry's main target demographic – 16–24-year-olds – particularly heavy
consumers of these products.

Music majors

The music industry is one of the sectors of the media with the highest concentration and internationalisation of capital (Sanchez-Tabernero in Albarran

et al., 2005). For the second half of the twentieth century five companies, the majors, have been responsible for over 75 per cent of the world market for recorded music. These organisations are some of the most internationalised in the media (Aris and Bughin, 2005). Until the advent of digital technology they were highly vertically integrated and active in all stages of the value chain apart from retailing, with activities stretching from recording and duplication to global distribution and marketing.

The industry continues to consolidate, in the main a response to falling profits. Vivendi merged with Universal Music in 2002, and in 2004 Sony Music and the Bertelsmann Music Group joined forces, leaving the industry dominated by four global players: Warner Music Group, Universal Music Group, EMI Group and Sony BMG. These players continue to acquire independent music labels to add diversity to their ranges in much the same way that large publishers have acquired smaller book imprints. And as with book publishing, the acquired companies normally continue in their area of specialisation, but benefit from greater critical mass in terms of marketing and distribution.

As with other sectors of the media, the increasingly large amounts paid to stars, or anticipated stars, have introduced significant structural problems for the music majors. The costs of guaranteed artists' royalties and marketing have become so high it is becoming impossible to achieve the sales necessary to support them (Vogel, 1999). As a result, less expensive mid-list artists get far less production or marketing attention, depressing their chances of success in the marketplace. This in turn creates a precarious situation for the music company whereby overall performance is disproportionately reliant on a few musicians. Less than 20 per cent of new releases provide a return on investment, meaning that those that do succeed must cover the costs of the unsuccessful products.

Music companies seek to share the risks of new products with artists through a long established and much disputed practice known as recoupment. This involves a record label giving an artist an advance to finance the production and marketing of an album and then keeping royalty payments due to the artist until it has recovered its investment. First albums by new artists seldom recoup their production and marketing costs so the unearned advance is carried over to the next album. This can mean that an advance is never earned out and musicians can be in debt to the music company for years.[31]

Many see this as an abuse of the system since record companies can manipulate royalty statements by inflating recoupable costs and reducing royalty payments. The industry estimates that an artist signed to a major label will need to sell over a million units in order to offset costs, and according to the Recording Industry Association of America (RIAA) only 10 per cent of albums achieve profitability. The band XTC, during an acrimonious fight to end their contract, claimed that the label Virgin made £30m out of the band, but that because of recoupment charges the band didn't make a profit for 18 years. In its defence, the industry argues that labels take an enormous risk in financing new albums and recoupment allows them to bring more music to the market.

Independent labels

Independent record companies are an established element of the sector, responsible for around a quarter of global music sales (Hesmondhalgh, 2002). Although there is an established progression whereby successful and well-known independent labels are acquired by the music majors – examples include Blue Note, Motown or Def Jam – their places will be taken by a new crop of small labels.

Indies focus on new or special interest genres and play an important role in finding new talent. Technological advances have breathed new life in the sector. Relatively inexpensive recording devices and instruments allow more musicians to produce studio quality music without professional recording studios. Sites such as Myspace.com or sessionsound.com allow musicians to upload their music to global audiences.

Business model

Music companies have traditionally had two principal sources of income: the sales of CDs, and royalties from music publishing. Now new income streams are developing including audio downloads, ringtones, touring, merchandising and sponsorship. Thus, while physical sales remain central to the business and will outstrip digital for many years to come, there is fundamental transformation at work.

CDs were first introduced in the early 1980s at a price of around $14, double the price of an LP. Record companies justified this on the grounds that CDs were more durable, provided superior sound, and required expensive new facilities to produce. While the cost of physically producing a CD has dropped dramatically since then, marketing costs have grown (not least because promotional music videos have now become standard practice), and prices have remained constant. Since the advent of digital downloading, the music companies have actually increased the average price of CDs to retailers each year, hoping to offset a decrease in unit sales they claim is due to illegal downloads. These price increases have been passed on to consumers.

Seventy-five per cent of music company revenues come from back catalogue sales which carry higher profit margins because production and marketing costs have been written off. Reissuing and reconfiguring back catalogue material for 'nostalgists' (who buy albums that remind them of their youth) and classicists (who build collections of classic music) now accounts for over 10 per cent of sales.

Music publishing   This involves exploiting catalogues of song rights for use in film, television, advertising and video games. Working with television advertisers to have an artist's songs placed in commercials is another marketing method that generates licensing income for the record company.

Figure 2.9 Value chain – the music industry

Music publishers originally dealt with printed music and scores. While this is still the case for classical music, music publishing for popular music involves matching new compositions with recording artists, collecting royalties and protecting against copyright infringement.

Music publishing is more predictable and less risky than the recorded music business. Publishers purchase songs with a proven track record that can be exploited over many years, and there is an established global infrastructure for collecting royalties. Music publishers also earn money from sales of CDs. They are, however, less dependent on that revenue stream and as a result have not been so badly affected by Internet piracy.

Other potential revenue sources are concerts and sponsorship. Traditionally music companies do not have access to these, but many are seeking to revise contracts to give them rights to portions of these income streams.

Value chain

The music industry's value chain, illustrated in Figure 2.9, has the following stages.

Content acquisition There are many parallels between the music and the book industries' value chains. Unsigned artists send 'demo' versions of their music to either a music company or a music publisher hoping to be taken on. As with writing books, there is a voluminous stream of new material coming from content creators, which has increased as a result of low-cost digital instruments and recording technologies. And as with book publishing, only a small fraction of these creations will be accepted.

Signing artists Should a record company decide an artist has talent and market potential they are put under contract and an in-house 'A & R' (artist-and-repertoire) manager will start developing their musical style, setting up the marketing strategy and planning recordings. These A & R managers are talent scouts who view live performances, trawl the Internet and listen to the demos submitted to music companies in search of new artists and songs. They require a basic set of skills centring on recognising talent, developing that talent by introducing artists to specialists – songwriters, recording engineers, etc. – and providing marketing expertise.

Production   This stage involves all activities concerned with preparing the record for the market, from rehearsing, recording and mixing musical tracks to budgeting and arranging copyright licences. It involves a wide group of individuals ranging from the artists themselves to songwriters, arrangers, sound engineers, and more, all of whom make a creative contribution to the finished product. Producers guide the overall process, acting as artistic and business managers. The complexity of production and the number of experts involved determine the production costs. The final outcome is a master tape which is delivered to the record company.

Publishing   This stage is largely unknown to lay music buyers but is central to the health of the industry. Sheet-music publishers promote and manage the sale and use of sheet music in recordings, on air and in live events. Each time sheet music is used a royalty is paid, and this income is divided equally between composer and publisher. There are many independent music publishers, but the business is dominated by affiliates of the music majors.

Marketing   The music industry is intensely competitive. Promotion and marketing are central to the success of new products and the marketing department is often the largest and most powerful of a music company.

The tasks at the marketing stage of the value chain include promotion, merchandising, and publicity and advertising. Promotion involves ensuring the new tracks are played on the radio. This stage used to be notorious for payola (bribing radio stations to play records) and rigging music charts, reflecting the fact that radio is one of the most influential promotional tools for the music industry and key radio stations can make or break new artists. Today such practices have been cleaned up but competition for airtime remains intense since the majority of stations play fewer than 40 titles in rotation each week while the industry produces several hundred new records. Merchandising includes tasks ranging from designing covers to store promotions. Publicity and advertising activities include the production of promotional materials as well as organising media appearances and shooting music videos.

Distribution   Music companies have a variety of distribution channels at their disposal. Retail chains are the traditional and still the major distribution channel for recorded music. Their mark-up is around 40 per cent. Distribution to retail outlets must be managed efficiently: the volatility of public taste means that recordings need to be shipped fast in large quantities. Some music companies such as Columbia Records and BMG have established record clubs to sell CDs directly to consumers.

Retailing   There are two types of physical retailers. Specialists concentrate exclusively on selling music and related products. They have been hard hit by online piracy, the decline in CD sales, and pricing pressure from discount retailers. Discount retailers include chains such as Target and Wal-Mart in the US and supermarkets such as Tesco or Asda in the UK. While music represents a small element of their entire product range they have disrupted music industry retailing habits because they use heavily discounted CDs to attract consumers. As with book retailing, this new outlet has hit independent stores hard. The Internet is an important sales channel for music, mainly through online retailers such as Amazon.com.

Strategic issues facing the music industry

The music industry is being battered by a range of issues that are affecting profitability and placing question marks over the long-term future of the sector. The two most significant issues are the Internet and piracy.

The Internet   The Internet is proving to be a fundamental force for change for the music industry – whether this will ultimately prove positive or negative remains to be seen.

On the plus side it offers new ways to reach consumers and promote music. It has created new formats for music delivery particularly digital downloading. The market for legitimate downloads is expanding rapidly and allows a more dynamic connection with fans. Research suggests a significant proportion of tracks are being bought by people who would not have bought the album, and that people who buy music online tend to buy more music overall. Mobile music sales for ringtones are an important growth area, and the Internet is re-creating the singles market, which in the 1970s formed 20 per cent of record company revenues. The Internet has also led to the emergence of niche audiences for specific types of music products, and global networks allow these to be aggregated into global niches that offer significant market potential.

However, the Internet is also highly disruptive for established industry practices. Digital distribution bypasses the value chain stages that have traditionally yielded the most value for record companies, CD pressing and distribution. Musicians can upload tracks and market these online, bypassing the music majors. New business models along these lines are emerging, for example record companies that use the Internet to discover and distribute artists' work, to create online markets for touring artists with an established fan base, or to build a fan base for as yet unsigned bands. While successful examples of musicians bypassing the music industry in favour of the Internet are still rare, the opportunities are substantial and relatively straightforward in comparison to the complexities of signing a deal with a major music label. However, since it is problematic as yet to secure an income for digitally distributed music, a hybrid model seems to be appearing whereby the Internet is used to gain exposure and a following, at which point artists shift to more conventional arrangements.

Piracy   Piracy has been a problem since the 1970s when the invention of the audio cassette unleashed the potential for home taping. However, with analogue products only a limited number of copies could be made before they became unusable. Piracy involving digital copying is a far more significant threat since the number of useable copies that can be made is unlimited.

Online piracy involves peer-to-peer networks that allow users to share music files bypassing the music companies. The music companies, as copyright holders, see these transactions as theft and file-sharing as the root cause of the recent decline in sales. However, users and service providers counter that the root problem is that the music companies have persisted in using distribution systems and formats that do not match customer needs – bundling tracks together in albums rather than selling them separately, as well as charging excessive prices.

The music companies have employed a variety of strategies to combat digital downloading. These include suing the peer-to-peer organisations in order to shut down the websites (a lawsuit against Napster forced it into bankruptcy), suing individual users, seeding peer-to-peer networks with fake files containing incomplete versions of songs and even acquiring peer-to-peer operations (Bertelsmann's purchase of the bankrupt Napster). However after years of fighting illegal downloading and piracy, attitudes are beginning to change. The growth of legal online record stores and the attractive economics of digital distribution are changing the way in which music companies find, promote and sell new music, and, as with preceding new platforms, the industry is gradually finding a way to accommodate the Internet into its business models.

Notes

1 For a full history of MTV and analysis of its brand strategy see Tungate (2004).
2 Nielsen Media Research, NTI Annual Averages.
3 World Association of Newspapers.
4 For a detailed history of the development of the newspaper industry see The World Association of Newspapers' 'Newspapers: a brief history', at www.wan-press.org. This section draws heavily on this source.
5 Majoribank's 'Strategising technological innovation: the case of News Corporation', in Cottle (2003) provides insight into how developments in information and communications technologies have had a profound impact on production and organisational processes in the newspaper industry.
6 In 2004 the benchmark of $1 billion revenue was reached for US online newspaper titles. However, the portals Yahoo!, Google, AOL and MSN generated over eight times as much advertising revenues as the entire online newspaper industry (*E-Marketer*, 18 August 2005).
7 Cited in 'I've had it with men', at www.media.guardian.co.uk/print/0,,329968015-105414,00 htm, accessed 04.06.06.
8 This book provides a valuable and detailed overview of the magazine sector and is a key source for the information in this section of the book.
9 *The Magazine Handbook*, at www.magazine.org.

10 www.mediainfocenter.org/magazine.
11 *Hall's Magazine Reports*, December 2002.
12 ABC, 2004; MRI, Fall 2004.
13 www.fipp.com.
14 *Hall's Magazine Reports*, December 2004.
15 *The Magazine Handbook*, at www.magazine.org.
16 Presentation by the US Postal Service to the International Federation of the Periodical Press, Bern, 2006 (www.fipp.com).
17 Jupiter Research Data.
18 Veronis, Suhler Stevenson, 2002.
19 Source: Nielson Media Research, NTI Annual Averages data ©2004 Television Bureau of Advertising, Inc.
20 Offcom study of the communications market 2004: *Television*: 72.
21 Tad Friend, 'Laugh Riot', *New Yorker*, 28 September 1998.
22 This list draws on a number of sources including Kuhn, 1984; McQuail et al., 1990; Blumler, 1992.
23 wwww.nab.org/radio/radfacts.asp, accessed 06.09.04.
24 European Commision (2002) *Eurostat Report: Statistics on Audiovisual Services*, p. 114.
25 M Street Corp., 2003, at www.mediainfocenter.org/music/radio.
26 For 1999 radio's share of revenue was 12 per cent against 41 per cent for television and 38 per cent for magazines (McCann-Erikson).
27 2003 Arbitron Inc. /Edison Media Research.
28 www.mpaq.org/anti-piracy.
29 *Financial Times*, 30 November 2004: 33.
30 For a fuller discussion of the role of agents see Bart and Guber's (2003) book on the movie industry, *Shoot Out: Surviving Fame and (Mis)fortune in Hollywood*.
31 For a discussion, see Hesmondhalgh, 2002, p. 169.

THREE

Common Trends in the Strategic Environment

The effective organization of industrial resources, even when considered in its rational aspects alone, does not approximate to one ideal type of management system ... but alters in important respects in conformity with changes in extrinsic factors. These intrinsic factors are all, in our view, identifiable as different rates of technological or market change. ... By change we mean the appearance of novelties: i.e. new scientific discoveries or technical inventions, and requirements for products of a kind not previously available or demanded. (Burns and Stalker, 1961/1994: 96)

This citation comes from a classic book writter in the 1960s on the management of innovation – one of the few that draws on the media industry for its examples. It is included here because it neatly underlines the key drivers of environmental change for the media today – changes in technology and changes in consumer behaviour – and also the enduring nature of these themes. These two elements have always driven the practice and content of strategy in the media, what is different in the current context is the velocity, intertwinedness and therefore complexity of these elements.

This chapter draws together the previous chapter's analysis of developments in the media industry's constituent sectors to highlight these and other common themes that are shaping the strategic environment of media firms and which are driving both the content and processes of strategy.

Ongoing technological change

Viewed longitudinally technological change has been a consistent and long-standing challenge for the media industry. The long-term erosion of traditional media products by new media ones is inevitable (Picard, 2003), although as Riepl (1913) and Fidler (1997) stress, new forms of communications media do not extinguish previous ones, but rather force them to evolve and adapt. This constantly shifting 'technological carpet' gives rise to one of the core strategic challenges for strategic management – adapting strategy and organisation in response to these developments. And it is skilled at responding to this challenge – when faced with major shifts, the constituent sectors of the industry have shown a remarkable ability to adjust their products and processes and carry on, albeit with different business models and lower revenues.[1]

However, from a strategic perspective, the changes experienced over the past 50 years represent, in the main, incremental alterations to the status quo. The strategic context of the media sector has remained 'mature' (Porter, 1980), with slow growth, strong competition between a known group of players and knowledgeable customers. The 1990s, which brought the full-blooded advent of the Internet and digitalisation, heralded a new era, one that emerged with unprecedented speed. At the time the Internet appeared to be the prime driver of change, although it is now clear that digitalisation is at least as important a development. Many of the threats and opportunities in the current strategic environment can be traced back to this single advance that has transformed the delivery system of virtually all media products. The Internet could not offer songs to download and newspapers could not provide online articles and podcasts, if those products had not already been transformed into digital code.

Once digitalisation and the Internet joined forces, the ensuing up was tremendous. It altered industry structures, accelerating the formation of network structures and creating new strategic interdependencies between organisations that might also be competitors (the UK's Freeview digital television consortium is a good example). It dismantled business models – think of the impact of peer-to-peer file-sharing for the film and music industries. At the same time, these changes have been a force for revitalisation, 'cleaning up' out-of-date products and business models and forcing sectors to reinvent themselves, enlarging income potential by allowing brands to be leveraged across more platforms.

Acceleration of the hit model

In the creative industries success always begets more success, but in an era of globalisation the success can be very big indeed. (Hutton, 2007: 24)

A constant strategic challenge in the media industry is that content is supremely unpredictable. Despite decades of research and increasingly sophisticated marketing techniques, it is impossible to predict which products will succeed. However, hard companies try to extrapolate formulae from past successes, at base it is a game of chance. Content involves alchemy – informational, creative and entertaining elements are combined in a way that may or may not strike a chord with public taste. It is not possible to fully explain why *Titanic* was a world-wide hit and *Waterworld*, released at a similar point with a similar theme and a similar budget, flopped. As we have seen, the music industry expects that 80 per cent of its new CDs will fail to cover their costs despite the experience of the executives who signed up the artists concerned, and during Katzenberg's decade at Disney, of the thousand plus projects he oversaw, just 10 per cent accounted for 91 per cent of the studio's operating income (Stewart, 2005: 2).

In response to these existential uncertainties the media industry has employed two strategic responses. The first, which was employed for decades and is still used in mature sectors with low margins that do not have the resources or infrastructure to play the blockbuster game, is known as the 'mud against the wall' formula. This seeks to increase the odds of success by increasing the number of attempts. In product terms it means generating high volumes of unique products in the hope that a number of these will spark random interest. Thus publisher Bloomsbury had no idea that the first Harry Potter book would be a bestseller, and its initial print-run was around 500 copies – a standard quantity in book publishing for a first novel by an unknown author.

The primary impulse to create content under this system is creative or artistic, and the underlying assumption is that 'cream rises to the top'. The market, prompted by critical acclaim and word-of-mouth recommendation, will find good products and sales will follow as positive word-of-mouth publicity spreads. From an organisational perspective this is a *laissez-faire* approach: all products receive a certain amount of time and investment until clear winners appear, at which point marketing attention scales up rapidly. The disadvantage is that resources are spread thinly over a wide range of diverse products and revenues and profitability are low. The advantage is that such systems allow a wide range of employees to work creatively, meaning levels of intrinsic motivation tend to be high. Historical accounts of 'the golden age' of book or magazine publishing often describe media organisations operating under this product strategy.

In recent years this model has been replaced by the 'hit' or 'blockbuster' model. This is a risk reduction strategy that is becoming both more entrenched and more extreme in the broadcasting and entertainment fields, where blockbusters increasingly dominate the revenues of the largest media firms (Aris and Bughin, 2005). In a blockbuster or hit environment a few media products – bestselling books, blockbuster films television shows or sports fixtures – generate the bulk of revenues for media organisations, which become disproportionately reliant on these products,[2] and it makes strategic sense to pay high advances and royalties to top content creators and then spur demand by spending aggressively on promotion (Vogel, 1999). Media organisations' product strategy, then, involves identifying in advance a handful of products that offer the greatest market potential and then devoting the lion's share of investment and attention to these.

The primary content-origination impulse under this approach is economic rather than artistic, and the creative and marketing strategies are closely intertwined. There are two underlying assumptions. First, that larger budgets – for talent, production and marketing – mean larger audiences, and, second, that those audiences choose products according to how heavily they are marketed, that audiences can be 'herded to the cinema' (De Vany and David Walls, 1999).

A blockbuster strategy imposes a template on content creation. A new concept should appeal to the largest number of audience groups and eliminate the risk that particular market groups might reject the project. Blockbuster movies illustrate this concept neatly (Schatz in Collins et al., 1993). Ideas for new film must have the potential to be reincarnated in different media forms and become a franchise. This dictates the creative components: narratives and characters are simple, plots explore broad universal themes, special effects are extremely sophisticated – to compensate for the simplicity of other elements (cynics have suggested blockbusters are designed to work for subliterate audiences with short attention spans). There must be soundtracks strong enough to support linked CD and music videos. The term 'blockbuster' is inextricably linked with the 'high concept', a term attributed to Steven Spielberg. High concept movies appeal to wide audiences and have plots that can be described in a couple of sentences that instantly convey the gist of the movie (thus 'Bus with a bomb' is the high concept for the movie *Speed*).

Why is the hit model escalating? Why is the dynamic getting more powerful in the current environment? There are a number of underlying factors. First, audiences have become more fickle as the range of entertainment and leisure options has increased. Against this backdrop, the appeal of stars who can guarantee audience attention grows. Second, technological advances in recording, processing and transmission have increased the number of multimedia reincarnations that are possible, meaning more outlets to recoup investments, and therefore greater leverage for successful products – that is, the potential for economies of scale. Third, globalisation and the borderless nature of media products mean that the potential market for media products has grown, that the potential for economies of scope has increased. Fourth, consolidation means corporate purses are larger: the media majors have more to invest in content and stronger distribution architectures to support their products. Fifth, what is known as 'killer content' has proved to be one of the most powerful means of persuading consumers to abandon existing patterns of consumption and adopt new technologies and products. This has intensified the bidding for certain categories of content such as key sporting fixtures or films. Finally, there is a growing recognition amongst creative talent of their power in marketplace and a desire on their part to negotiate the best deals they can. This is related to the increasing prominence of agents and attorneys in the media and entertainment industries.

Demassification and the emergence of the niche

While the largest entertainment organisations continue to seek to perfect 'one-size-fits-all products' – the blockbusters that will appeal to the largest

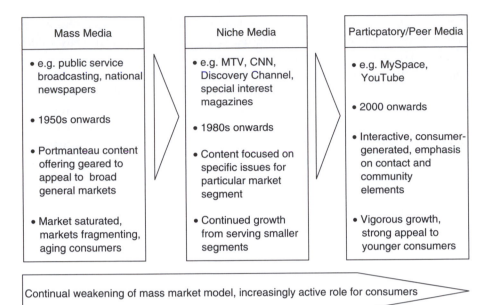

Mass Media	Niche Media	Particpatory/Peer Media
• e.g. public service broadcasting, national newspapers	• e.g. MTV, CNN, Discovery Channel, special interest magazines	• e.g. MySpace, YouTube
• 1950s onwards	• 1980s onwards	• 2000 onwards
• Portmanteau content offering geared to appeal to broad general markets	• Content focused on specific issues for particular market segment	• Interactive, consumer-generated, emphasis on contact and community elements
• Market saturated, markets fragmenting, aging consumers	• Continued growth from serving smaller segments	• Vigorous growth, strong appeal to younger consumers

Continual weakening of mass market model, increasingly active role for consumers

Figure 3.1   Evolution of media content models

audience possible – some of the most energetic growth in the sector comes from a contradictory trend, the emergence of the niche.

Mass media products are designed to reach large cross-sectional audiences and are based on technologies that allow massive duplication at low cost for huge audiences (newspaper or printing presses, radio or television networks). Advertisers tend to prefer products that are moderately popular with many and actively disliked by none – expressed in the television industry as the concept of the 'least objectionable programming' (LOP). This can only work, however, when the choice of viewing options is limited. Technological advances have reduced the barriers to entry in content creation, made professional-level production tools widely available, and provided global distribution and promotion architectures. The result is that across all segments, the mass media products – the television channel, the daily national newspaper, the general interest magazine – which owed their success to catering to many different groups of consumers simultaneously, are declining in favour of specialised products aimed at specific segments – a development broadcasting analysts term as a shift from broadcasting to narrowcasting. The stages in this development are shown in Figure 3.1.

Technological advance has allowed specialised content to be matched with specialist audience niches, and audiences have embraced this possibility. It appears that in many fields they prefer targeted products over generalised ones. Thus in the UK the between 1993 and 2003 the viewing share of non-terrestrial channels (i.e. niche or specialist ones) increased from 6 per cent to

33 per cent, at the expense of the dominant mass market networks, BBC 1 and ITV1.[3] Similarly, in the US, increasingly specialist niche magazines are growing in popularity while general news publications, *Time* and *Newsweek* for example, continue to lose market share.

This may not, however, result in the contraction of the mass media system that some observers predict (see, for example, Meyer, 2004). First, customers can now consume media in more ways and more places, which has expanded the market – for example, many people listen to Internet radio while at work. Plus, when niche products are combined with a global distribution architecture, then global niche markets can emerge – reality shows such as *Big Brother* are an example of this trend.

Personal and participatory content

But while the markets for mass media products such as television channels and national newspapers do seem to be splintering or 'demassifying' as it is sometimes put, at the same time substantial markets are aggregating around new types of media products, particularly those involving user-created social-network-spawned media content – participatory media or peer content (see Figure 3.1).

A vast amount of information is now being created, stored and shared by users often in social networking sites that combine personalised content with a participatory context. The type of content to be found on such sites spans a broad spectrum from restaurant and film reviews to more complex products such as blogs, wikis, discussion forums, photo blogs and podcasts. Audiences for participatory content models are often very small, but some products have very substantial numbers of users indeed. YouTube.com, where members can post home-made video clips (bought by Google for $1.65 billion in 2006) and MySpace.com, a social-networking and blogging service (bought by News Corporation for $580 million in 2005) are leading examples.

These products are hybrids and hard to categorise. They are communications products as much as media ones. They are designed to look and feel amateur and be extremely easy to use (anyone who can send an e-mail attachment can upload a video to YouTube), but involve high levels of investment and expertise.

Not surprisingly, they have led to a surge in consumer content – in 2007 it was estimated that over 45 per cent of all Internet users in the US read blogs (although it is also frequently claimed that the majority of blogs have only a handful of readers). For some this development represents a loosening of the big media's stranglehold. Certainly their popularity poses a challenge for the established media industry which depends on the aggregation of mass audiences, especially as major consumer brands are beginning to advertise on the most popular sites. But they are not unproblematic for users either. This type of content is certainly fresher and more spontaneous than professional content, but these sites and products do not necessarily subscribe to the public interest strictures of the traditional media. The content is unedited and they provide a personal voice – indeed that is part of their appeal. But the filtering, editing and quality control systems employed by the established media (and demanded by the market and regulators) are often absent except in the largest sites.

Media overload, multi-tasking, time-shifting and space-shifting

The trigger is technological, but the impact is behavioral. (*Blueprint for Transformation*, American Press Insitute, 2006: 6)

As niche products compete with mass market ones, as peer content increases, and as blockbusters become more intensively marketed, the media options available to consumers grow inexorably. Mobile telephony is moving into the field of content provision. Digital television is increasing the range of options for both television and radio. However, while we are certainly managing to consume more media (in 2005 Medill's Media Management Center found that young people consume 20 media hours in seven clock hours), this process cannot continue indefinitely – consumers' time and financial budgets are not limitless. There is evidence that readers are reading fewer publications and spending less time reading overall, and while the supply of television programming in Europe proliferated during the 1990s average television viewing times increased by an average of only two minutes per year (Picard, 2003).

Indeed, beyond a certain point the number of media options available ceases to be enriching and starts to become counterproductive. Simon (1955) pointed out that a wealth of information creates a poverty of attention: when information input becomes excessive, consumers become anxious and start to actively avoid additional information.[4]

Thus, competition is increasing not only between players but also for audience attention. Competition has not only brought many more new players and product offers into the market, but it has also heightened the battle for consumer 'eyeballs'. It is unlikely that available hours for media consumption will increase as dramatically as the number of products and channels available and organisations providing them.

None of these developments – increased competition, an associated decline in prices and media overload – bode well for the established mass media. In addition, there are significant changes in how media are consumed, specifically those concerned with time-shifting and space-shifting. In the analogue era different types of content were linked to specific appliances or distribution media and distributed according to fixed schedules. Television programmes were broadcast on a television set at set times, newspapers printed on paper were delivered in the morning, etc. Digitalisation, the increasing use of the PC, the Internet and the computer technology in set-top boxes, means that consumers can consume content on different devices, in different locations, when they want to, and select only specific elements from composite offerings.

Time-shifting is particularly significant for the mass media model. This occurs when consumers record and store broadcast content such as television and radio and consume it at a time more convenient for them. It clearly affects the packaging or scheduling function of the media firm – in extreme cases rendering it redundant. It also creates challenges concerning advertising, since the majority of personal video recorder users appear to choose to blend out advertising.

New strategic environment

Companies in the digital marketplace face a complex business environment full of ever-changing technologies, regulations and competitive threats. Investment risks, including billions of dollars set aside for the development of new products and services, acquisitions and new markets expansion, are daunting. Gone are the days companies ... could develop and unwaveringly adhere to a long-term corporate strategy. (Arthur Andersen, 1998)

From a management perspective, these changes mean a very different strategic environment, an 'emergent' one. Emergent environments are typical of the high-tech and biotech sectors. They are in essence highly uncertain: industry boundaries are unclear, business models are evolving, consumer preferences are not well known, and competition can come from hitherto unknown players (Eisenhardt and Brown, 1999; Robins and Wiersema, 2000).

Emergent contexts present a complex management challenge, particularly for incumbents encumbered by their legacy systems and processes. They will need to embrace new strategic directions that will lead to corporate renewal, if not transformation. They will require new domain-relevant skills – new fields of expertise. They will need to master new product areas that involve different types of content and different content competencies. They will need to be able to strategise more rapidly and make their organisations more flexible – but important business decisions regarding strategic priorities, technological choices and capital investments must be made with imperfect information.

But at the same time as they are damaging existing business models, technological advances are also creating opportunities. The Internet has lowered barriers to competition, allowing new types of players into the industry – players like MySpace, YouTube and Facebook are obvious examples of this phenomenon. Products for specific audiences from certain demographic niches and particular interest groups are emerging. Online bookselling has revitalised sales of backlist titles and digital printing means that titles need no longer go out of print. Digital recording technologies coupled with social networking sites mean new and greater opportunities for musicians to find markets for their compositions.

As this chapter has shown, the media industries are operating in mature sectors with rising costs, declining revenues, increasing competition for audience attention and evolving technological platforms. To ensure future survival and growth they must adjust to this strategic environment and this will require organisational transformation – the second part of this book explores various strategic and organisational tools which can help achieve this.

Notes

1 However this chameleon-like ability to adapt to habitat makes it very hard to undertake longitudinal studies in the sector, since boundaries and definitions shift so frequently.
2 Such 'winner-take-all markets' have long existed in the unmediated content markets – the performing arts, entertainment and professional sports (Frank and Cook, 1995), and began to take root in the media field back in the 1940s when the Hollywood studio system began to crumble. As their control over actors and distribution fell, the pressure on studios to produce hits, and to invest disproportionate amounts to ensure this happened, grew (Croyteau and Hoynes, 2001). Many factors underlie the emergence of this appraoch in the media field, with technological advances, particularly improvements in information processing and transmission, which has increased the leverage for key products and individuals, particularly important. This trend has significant social and cultural consequences, not least on cultural diversity, which are, however, outside the scope of this book.
3 BARB statistics presented to the Select Committee on Culture Media and Sport. Available at www.publications.parliament.uk/pa/cm200405/cmselectcmcumeds/82/8205.htm.
4 Picard (2006) points out that in 1900 *the New York Times* had 14 pages daily. By 2000 the average was 88, and this rose to over 100 pages regularly. Similarly, 800 MB of recorded information is produced per person per year.

FOUR

Convergence and its Causes

The next decade presents the most significant international business opportunity in history.
(Gerald Levin, cited in Mitchell, 1997)

This chapter explores one of the most widely hyped and fiercely debated concepts in the media industry over the past two decades, convergence. It is hard to overstate how profound a development convergence was expected to be in the late 1990s when the concept was first mooted. It was presaged as 'a second industrial revolution' (Henzler, 1998), 'comparable in scale to the biggest changes ever experienced by humans' (Barwise and Hammond, 1998), something that would herald a new industrial era described variously as 'The Era of Networked Intelligence' (Tapscott, 1996), 'The Network Economy' (Kelly, 1997), 'The Networked Economy' (Schwartz and Leyden, 1997) and 'The Age of Digital Convergence' (Yoffie, 1997).

Having taken a severe knock after the dotcom crash, convergence has resurfaced, albeit in a slightly different form from that originally envisaged, and with characteristics and consequences that are somewhat different to those anticipated previously. This chapter will explore convergence from the perspective of the changes that were expected, and contrast these with those that have actually taken place. Its goal is to provide a broad overview of the nature of convergence and its implications for organisations in affected sectors. The broad scope of this task in terms of the range of industry sectors covered, the variety of different types of organisations within each sector and the diversity of the various business tasks carried out, not to mention international differences between sectors, mean that it must inevitably concentrate on the broad picture. This, it is hoped, will deepen the understanding of the strategic environment discussed in the previous chapter, and provide a basis for the discussion of the complex interdisciplinary strategic challenges covered in the second part of the book.

The chapter falls into three parts. First, the phenomenon of convergence is discussed. Second, the various environmental factors and technological developments which have together provoked the phenomenon are explored. And finally, the chapter closes by assessing the current status of convergence and its implications for media organisations.

Constructs of convergence

The term convergence is both ubiquitous and poorly defined, more of a buzzword than a formally expressed concept. Although a fundamental element of business and policy discourse, scholarly definitions display little consistency. Indeed, in its field, convergence stands out as an impressively imprecise concept (as one academic pithily observed, 'uses of the term convergence have not converged'). It appears that in the field of convergence constructivism rules – what you understand by the term depends on who you are and where you stand. But while there is no commonly agreed objective definition of what is taking place, there are three discernible approaches towards interpreting the phenomenon which vary according to context and standpoint, described below.

Convergence of delivery platforms – network-focused definitions

This view of convergence is favoured by the telecommunications sector. The telecoms sector is of course responsible for supplying the 'conduit' for the new products and services arising from convergence. The intellectual roots of this type of definitions lie with the idea of the 'information superhighway', the concept of a universal information pipeline that was so popular in the 1980s. This concept itself was probably connected to the deregulation of the telecommunications industries worldwide, particularly the US Telecommunications Act of 1996.

This understanding of convergence sees advances in digital transmission technologies as a prime driver of change, the assumption being that once a variety of different messages are in a common digital format they can be transported and processed similarly. For example, Katz and Woroch (1997: 2) describe a 'Swiss army network: a single integrated infrastructure capable of delivering voice, video, and data services', Shepard (2000: xv) of 'all things over IP'. Baldwin et al. (1996: x) talk of 'an ideal broadband communications system that would integrate voice, video, and data with storage of huge libraries of material available on demand with the option of interaction as appropriate'.

Network definitions are also favoured by policy makers. Thus, at the close of the millennium, UK regulators proposed that 'Convergence will have taken place when all networks (broadcasting, satellite, cable, telephony) are each capable of providing all the different services (radio, television, voice telephony, data) and when each network (or platform) has a roughly equal share of consumer patronage' (Hooper, 2000).

Convergence of devices – product and service-focused definitions

Rather than a universal pipeline, product/service-focused definitions view convergence as leading to a universal convergence device, a multi-purpose 'information appliance' which combines the functions of converging sectors – Microsoft's 'digital home' concept reflects this view of convergence. This group of definitions approach convergence from the demand side, from the perspective of products and services. For example, Yoffie (1997: 2) defines it as 'the coming together of previously distinct products that employ digital technologies ... the uniting of the functions of the computer, the telephone and the television set', whereby, for example, 'a computer begins to incorporate the functionality of a communications device, and the telephone takes on the functionality of a computer'.

Convergence of industries – sector-focused definitions

This set of definitions view convergence as the technologically driven fusing of the content (i.e. media), computing (i.e. information technology) and communications (i.e. telecoms and broadcast distribution) industries into a mammoth new 'media and communication' sector' (Bradley and Nolan, 1998; Chakravarthy, 1997), commonly expressed in the so-called '3-C Model of Convergence' (see Figure 4.1). A subset of industry-level convergence is corporate convergence – whereby companies from one sector acquire or ally with other firms, or start new ones, in another of the converging industries.

Nicholas Negroponte of the MIT media lab is credited as the originator of this view of convergence. He predicted in 1979 that communications technologies will undergo a joint metamorphosis whereby the broadcast and motion picture industry, the computer industry, and the print and publishing industry would

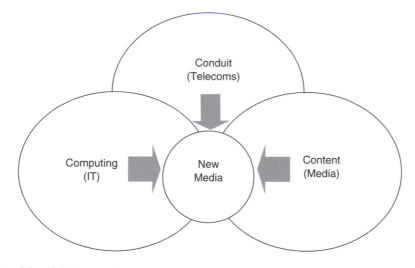

Figure 4.1 '3-C' Model of convergence

come together to create a new sector and new forms of communications (cited in Fidler, 1997). The consultancy KPMG developed a definition of convergence which captured the intricacies of the process from the perspective of media firms. This viewed convergence as:

> an on-going process which entails the coming together of content from the audiovisual and publishing industries, potentially separate physical infrastructures (such as those supporting broadcast television or telecommunications services) able to carry similar sorts of information at increasingly lower costs, the interactive storage and processing capabilities of the computer world and the ubiquity, improving functionality and ease of consumer electronics.[1]

Convergence in phases   Andersen Consulting (Shillingford, 1999) suggested that convergence would have three identifiable stages:

Stage I   Convergence happens between market segments within a sector, such as alliances between fixed-line and mobile telephony operators. At the point of writing this stage of convergence is well established in most markets. It has encouraged new entrants as well as growth across the segments. Decisions taken at this stage do not affect immediate performance but are important to long-term strategic position. Examples of Stage I convergence include IP voice, fixed-mobile, Internet devices and network PCs.

Stage II   Structural barriers between industry sectors start to disappear, for example mobile telephones become capable of receiving television programming, and telecoms players form content alliances with television broadcasters. This stage of convergence has also been reached in many developed economies. Strategies are often primarily defensive as companies seek to prevent the potential erosion of their markets. Competition is intense as they seek to ensure they can remain active at all stages of an expanding and ever more complex value chain. Customers benefit as prices fall, partly due to competition between providers, and partly to attract customer volumes.

Stage III   Applications are developed that require key success factors from communications, content and computing. At this stage traditional industry definitions become hard to apply. The iPod that straddles computing and the music industry, Facebook, MySpace and YouTube are examples of a Stage III convergence product.

Causes of convergence

In order to understand the concept of convergence, and its implications for strategic management in the media industry, we need to examine its underlying drivers – the various closely intertwined developments which are together provoking the phenomenon. The keyword here is intertwined. Trying to separate the various elements which together have triggered convergence imposes a somewhat artificial order on complex data. The various elements discussed below should therefore be viewed as pieces of a jigsaw: alone they do not reveal much; together they form a more complete picture.

The Internet and the World Wide Web

The exponential growth of the Internet and the World Wide Web is one of the main catalysts of the blurring of borders that characterises convergence. At root, the Internet is a loose matrix of interconnected computer networks which enables PCs to communicate globally at low cost. It has blurred the distinction between computing and communication and also between the communications and media sectors – since as a hybrid between a broadcast and a point-to-point medium, the content it carries combines elements of communication, information and entertainment.

The Internet dates back to 1969. It was created at the behest of the US Department of Defense as a computer network of defence-related research networks. The goal was to create a network that was highly distributed rather than hierarchical and which would not be interrupted in case of military attack. The system developed used packet-switching to ensure that it was indestructible – anything sent over the net is broken down into small packages and routed from one computer to another. The resulting system was both completely decentralised and entirely open. Since then it has been continually enhanced in response to developments in digital technology such as high-bandwidth communications and powerful software for sharing information.

Before the development of the World Wide Web (WWW), the Internet was essentially an e-mail service for the academic world – the TCP/IP protocol enabled universities in the US to exchange data. Mass uptake only started after the creation of the dynamic graphical interface the World Wide Web and the software browser Mosaic. Thereafter, uptake spread fast and the Internet became increasingly commercial. Kelly (1997: 31) attributes this growth to two elements in particular – cheap 'jelly bean processing chips' (see Moore's Law, below) and falling telecommunications charges.

The Internet is multiply significant for the media industry. It represents a new mass media platform, one that has grown faster than any other platform in history and that looks set to expand until it encompasses a major part of the world's population. It is also an instantaneously global distribution and communication channel. This allows traditional mass media content to be distributed in new ways, direct to home in digital form for example, as well as new types of content, user-generated content for example, to flow unmediated from producer to consumer.

Digitisation of information – from atoms to bits

At the heart of this frenetic business is the great enabler of digitisation. While past technical advancements merely mimicked old technologies and processes ... digitisation is creating completely new modes of work, play and personal development. (Arthur Andersen, 1998)

Digitisation and the Internet – as inseparable as Siamese twins – stand at the gateway to the turmoil under way in the media sector. Digitalisation is at least as important as the Internet in terms of driving convergence – some would argue more so.

The world's television and telecommunications industries have since their inception been based on analogue technologies. Now digitisation, coupled with the development of the computer as an interactive medium, means that digital technology is replacing analogue technology and the mass media are 'going digital'.

Digitisation simply means mathematically reducing all types of information (video, still pictures, audio, text, conversations, games or graphics) into binary form. Once in this format it can be manipulated and stored by computers, transmitted by networks in perfect fidelity to the original, and used immediately by another party on the network or stored for later use. Further once information is digitised, new possibilities for new products and services result. Different forms of information – pictures, sound, text – can be combined to produce multi-media products and these can be stored, transmitted and retrieved instantly from any point on the globe.

For the media industry digitisation has significant implications. First, content becomes 'platform agnostic', a 'liquid asset' which can flow anywhere (Wolf, 1999). Second, it becomes possible to customise content to match individual tastes – a development which undercuts a basic characteristic of the mass media, namely the distribution of an identical message to many recipients. Third, it is possible to create 'rich' media products – i.e. products combining many different types of content simultaneously.

Computing power – faster, cheaper and ubiquitous

Constant improvements in computer performance coupled with falling prices are another factor behind convergence. 'Moore's Law' (named after the founder of Intel, Gordon Moore) has been proposed as the governing dynamic. Moore's law isn't a law in any physical sense, but nonetheless has driven and will continue to drive developments in the IT and communication industries. This observes that every 18 months processing power doubles while the cost of generating that power holds constant, thus when personal computers were introduced in 1985 they cost $3,000 and by 1998 the price had fallen to under $1,000 and they had become significantly more powerful (Downes and Mui, 1998).

These developments meant that the cost of participating in the global networked electronic platforms fell and continues to fall. They also mean that it became feasible to extend digitisation of information beyond data to include voice, video and audio forms of content. The net result is that the potential performance and benefits of computing power increase further, which in turn attracts ever more individuals to participate in the new information networks, enabling performance and benefits to be further improved (see discussion of the economics of networks on).

Dramatic increases in bandwidth capacity

While there has technically never been a true shortage of bandwidth – more data could always have been transported using more sensitive and more expensive equipment – the media industry has nonetheless grown up in a world where bandwidth has always been expensive and, because of rationing by regulators, scarce or simply not available. Now, in parallel to the advances in computing power, technological developments in wireless technology, coaxial and fibre optic cable, routers and digital compression, mean that telecommunications bandwidth, the speed at which data can be moved through the phone network, is increasing rapidly while prices are falling. The phenomenon here has been expressed in the form of Gilder's Law (named after George Gilder, a futurist and economist), which states that the total bandwidth of communications systems will triple every 12 months, meaning that more data can be transported more quickly and at lower costs.

Standardisation of network architecture

The emergence of universal technical standards for communication is improving the exchangeability of signals of all kinds and also allows information to be 'disconnected' from the proprietary channels upon which it has hitherto been carried (Evans and Wurster, 2000). This can be seen as the third stage in a progression from proprietary systems (1950s–1990s) which featured closed networking standards (such as IBM's System Network Architecture), to standard platforms (1980s–2000s), typified by the IBM PC or DOS/Windows, and finally to universal standards. In the era of standard network computing which is developing, each computer is autonomous and functions as a peer of its 'colleagues', and there are de facto open public standards which were not established by companies or governments but emerged from widely used applications – examples include TCP/IP, HTML, WWW and PDF.

Open standards ensure compatibility between devices, which in turn means the exchange of data between members of the network becomes easier. This, combined with a rapid increase in the number of people and organisations connected by networks, allows 'everybody to connect with everybody else at essentially zero cost' (Evans and Wurster, 2000: 74), it also lowers communication and process costs, allowing the linkage of systems which were not compatible before.

Networked open electronic platforms

A crucial development arising from these various technological advances, ranging from the standardisation of network architecture to advances in distribution technology, is the development of new media platforms, namely high-speed, open multi-media communications networks. Telephone communications, mass media transmissions and computer data exchanges are gradually combining to create an integrated, interconnected system of multiple digital broadband networks that provides a global infrastructure – not least for the delivery of media content.

Indeed, networks are emerging as the dominant metaphor for the digital economy – as indicated by the number of names for convergence that feature the word 'network' (see the opening to this chapter). As Noam (1998) points out, we are witnessing the emergence of a 'network of networks', where in essence everything is connected to everything else. The increase in networks has three facets. First, we are seeing more networks – analogue and digital infrastructures, wired and wireless, point to multipoint, point to point, overbuilding of networks (cable, satellite, terrestrial, etc.) – offering multiple means of networking to homes and businesses. Second, we have better networks, partly due to the constant upgrading of broadband and narrowband infrastructures (fibre optic, satellite backbones, HFC, DSL), and partly due to improved performance (digital compression) and more flexible software. Third, there are more devices connected to networks (PCs, mobile phones, Blackberries, and so on).

Metcalfe's Law and network externalities

Networked electronic platforms are developing into the backbone infrastructure for converging industries, and networked environments exhibit particular characteristics which influence strategic options (Arthur, 1994; Kelly, 1997; Shapiro and Varian, 1999).

The 'economics of networks' dictate that when the value of a product to one user depends on how many other users there are, the product exhibits network externalities or network effects. Communications technologies are a prime example: telephones, e-mail, Internet access, fax machines, all exhibit network externalities. The driving force is positive feedback, encapsulated by Metcalfe's Law (named after Robert Metcalfe, the founder of the 3Com Corporation), which rests on the somewhat self-evident observation that new technologies are valuable only if people use them. Metcalfe's Law concerns the fact that the more people who use a particular type of software, mobile phone network, etc., the more valuable it becomes, and the more new users it will attract, increasing both its utility and the speed of its adoption by new users. This creates a virtuous circle, whereby the increase in value attracts more members, and the addition of more members dramatically increases the value for all members, in turn attracting even more members, and so on. This can be expressed in abstract terms in the form that for any communications network (not just computer networks) the number of nodes on a network yields that number squared in potential value. Therefore the sum of a network increases as the square of the number of members, or as the number of nodes in a network increases arithmetically, the value of the network increases exponentially.

Technologies subject to strong network effects tend to exhibit long lead times followed by explosive growth. Both fax machines and the Internet followed this pattern. It results from the positive feedback created as the installed base of users grows and more and more users find adoption worthwhile. Eventually a product achieves critical mass and takes over the market (known as the tipping point). Some of the most successful players in the IT, Internet and telecoms industries have been propelled forward by such dynamics. As a result, achieving critical mass becomes *the* strategic goal, since once the customer base is large enough, the market will build itself.

The innate characteristics of networked environments, therefore, have strong implications for those managing businesses in the converging sectors, particularly concerning the introduction of new products and services, pricing, and production and distribution strategies.

Deregulation

Forces of industry deregulation have served both as a backdrop to and a catalyst for the digital revolution. Over the last decade, deregulation has affected a wide range of industries, ranging from banking and aviation to public transportation and utilities, but it is the deregulation of national telecommunications monopolies that has acted as an important catalyst for the digital revolution. The US Telecom Act of 1996 led to a restructuring of the telecoms sector and a flurry of consolidation activity in the broadcasting field. The World Trade Organisation's Telecommunications Accord (1998) triggered a wave of competition in every world market by removing artificial barriers to entry and led to a wave of privatisations – for example in the telecommunications sectors between 1993 and 1998 privatisations valued at over $100 billion took place (Arthur Andersen, 1998).

Detailed discussion of this phenomenon is beyond the scope of this chapter, but it is worth noting that the removal of existing regulatory infrastructures, coupled with the radical market restructuring taking place in the sectors affected by convergence, has led to regulatory uncertainty – for organisations and for policy makers. Regulators face serious challenges in designing a regulatory structure for the emergent media and communications sector.

Globalisation

The globalisation of business is a defining feature of the current industry environment. This represents far more than the development of global organisations that operate in geographically dispersed regions. Rather, it represents the emergence of global markets, a phenomenon which is closely linked both to the development of the media and communications industries and the revolution in production and distribution they have precipitated. Indeed, in some respects globalisation can be viewed as the development of one large global network for trade and business.

As customers become increasingly accustomed, on the one hand, to sourcing goods from all over the world and, on the other, demanding access to the same brands and goods from any point on the globe, organisations must compete across geographic divides and meet the needs of customers, wherever they are. This in turn has created a highly competitive environment which has forced the pace for the development and adoption of digital technologies.

Status of convergence

Convergence was seldom out of industry headlines at the turn of the millennium. It has fallen out of the limelight since then, but has not gone away, indeed it is probably more tangible a phenomenon than it ever was. In order to assess the status of convergence, we can turn back to the three definitions of convergence outlined at the beginning of this chapter and see how accurate have these proved to be.

Network-focused approaches

Network convergence in the 'pure sense', where all networks are capable of carrying all types of content, *and* share similar consumer patronage, is not yet reality. One reason is that concepts of network convergence contradict an important received wisdom in telecommunications engineering, that particular networks are best suited for particular types of information. Similarly, consumers demand different functionalities for different forms of information – and one network cannot guarantee to meet all of these.

Product and service-focused approaches

From the perspective of consumer products and services, a convergence of functions is clearly taking place. It is commonplace for mobile phone to offer the functions carried out by radios, cameras and even televisions. Digital television systems combine functionalities from the PC industry (the set-top box), telecommunications (the cable) and the media industry (television programming).

That having been said, a single multi-purpose, multi-function information device has not yet emerged. Indeed, rather than the emergence of a multi-purpose 'information appliance', a plethora of new digital devices and applications have emerged to meet the increasingly sophisticated needs of digital consumers. Thus, from a device standpoint, the term 'divergence' may be more accurate than 'convergence'. This means that media firms are likely to need to revision content for a number of different platforms for the foreseeable future.

Industry-sector focused approaches

What we call 'Large C convergence' has not evolved as quickly as, or in the way, originally anticipated. Tom Price, Global Managing Partner, Andersen Consulting Communications-High Tech Practice. (Cited in *Financial Times*, 18 March 1999)

While, in immediate terms, the media, telecommunications and IT sectors are all clearly distinguishable, there is evidence of a blurring between the industry groupings. For example, the majority of companies in the telecoms sectors are actively engaged in the creation, packaging and transmission of forms of content other than voice, especially entertainment-related content.

Similarly, at a corporate level, there are many examples of convergence. Microsoft has for many years been actively exploiting the potential of convergence (Chakravarthy, 1997), and is active in video games (via an alliance with Sega), in filmmaking (an alliance with Dreamworks), in television (through its joint venture MSNBC) and in book publishing (through its acquisition of Dorling Kindersley). British Telecom and Telefonica are good examples of telecommunications players which have invested in the content sector.

Nonetheless, progress has been slower than anticipated and as time passes commentators are becoming markedly less confident and 'global' in their predictions. It has been suggested this is due to a number of barriers which were underestimated by those making early predictions (Shillingford, 1999):

- *'Sticky' consumer habits.* We adopt new products and services and change our habits of media consumption more slowly than expected. Many 'time poor' consumers are close to the limit of the amount of media they can consume.
- *Replacing existing technology takes time.* The complex ecosystem of phone lines, telephone poles, legacy computer systems, household brown goods can take many years to replace.
- *Deregulation is distracting companies.* Continuing changes in public policy, bandwidth auctions, digital switchover, and so on, are reshaping traditional competitive environments and adding complexity to strategic decisions.
- *Traditional media businesses have proved more resilient than commentators expected.* Despite some dramatic predictions traditional media businesses have withstood the arrival of the Internet surprisingly well. For example, in the US TV broadcasters actually experienced an increase in overall viewer numbers at the turn of the century (largely as

a result of changing demographics), and the appeal of peak-time advertising slots on the major networks actually increased, partly due to audience fragmentation, partly due to a surge of advertising from new economy firms on old media. As a result they experienced far less pressure to change radically than was widely anticipated. Now, however, it has become very clear that the Internet, and associated changes, will undermine traditional mass market business models. Traditional media firms appear to be open to engaging in the types of transition strategies predicted nearly a decade ago.

Conclusions

The term convergence was as common a term as the 'Millennium Bug' at the turn of the century. At this time it was generally viewed by the media industry to mean the technologically driven blurring of the media, telecommunications and information technology sectors. A decade into the process it is clear that, like many predictions, while it was not exactly wrong, it also did not fully capture the reality of developments. This chapter does suggest that some type of convergence is taking place, but this is far from a neat linear or clearly phased process. The tidy depiction of convergence provided in the 3-C model belies the chaos of reality. The content, communication and computing sectors are coming together, but the process is taking place at different levels and at different speeds. While there is a 'coming together' of distribution architectures, convergence increasingly seems to involve a subtler type of blurring, particularly between products and services.

Indeed, the most promising place to look for convergence may be at the level of business model and product. Thus, the most important new textbook publications are not simply just books, but have evolved into entire educational support systems for academics, spanning lecture plans, assessment and grading. Online sites such as MySpace combine content with communication functions. Specialist magazines are extending their brand into 'people media' – conferences, breakfast briefings and even job search services. Endemol's business models lay as much stress on mobile revenues as they do on the content of television formats.

Because the concept of convergence remains profoundly confused, both in terms of definition and of effects, it is difficult to draw anything but the most broad conclusions about its implications for media organisations and their strategic management. This task is complicated further by the fact that each sector has its own business model, technological platforms, product characteristics and potential substitutes: a licence fee funded public service broadcaster is affected differently from a satellite television broadcaster, a newspaper publisher differently from a school textbook publisher.

It is clear that the proliferation of technological possibilities, the profusion of alliances, the high capital investments required to participate in the digital arena, and the uncertainty about customer reactions to the new products and services have created high levels of strategic uncertainty. New players, new business models, and new forms of competition are emerging and providing an impetus for change in every sector of the media industry. From the perspective of practitioners on the ground the gradual integration of the media industry with those of information technology and telecommunications constitutes a reorganisation of existing market and industry structures and ongoing turbulence.

In the midst of this maelstrom, managers must continue to manage, and at the same time design strategies to ensure that their organisations make the transition from a classic to a digital media environment. In a world where much is uncertain they must identify the structures, competencies, processes and cultural characteristics that will determine success in a digital environment, and link these together into a cohesive strategy that creates a sustainable model for long-term successful performance. In addition, they must avoid falling into the trap of assuming that in a converged world nothing will be the same. Indeed, a critical challenge is to determine precisely which of the 'old' rules of the game still apply and which will be usurped by radical new concepts. Is convergence rewriting the whole rule book or just a few particular regulations?

This first part of the book has providing a broad outline of the media industry, its constituent sectors, and the changes convergence is bringing. Part II looks at the various strategic levers that can be employed to gain mastery of this environment.

Note

1   KPMG: *Public Issues Arising from Telecommunications and Audiovisual Convergence for the European Union* at www.ispo.cec.be.

Part II

From Context to Concepts

FIVE

Strategy in the Media Industries

Part I of this book dealt with the industry context, the strategic environment. It demonstrated that the media industries are far from monolithic, but rather a collection of highly individualistic sectors. Part II will demonstrate that strategic theory, too, is far from monolithic but is also a rich and variegated field.

This section builds upon the basis provided by Part I to explore a variety of different strategic approaches and tools that managers can use to respond to, and hopefully master, the media industries' strategic environment. It deals primarily with concepts, with theoretically driven approaches than can be used to guide strategic activities in the media sector. Its goal is to build a bridge between the general discipline of strategic management and the specificities of the media industries and media organisations. On paper this sounds like a relatively straightforward exercise; in practice, however, it is complex, due to a number of intrinsic aspects of the field of strategy.

First, there is the problem of breadth. The body of scholarship relating to matters of strategy is quite simply enormous. As Starbuck (1965) pointed out over 40 years ago – since when the field has continued to expand massively – potentially every single thing ever written about organisations can theoretically be described as concerning strategy.

Second, there is the problem of fragmentation or pluralism. Research in strategic management started in the 1960s. At this point the foci were business policy and general management, and the primary emphasis in research and teaching was single case studies (Hitt, 1997). Gradually, however, the themes of corporate strategy and firm performance rose to prominence, and with the publication of an influential book by Schendel and Hofer (1979) the name of the field changed to strategic management, a shift that was reinforced with the publication of Porter's equally influential book (1980) a year later (Hitt, 1997).

In subsequent years the field remained manageable, with investigations centred on three issues in particular: the effects of the environment on strategy, the importance of the fit between strategy and the environment, and the effects of strategy on performance; with most of these involving large samples using secondary data and statistical techniques (Hitt, 1997). Over this period the MBA course developed, and business policy or corporate strategy was often a capstone course in such programmes. These benefited from the fact that the field of strategy was still relatively coherent and rested on a widely accepted set of premises, assumptions, instruments and techniques. In subsequent decades, however, successive waves of research and critical reflection have generated a profusion of different concepts, approaches and schools. This has left the field richer, more mature and more subtle, but also differentiated and complex.

The third problem concerns compartmentalism – or incommensurability as it is expressed in scholarly literature. The various concepts and theories contained within the field of strategy are not only diverse, but in many cases inconsistent, if not contradictory. This is problematic for researchers and managers: 'accepting' the legitimacy of one particular model can often imply recognising alternative approaches as invalid (and also creates tremendous problems in terms of designing and teaching strategy courses, in that providing a thorough overview of the field can mean teaching a series of mutually incompatible theories).

A fourth problem concerns a fundamental difficulty establishing the boundaries to the field. Indeed, one of the rare areas of agreement in the strategy field is that there is little consensus concerning exactly what strategy is. If Starbuck is correct in asserting that virtually everything ever written about an organisation can theoretically be classified as strategy literature, then where, for example, does the discipline of strategy stop and organisational theory start? If we accept the assertion made by some scholars that all strategy is about change, does organisational change differ from strategic change, and if so, how? Translated into practical terms, which concepts and theories should be included in a book such as this, and how should they relate to each other?

There are, therefore, fundamental challenges in deciding what constitutes strategy, and, further, which of the many tenets and tools in the field are most relevant to managers in the media industries. One obvious selection criterion is to choose those most relevant to the field of media management. This is, however, problematic: media management is an emergent discipline and there is as yet no consensus concerning where the boundaries of the field should be drawn. Plus, although managers and researchers use the collective term 'the media and entertainment industries', as shown in Part I, in reality this comprises a broad range of sub-sectors, ranging from academic journal publishing to radio broadcasting, from textbooks to Hollywood movies, and each of these sub-sectors have very different environmental contexts, underlying technologies and regulatory influences, and so on. Thus the relevance of strategic tools can vary greatly.

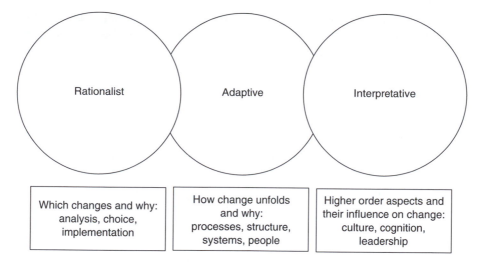

Figure 5. 1 'Organising' strategic theory (adapted from Chaffee, 1985; Johnson, 1987)

Dimensions of the strategy construct

One way to reduce the complexity in the field of strategy is by categorising or organising the theories within it. A number of researchers have developed proposals for organising the field of strategic theory (see, for example, Whittington, 1993; Rajagopalan and Spreitzer, 1996; Mintzberg et al., 2003). This book uses a categorisation which has been adapted from those of Johnson (1987) and Chaffee (1985). This views strategic models as falling into three core schools which are situated on a continuum moving from rationalist approaches on one side to interpretative approaches on the other, as depicted in Figure 5.1. It provides a means of reducing the complexity prevailing in the field, and accommodating the various, divergent, key concepts. These approaches are described below.

Rationalist approaches

Just about all typologies of strategy literature start with some variant of this category. It includes analytic approaches to the task of strategy, and concepts which assume firms and individuals behave in the main rationally (they can also be termed 'positivist' because of their reliance on analytical reasoning). Rational or classical approaches draw on industrial organisation (IO) economics and have a deterministic view of organisational behaviour. They focus on the strategic behaviour of firms, the structures of markets and their interactions.

Morgan (1986) uses the metaphor of 'organisations as brains' to describe rationalist approaches: organisations are rational systems that operate as efficiently as possible with standardised processes, mechanistic designs and clear goals. Chaffee (1985) describes such approaches as 'linear' to denote the methodical, directed, sequential action they entail. Rationalist approaches have also been termed the 'external environment school' because of their focus on the external factors that provide competitive and comparative advantages and limitations.

The strong influence of this school reflects the development of the discipline of management in general. In the 1960s formal business education grew dramatically in the US, business strategy grew as a field of study, as did the strategic planning function in firms. The business environment in the US at that time was remarkably stable and uncomplicated: US companies faced relatively little competition from abroad and the economy was growing strongly (Fulmer, 2000). During this period the foundation stones of rational approaches to strategy were laid which were to be extended and enhanced in future years and still provide the cornerstone of undergraduate and MBA management courses today, as well as the activities of management consultants (who have created some well-known models in the field, such as the Boston Consulting Group's growth/share matrix or Bain's Structure-Conduct-Performance (SCP) paradigm).

According to the rationalist school, strategy is essentially a plan, formed through the methodical, sequential analysis of the environment and the evaluation of the extent to which organisational resources can be utilised to take advantage of environmental opportunities or to address environmental threats (Minzberg et al., 1998). Some of the strongest and most enduring theoretical influences are Chandler's work in the distinction between strategy and structure and Porter's (1980, 1985) work on competitive strategy and competitive advantage. So, according to Chandler (1969: 383) strategy is 'the determination of the basic long-term goals and objectives of an enterprise, and the adoption of courses of action and the allocation of resources necessary for carrying out these goals'. The underlying assumption is that competitive forces in the marketplace determine the success and long-term viability of the media firm.

Thus, the external environment is the starting place for strategy, and the uncertainty and complexity present in the strategic environment can be reduced through comprehensive analysis. The models within the rational school focus on the content of strategy, on how plans should be formulated that provide a clear basis for strategic decision and action. They would, for example, help managers in the media and entertainment sector review the attractiveness of particular sectors or products and evaluate whether to enter or exit a particular field, or grasp broadly how environmental developments are changing the dynamics and structure of their industry – for example the impact of the Internet on the music sector, or of digital delivery systems on broadcasting. Key concepts include Porter's Five-Forces Model (explained below p. 111), Porter's Value Chain (explained in Chapter 2), the Boston Consulting Group's growth matrix and experience curve, and the resource-based view (also discussed below p. 115).

A large proportion of existing research into strategy in the media works with rationalist approaches (see, for example, Croteau and Hoynes, 2001; Doyle, 2002b;

Hesmondhalgh, 2002; Sanchez-Tabernero and Carvajal, 2002). In broad terms these studies tend to explore whether a variance (change in state) has occurred in the media sector and if so which causal factors may be responsible – for example, whether the number of joint ventures and alliances by media firms has increased and if the search for specific strategically relevant resources can explain this.

This is understandable. For researchers whose primary scholarly interest concerns industry conditions and structures, regulatory and policy issues, or the impact of media content on media and society, an aggregate level of enquiry makes sense. This research has provided fine-grained insights into shifts in the media landscape and into the drivers of firm behaviour. However, it has meant that the processes of management within the media organisation and that the complex interplay of organisational phenomena at play have received less attention.

Further, rationalist models lose validity in rapidly changing industries where structural boundaries are breaking down. Fulmer (2000), for example, discusses the challenges of applying the Porter Five-Forces Model to organisations such as Sony or Microsoft since it is almost impossible to decide which industries they are competing in. Indeed, classic approaches to management in general do not adapt well to changing circumstances (Morgan, 1986). Essentially, they involve exploring the logical consequences of various strategic options within a given set of circumstances. Increasing dynamism and complexity of the media industry's environment, the fact that markets become increasingly 'fuzzy' – that is, key aspects of the market structure, such as the probability of substitution, the number of firms in a market and barriers to entry, are difficult to identify, describe and define (Lacy and Simon, 1993) – mean that it is difficult to make the assumptions necessary to apply these models. Although it should be noted that key architects of the school dispute this conclusion (see, for example, Porter, 1996).

One aim of this book is to demonstrate the relevance of concepts from the adaptive and interpretative schools to the media industries, and underline how these might complement insights gained through the application of the rational frameworks. For this reason the subsequent chapters, in the main, focus on concepts and tools from these two schools (for a detailed breakdown see the 'Conclusions' to this chapter). In order to balance this out, two important models from the rational school are discussed below and applied to the media sector. A third model from this school, the value chain, is applied in the sector by sector analysis, discussed in Chapter 2.

Porter's Five-Forces Model

This is probably the single best-known model from the 'rational' school. The base assumption is that above average performance requires determining an optimal strategic position through close analysis of the dynamics of competitive rivalry in the industry concerned. The state of competition depends on five competitive 'forces', and the collective strength of these determine the ultimate profit potential in, and attractiveness of, the industry (Porter, 1980). The forces are: the threat of entrants, buyer power, supplier power, the threat of substitutes, and rivalry among existing firms. Application of this framework will support an organisation in finding a product-market position that allows it to exercise bargaining power over suppliers and customers while excluding new entrants and rivals from its product-market positions.

If we apply this model to the *Encyclopaedia Britannica* case which will be discussed in Chapter 6 we can see that before the advent of the CD-Rom and the PC, rivalry in the multi-volume encyclopaedia sector was relatively benign (see Figure 5.2). High entry and exit barriers brought stability, and the *Encyclopaedia Britannica* enjoyed a premium position with no obvious competitor. It had strong bargaining power over both suppliers (authors were plentiful and there was no threat of forward integration) and buyers (the *Encyclopaedia Britannica* had a highly differentiated brand and switching costs were high – it was unlikely that customers would shift mid-series to another encyclopaedia, or replace *Encyclopaedia Britannica* with another publication). The threat of new entrants was low (the capital requirements for creating a competing product were substantial, especially if the cost of the direct sales force was factored in), as was the threat of substitute products (the *Encyclopaedia Britannica* was the only one of its kind).

Encyclopaedia Britannica failed to fully understand how the CD-Rom, which was introduced in the late 1980s, would transform competitive forces within its sector. The threat of new entrants increased because it was far less expensive to produce encyclopaedias in CD-Rom format, and customers were less fussy about the brands producing them. Distribution channels – retailers – were easy to access in comparison to the complexities of establishing a door-to-door sales force. The threat of substitutes also increased. Not only was this a relatively easy field to enter, but CD-Roms offered functions that books could not match – sound, video, search functions, and so on. And while supplier power remained low, the bargaining power of buyers increased dramatically – there were now many alternative products and low switching costs. The result was a far more competitive environment, with more competitors, fast growth, low fixed costs, high exit barriers and high strategic stakes, as shown in Figure 5.3.

If we apply the Porter Five-Forces model to the newspaper industry and its current strategic threats (see Chapter 2) we see a similar picture. The attractiveness of the sector is declining: the threat of new entrants is high, since barriers to entry are falling; buyer power is increasing since they have many substitutes, including free newspapers; the threat of substitutes – chiefly from the Internet – is very high (the biggest problem); and rivalry between existing firms who face high exit barriers, emotional and physical, is intense.

In his book on the future of the newspaper industry, Meyer (2004: 40–1) applies Porter's theories to identify two basic strategic scenarios open to newspaper proprietors in this situation. The first is what Porter (1985: 311–12)

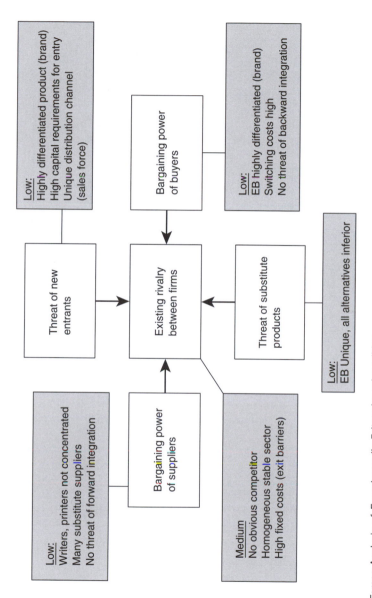

Figure 5.2 Five-Forces Analysis of *Encyclopaedia Britannica* print edition

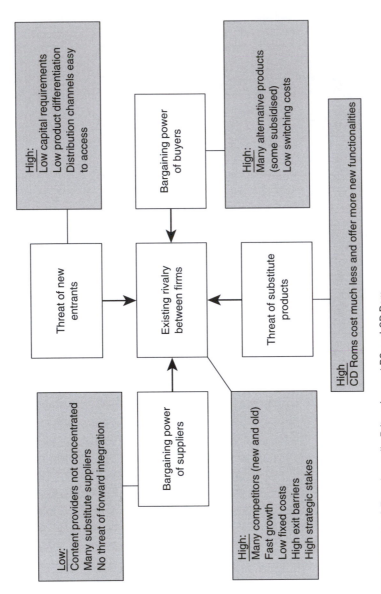

Figure 5.3 Five-forces Analysis of *Encyclopaedia Britannica* post-PC and CD-Rom

terms 'harvest instead of defend'. This is a short-term strategy with the goal of maximising returns now. It involves concentrating on segments where the threat of substitution is slowest, raising prices, cutting costs and postponing capital investments. The second strategy is to 'enter the substitute industry'. This entails accepting the new competitive situation, viewing the substitute (the Internet) not as a threat but as an opportunity, and for newspapers establish to online editions and seek to reap competitive advantages from their existing competencies and relationships with readers and advertisers.

Resource-based view

Porter's Five-Forces Model argues that a firm should design strategies that allow it to exercise bargaining power over suppliers and customers while preventing new entrants and rivals from entering its market. An alternative approach argues that competitive advantage comes from owning unique, valuable, inimitable, non-substitutable capabilities that allow the firm to offer its customers better value than its competitors. This 'resource-based view' (RBV) of strategy can be traced back to the late 1950s (Penrose, 1959), although it developed into a substantial stream of research during the 1980s where it was recognised as a very significant development in the field (Hitt, 1997).

It focuses on the perspective of the resources and capabilities a firm possesses and the competitive advantage they can or cannot create in a particular strategic environment (Wernerfelt, 1984; Prahalad and Hamel, 1990; Barney, 1991; Hitt et al., 2001). Firms can achieve sustained superior returns only when they possess resources other firms do not have (Peteraf, 1993; Miller and Shamsie, 1996). Strategically relevant resources need to meet the 'VRIN' criteria, that is, they need to be:

1. *Valuable*: a resource is only strategic if it is rent-generating and makes a substantial difference to a firm's cost-base or provides a source of differentiation
2. *Rare*: possession of the resource must be exceptional rather than standard. A standard resource is a threshold resource, a resource that is not strategic but necessary to compete in an industry
3. *Non-substitutable*: there must be no freely available substitutes for this resource
4. *Inimitable*: it must be difficult for other firms in an industry to acquire or copy. This can be because rivals cannot understand how they were created or are unable to replicate this process. (Bowman and Collier, 2006)

Resources that meet these criteria influence which markets a firm may enter and the levels of profit it may expect (Wernerfelt, 1984). In the media industry, the best types of content – the Harry Potter franchise, or Pixar's mastery of digital animation technology, meet these criteria: they are a valuable source of differentiation, are rare, have no substitutes and cannot be imitated.

A number of alternative categorisation systems have been proposed for classifying the resources identified using these criteria (see Chan-Olmsted,

2006, for a discussion of these). Miller and Shamsie (1996) divide resources into two categories: property-based resources and knowledge-based resources, either of which can stand alone (discrete) or as part of a network of resources (systemic). They see inimitability as central to competitive advantage.

Property-based resources are inimitable because they are protected by property rights (Miller and Shamsie, 1996). Discrete property-based resources include legally protected 'scarce and valuable inputs, facilities, locations, or patents' (Miller and Shamsie, 1996: 524) – for the media industry content libraries clearly qualify as examples, and indeed many of the acquisitions discussed in this book from the perspective of the RBV would be described as attempts to secure rare property-based discrete strategic resources. Systemic property-based resources include unique constellations of facilities, process and systems that are too complex for competitors to imitate, for example Sky Digital's marketing infrastructure which encompasses call centre, retail sales team and customer sales team.

Knowledge-based resources – tacit, implicit know-how and skills – cannot be imitated because they are protected by knowledge barriers. A creative team's network of freelance suppliers and a relationship built up over decades of collaboration, and reinforced by market success, is an example of a discrete knowledge-based resource. Systemic knowledge-based resources, on the other hand, involve knowledge-based resources that are integrated throughout an organisation, and would therefore also qualify as core competencies – for example Disney's ability to leverage the value of one content source across the company's many divisions.

The RBV research stream has been applied frequently to the media sector. Chan-Olmsted (2006)[1] proposes that because competitive advantage in the media industry derives so heavily from unique properties (exclusive content) and expert knowledge (the intangible 'know how' concerning audience appetites and creative processes), so the property/knowledge-based typology is valuable for classifying and analysing media firms' resources, and, by extension, understanding performance differences.

Resources can be created in four ways (Bowman and Collier, 2006). First, through luck, that is acquiring or creating a resource without knowing its future value: publishers' mud against the wall acquisition formula falls into this category. The second is resource picking – to do this a firm must have a view of the future that is not shared by other firms, which in turn relies on skills in analysing the external environment and firm information (Makadok, 2001). BSkyB's recognition of the role of killer content in driving uptake of pay-television offers, which led to an early lead in acquiring exclusive rights to key sporting fixtures in the 1980s is an example of resource picking. Third is internal development. This is a path-dependent process, by which over the course of its unique history a firm acquires rare and valuable resources and can exploit these in unique ways. Disney's library of animated films and characters, which provide a basis for content re-exploitation in many formats is an example of path-dependent resource creation. The last method of acquiring resources is alliance activity. An industry example of this is media firms' extensive use of joint ventures as a means of entering the Internet, broadband and wireless markets (Chan-Olmsted and Fang, 2003).

While the RBV has become an important element of strategic theory, shortcomings have also been identified. As with many of the frameworks discussed in this second half of the book, definitions are imprecise, making them difficult to operationalise in research. Barney (1991: 101), for example, defines resources very broadly indeed as 'all assets capabilities, organisational processes, firm attributes, information, knowledge, etc. controlled by a firm that enable the firm to conceive of and implement strategies that improve its efficiency and effectiveness'. The RBV can also be difficult to test empirically because idiosyncratic resources are hard to measure (Hitt, 1997). It has also been suggested that the approach is inappropriate for dynamic and volatile environments (D'Aveni, 1994b; Eisenhardt and Martin, 2000) and fails to accommodate the influence of firm evolution over time (Wang and Ahmed, 2007). Finally, some criticise the lack of prescriptive guidelines arising from the theory (Bowman and Collier, 2006).

Core competencies and dynamic capabilities

The core competence is a somewhat more pragmatic 'sister' to the RBV which has achieved greater resonance with practising managers. A core competence is also imprecisely defined, but is generally understood as a distinctive organisational attribute that creates sustainable competitive advantage and provides a platform for future growth – a 'gateway to tomorrow's opportunities' (Prahalad and Hamel, 1994). A competency is understood as a 'bundle' of individual skills and technologies that is integrated and company-wide, is unique to the organisation concerned, cannot be easily reproduced by competitors, delivers real and meaningful customer benefit, is extendable, is sustainable and is appropriable (that is, the added-value created by the competence is retained by the organisation – if this value accrues to the individual who possesses the competence, then the competence concerned is not 'core') (Prahalad and Hamel, 1990; Quinn, 1992; Kay, 1993).

The distinction between a strategic resource and a core competence is not easy to draw: competencies, capabilities and strategic resources all fall into resource-based theory. However, the critical distinction appears to lie in the fact that a capability or competence is a more complex phenomenon that is embedded in the wider organisational system. It is home grown (and therefore hard to acquire), involves organisational routines that have been acquired over time, are embedded in its architecture and culture (Teece et al., 1997), and has a high knowledge component. Further, the roots of distinctive capabilities often extend back to the organisation's founding circumstances, emerging in the first place as a means by which an organisation could fulfil its primary mission. They are thus intrinsic to a company's identify, deeply rooted in its culture, and contribute not only to competitiveness but also to the psycho-social 'glue' that creates identity, differentiation and cohesion (Schein, 1992), and form part of an organization's personality (Drucker, 1994).

CNN's breaking news as a core competency In approximately the first 15 years of its life (from 1980 to 1995), in the period before it was acquired by Time Warner and before it became part of the AOL Time Warner empire, CNN was worldwide leader in broadcast news. A core competence in covering and transmitting breaking news on a global basis, faster than any other news organisations at the time, contributed greatly to its leadership position. Analysis using the core competency framework allows the individual components, the routines embedded in CNN's architecture, that together make up this competence, to be identified:

1. *Organisational infrastructure.* CNN was a news network, and also a geographically diffused network organisation, a response to the requirements of its newsgathering and broadcasting activities. The hub was in Atlanta, Georgia. There were production facilities in Georgia, Washington, London and Hong Kong, ten national and 21 international news bureaux. It had a 32.6 per cent stake in n-tv (Germany) and 50 per cent of TV-6 Moscow, was a subscriber to Worldwide Television News, Reuters TV and APTV, and a participant in news pools covering the Far East, Europe, North America and the Middle East.

2. *Distribution infrastructure.* CNN's broadcast infrastructure was difficult for competitors to replicate because it had been created in a path-dependent way. Domestically it was the first cable news service and therefore had locked-in 'must carry' agreements with most cable operating firms in the US. Internationally it had blocked space on eight satellites that carried its signal. This gave it the largest and most flexible footprint of any broadcast service and by splitting its signal up in so many ways, CNN, uniquely, could offer both global advertising and regionally targeted advertising.

3. *Newsgathering infrastructure.* CNN had achieved its success through alliances. In addition to its relationships with cable operators, it had reciprocity arrangements with local stations all over the world to exchange its news coverage in return for significant local stories of global interest. This created a worldwide newsgathering system – albeit an unorthodox one for the industry at that time which had a strong bias for homegrown news. CNN invested consistently in developing overseas newsgathering, by increasing both alliances and the number of international bureaux. It also invested in the technology for international newsgathering, thus making its own operations faster and easier. It pioneered the use of collapsible satellite dishes that could be taken on commercial aircraft – this allowed it to get its journalists on site and broadcasting far faster than competitors. It used a network of high level relationships to further these activities, particularly through Ted Turner's friendships with heads of state which enabled CNN to extend its newsgathering network into parts of the world that were closed to other broadcasters (Rosenstiel, 1994). As a result of this newsgathering capacity, CNN became *de rigueur* viewing for world leaders, opening whole new communications systems between governments (Whittemore, 1990).

4. *100% control of airtime.* Unlike its competitors, CNN did not depend on advertising for the bulk of its revenues (its main income was from cable providers). This meant it could suspend normal schedules at any point should a new story break. Its advertising-financed competitors could not in the main do this, since they would forfeit both revenues from, and credibility with, their advertising customers.

5. *Real-time decision-making skills.* The news journalists' emphasis on speed infused the entire organisation. Even staff in non-broadcast areas became skilled at making fast decisions.

6. *Track record of success/news coups.* CNN's track record of news coups helped create a powerful brand associated globally with immediacy and drama. This again was a product of its history and therefore difficult for competitors to copy. In 1986, when the Challenger Space Shuttle exploded, CNN was the only television channel to cover it live. It then sold its footage to broadcasters all over the word, creating an awareness of CNN, particularly in Europe, which would have been hard and expensive to achieve through marketing campaigns. As a result, a few months later CNN was available in over 150,000 households. In subsequent years, CNN's consistent investment in its international newsgathering infrastructure meant it could repeatedly score against its competitors by being the only news service to broadcast exclusive live coverage of events such as the Tiananman Square Massacre (1989), the US invasion of Panama (1989), the release of Nelson Mandela (1990) and the 1991 Gulf War bombing of Baghdad.

CNN's abilities with breaking news classify as a core competency. But illustrating the overlap between the two theories, this 'skill bundle' also conforms to the VRIN criteria used to identify a strategic resource according to the RBV. Thus CNN's competency in breaking news was also rent-generating and a source of differentiation (valuable), comprised an exceptional combination of elements (rare), had no obvious alternatives (non-substitutable) and was challenging for competitors to replicate (inimitable). Applying Miller and Shamsie's (1996) property-knowledge resource typology shows that this core competence combined property-based resources (the organisational and distribution infrastructures were property-based systemic resources, and 100 per cent control of airtime was a property-based discrete resource) and knowledge-based resources (the real-time decision-making skills and the track-record of success/news coups were knowledge-based systemic resources, the newsgathering infrastructure was a property- and knowledge-based systemic resource).

Adaptive approaches

A core distinction in strategy literature is between strategy content and strategy process (Chakravarthy and Doz, 1992; Pettigrew, 1992). Rationalist approaches focus on the content of strategy, crudely put, the contents of the strategic plan. They seek to find a strategic position that will lead to optimal performance under varying environmental conditions (Chakravarthy and Doz, 1992). They argue that the growth and survival of organisations is influenced by the structure and dynamics of an industry and the quality of response to environmental factors, particularly the economics of business cycles. Strategy involves maximising returns from resources and establishing equilibrium within this context.

An alternative perspective is that equilibrium is rare. Change is endemic to organisational environments, and, echoing Schumpeter's concept of 'creative destruction' (1934), an ultimately positive force. Researchers sharing this viewpoint began to study the interplay between the structure and dynamics of an industry and the structures, strategies and processes inside organisations. They recognised that the interrelationship between these elements needed to be explored, and that an important aspect of strategic activity involved reconciling and integrating these external and internal elements. They also recognised that environmental change, particularly technological change, can erode the strategic value of an attractive product-market position or of distinctive resources or capabilities.

Such considerations lie at the heart of the 'adaptive' school. This views strategy as 'a process not a state' (Pettigrew, 1992) and is concerned with 'how effective strategies are shaped … validated and implemented effectively' (Chakravarthy and Doz, 1992: 5) to ensure that organisations master complex and uncertain environments. An important emphasis is on adaptation and self-renewal: 'strategies must change in keeping with both new opportunities and threats in its environment and changes in … strategies and strategic intent' (Rajagopalan and Spreizer, 1996). Thus strategy is not primarily about planning, rather it is about trying to see the world as it really is, and preparing the organization so that it has a chance of a successful future (Fulmer, 2000), and the reality of strategy lies in strategic actions, rather than strategic statements (Burgelman, 2002).

So change (or adaptation) is intrinsic to strategy, and by extension strategy is intimately involved with the organisation. A shift in the content of strategy must mean shifts in the organisation – in structure, people and processes. Indeed, for Mintzberg and colleagues the field of strategy is subsumed within the broader one of strategic change, thus 'to manage strategy is to manage change – to recognise when a shift of a strategic nature is possible, desirable, and necessary, and then to act – possibly putting in place mechanisms for continuous change' (Mintzberg et al., 2003: 166).

If rationalist approaches see strategy as a plan, then adaptive ones see strategy as an evolutionary process where change takes place progressively as firms undertake a series of strategic readjustments in response to a changing environment. While the devising of the content of a strategy can be structured and formal, the actual process of strategy is gradual and messy, triggered by learning taking place in various parts of the organisation. Strategy can sometimes be visible only in hindsight as a 'pattern in a stream of decisions' as Mintzberg (1987) famously described it.

Critically, strategy is not decided, then carried out, but emerges in the process of being implemented. Monitoring the environment, analysing developments and making changes are continuous and contiguous activities. The boundary between the organisation and its environment is highly permeable, and the environment is a major focus of attention in determining organisational action.

If the frameworks in the rational school seek to support organisations in their search for a strategic position that will guarantee sustainable advantage, the concepts in this school seek to enable dynamic strategic positioning, for example in the design and redesign of the structures and processes by which an organisation can respond to changes in the environment.

Concepts particularly relevant to the media sector from this school are those concerning responses to technological advance. For example, those that allow organisations to distinguish between different types of technological change and understand their respective implications for different types of organisations, or models that provide insight into which technology will dominate after a technology transition, and explain why an 'inferior' technology may become an industry standard, or concepts that help incumbent organisations resist inertia and establish new ventures based on new technological platforms (these are discussed in Chapter 6).

A further distinction in this field is between incremental change and transformational change. The pace and velocity of environmental change are not constant. Organisations need to be capable of both incremental and transformational change (Tushman et al., 1986). Transformational change itself has more than one incarnation, and can involve a quick dramatic revolution, or renewal – a more gradual process. Transformational strategic change – such as is currently required in many sectors of the media in response to the Internet and digitalisation – is recognised as one of the most challenging for leaders and uncomfortable for those inside organisations, since it involves moving from the known to the unknown, and requires existing success formulas to be abandoned and new competencies and attitudes to be developed (Mintzberg et al., 2003). These aspects of adaptive approaches to strategy are discussed in Chapter 8.

Interpretative approaches

Rationalist approaches in particular have been criticised for failing to accommodate the diversity and disorder of organisational life – Mintzberg once famously claimed that 90 per cent of rational strategies are never implemented successfully – and also for failing to address the habits of mind that so often prevent strong players from making a bridge between one type of environment to another.

The interpretative school of strategy focuses on exactly those elements that often prevent strategic plans being implemented, namely the deeper 'hidden' aspects of the organisation, such as mindset, belief systems, values, motivation and emotions. These elements are often underplayed or even ignored in strategic plannning, partly because they are highly subjective and somewhat ethereal, and partly because they concern subjective and unconscious phenomena that are difficult to access and interpret. Researchers in the field, however, argue that interpretative elements can both help and hinder strategic change, and that successful strategic initiatives have found a way to take these powerful but hard to manage forces into consideration.

The interpretative approach seeks to understand organisations from the perspective of those working in them with a focus on how meaning is constructed out of events and phenomena, the influence this meaning has on the behaviour of the firm, and the outcomes of that behaviour. A basic assumption is that organisational members actively create or enact the reality they inhabit (Weick, 1979), thus reality is understood as 'socially constructed'.

The adaptive and interpretative schools are closely linked. If all strategic activity is ultimately about change, the adaptive school looks at the changes that need to be made in routines, systems and technology. But congruent changes also need to be made in the organisation's overt and covert cultural and social systems, in its interpretative phenomena, and these issues form the focal point of the interpretative school.

A number of levers can be used to achieve strategic change. While rational approaches tend to focus on tools such as education and communication, the interpretative school looks at how socio-cultural, symbolic, cognitive and political processes can be employed to speed processes of transformation and signal the types of changes required from organisation members. Thus, interpretative approaches focus not only on how an organisation might be restructured (a focus of the adaptive school), but also on the meaning created by the events staged to publicise the change, by the choice of individuals to head up the new structure, by the individuals marginalised through these actions, and how these flag up the changes that are required on an individual level (Johnson and Scholes, 1989).

Of all the schools outlined here, the interpretative school is the least cohesive – indeed some would dispute whether it even constitutes a school. However, the concepts in this approach have a common starting point, the 'higher order', or deeper psychological and often unconscious, aspects of organisations such as underlying beliefs, mindset, mental models and motivation.

Interpretative approaches also consider how the emotions expressed by the change leader allow those in the organisation to frame and 'make sense' of the changes (Gioia and Chittipeddi, 1991). Academic understanding of the role of emotions in strategic change is still in its infancy, but the emotional capability of an organization has been identified as important in processes of radical change in that it affects its ability to acknowledge, recognise, monitor, discriminate and attend to emotions at both individual and collective levels (Huy, 1999).

Symbolic, cognitive and cultural elements are particularly important in media organisations, partly because the individuals who choose to work in the sector are often motivated to do so because of their own 'higher order' needs, and partly because of the tremendous influence that the media industries exert over our lives and societies. And there is ample evidence of the strategic relevance of concepts from this school to the media industries. Culture is an important factor in established firms' ability to respond to new technology.

Meyer for instance (2004) sees the high levels of cash traditionally generated by the newspaper industry as generating a complacent culture that slowed its ability to respond to the threat of new technology, and notes that the new content forms that seize the potential of new technologies are being created by non-journalists who have worked outside the journalism culture.

Staying with the entertainment sector, the past years have shown how mental models have influenced the music majors' responses to the Internet, and indeed to a raft of earlier advances including compact cassettes, VCRs, CDs, and so on. Similarly, the blockbuster strategy is a good example of the impact of cognitive assumptions on investment decisions. The movie industry steadfastly clings to the beliefs that big budgets mean big audiences and that consumers respond to saturation advertising, even though the statistical correlation between stars and success in the film industry is disputed (Ravid, 1999).

Conclusions

Part II of this book draws heavily on models from the adaptive and interpretative schools, and far less on rationalist approaches. The latter have been applied extensively to the sector, as already discussed, while the other two, appear far less frequently in research. Concepts from the adaptive school are to be found in Chapter 6 (on technology), Chapter 7 (on creativity and innovation), Chapter 9 (on structure) and Chapter 10 (on leadership). Interpretative models recur frequently throughout this second part of the book. In addition Chapter 8 (on culture and cognition) draws explicitly on such approaches, as do Chapter 7 (on creativity and innovation) and Chapter 10 (on leadership).

Note

1   This discussion of the RBV's application to the media industry draws heavily on Chan-Olmsted in Albarran et al. (2006).

SIX

Managing Technological Change

A critical pattern in the dynamics of technological innovation ... is the disturbing regularity with which industrial leaders follow their core technologies into obsolescence and obscurity. (Utterback, 1994: 162)

The media sector and its observers tend to discuss the industry in terms of content and its creation, with technology entering discussions as an enabling, contributory or disruptive factor. The secondary status accredited to technology is surprising since media industries are symbiotically linked with technology and technological change, and viewed longitudinally, technology is a powerful influence on both organisational behaviour and strategic outcomes. Each of the three core dimensions that constitute the sector – content, distribution systems and the devices that display content (Wildman, 2006) – came into existence because of technological invention and continue to be subject to technologically induced change.

While the industry may underplay its dependence on technology, advances in technology have long been used to give products a competitive edge. Walt Disney, for example, was a pioneer in exploiting new technological possibilities to make his animated films more striking (Bennis and Biederman, 1997). His studio was the first to synchronize sound with movement on film in 1928 and the first to use a new three-colour process from Technicolor in 1932. It invented the multiplane camera which allowed more realistic depth effects in animated film as well as the feature-length animated film *Snow White and the Seven Dwarfs* (1938). In the 1950s it was one of the only major Hollywood players to embrace television as a growth opportunity.

Research on technological advance in the media industries has concentrated primarily on two issues: the adoption of new technologies by individuals, and the introduction of new technologies on media markets (Chan-Olmstead in Albarran et al., 2006). The substantial body of research into firm-level responses to technological innovation does not seem to have permeated media industry or media management academic discourse very far, and one goal of this chapter is to address this shortcoming, since this research stream has many significant insights for strategic managers in the sector.

This chapter explores the often intricate relationship between technology, technological change, organisational strategy and the media industry. It explores the industry's symbiotic relationship with technology by tracing the key developments that have shaped, perhaps even given birth to, its various sectors. It reviews theoretical understanding of the relationship between firm strategy and technology, and the distinguishing features of different types of technological change. It then looks at the requirements these various types of innovation place on firms, and at the factors that help or hinder effective responses. These issues are developed further in Chapter 7, which deals with creativity and innovation.

Technological change and the media industry

Increasingly, the time period that an innovation can last is [getting] shorter. Look at the home audio music business. The music box controlled that market for 100 years. The phonograph controlled the market for 70 years. Cassette tapes dominated for 25 years until the arrival of CDs. Now, after 10 years, CDs compete with mini-disks, DVDs, MP3, and the Internet. (Mauzy and Harriman, 2003: 3)

A retrospective glance at key events in the media industry over the last 100 years shows a persistent pattern: technology gives, and technology takes away, but it seldom takes everything away. As Figure 6.1 shows, technological advances create new products and segments of the industry, fuel increases in usage and spending on media products, but at the same time erode existing markets, segments and business models. The commercialisation of printing with moveable type by Gutenberg in 1448 disrupted the then print media sector that used carved wooden blocks. The microphone, radio and the technology of sound recording led to the emergence of radio broadcasting and recorded music, but meant reduced audiences for music concerts. The emergence of television added a new pillar to the media industry, but contributed to the demise of Hollywood's studio system, spelt the end of the comic as a major leisure product for children in the US. In the UK it caused newspapers' share of total advertising revenues to fall from 90 per cent in the 1940s to 20 per cent by the 1960s. The emergence of the CD-Rom boosted the sales of home computers but undermined the reference book industry, particularly the print encyclopaedia. Desk-top publishing systems improved the economics of newspaper publishing but rendered traditional craft newspaper printing skills redundant.

The fact that the media industry owes its existence to technological advance, and that technology is a permanently moving carpet under its feet, is surprisingly seldom acknowledged by the industry itself. It repeatedly greets

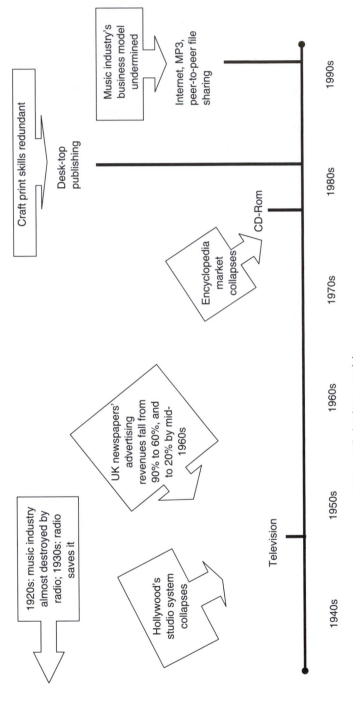

Figure 6.1 Technology's track record of undermining media business models

Table 6.1 Technological developments and the media – an historical perspective

Time	Technological development
1450	Book printing press based on interchangeable type
1826	Black and white photography
1873	Colour photography
1876	Telephone and microphone
1877	Phonograph
1888	Box camera and roll film
1895	Cinematograph invented by the Lumière brothers
1910	Silent film
1920s	Cinema, radio
1927	*The Jazz Singer* – first talking picture, first radio licences granted
1930s	Film with sound, FM radio
1940s	Colour film, RCA markets television sets
1950s	Black and white television and television networks fully established in the US, cinema and library visits show decline
1960s	Colour television, long-playing records
1970s	Teletext, VCR, cable television (US)
1979	Sony Walkman
1979	CompuServe bulletin board
1980s	Personal computer
1983	Internet
1984	Apple Macintosh
1989	World Wide Web, compact discs, satellite transmission (Europe), cable transmission (Europe)
1990s	Penetration of home PC
Mid-1990s	Netscape Navigator, digitalisation, digital broadcasting (Europe), Internet
Late 1990s	Wireless telecommunications, broadband technologies, fibre optic infrastructure, on-demand television services, personal video recorders

new technologies with dismay – forgetting that the products its business is currently based around once represented radical alterations to the status quo of existing industries.

Fear of the new is a longstanding feature of incumbents' responses. Hollywood was hostile to television. Both the television industry and Hollywood feared the VCR. The music industry tried to block the compact cassette, the compact disc and more recently the Internet. Looking further back still, book publishers were concerned that circulating libraries would reduce their sales. However, despite their forebodings, in each case the new technology led to new markets and increased revenues for incumbents: the consecutive introduction of video, cable/satellite, video on demand, DVD and home cinema technology have ensured continued growth for the film industry over past decades.

Technological innovations tend, therefore, to supplement, rather than replace, previous technologies. The previous medium is not destroyed, but progressively undermined, more often than not slipping down the food chain with lower revenues and smaller market share. This dynamic was observed by Riepl (1913), chief editor of Nuremberg's biggest newspaper, who proposed that established media never die, but adjust to a new technological environment, perhaps being used in different ways and with different formats.

Technology and strategy

The field of strategy is concerned with how an organisation orchestrates a successful response to its environment. Strategy is challenging because that environment is never static. Rather like all complex systems it is in a constant state of flux. The nature of this change can vary. At some times it can represent relatively benign and easy to accommodate alterations to the status quo, at others it can be rife with many different developments, the dimensions of which are far from clear, and the implications of which are hard to predict.

As we have seen, technological change is always present in the media field, and as with many sectors, the need to adapt to this is a long-standing strategic requirement (D'Aveni, 1994b; Bettis and Hitt, 1995; Christensen and Overdorf, 2000). However, it can be argued that the volume and velocity of the changes now underway – broadband, WiFi, the Internet, mobile telephony, social networking sites, MP3 players and so on – have created a peculiarly challenging environment for the media industry, one where existing business models are clearly expiring, and where the volume and velocity of change makes outcomes non-linear and unpredictable.

This chapter explores strategic and organisational responses to such developments. Technological change can clearly be analysed from a rational strategy perspective – for example its ability to lower entry barriers, to create substitutes, to alter value chains and affect competitive positioning. But as an ongoing phenomenon, an emergent one and a complex one, it can also be viewed through an adaptive lens, which would highlight the iterative processes by which an organisation aligns itself with its environment (Drazin and Schoonhoven, 1996), and the ways in which organisations alter structures, processes and systems (see, for example, Kanter, 1983, 1992).

It is important not to oversimplify the relationship between technology and strategy, to overemphasise technological factors at the expense of other factors in the cultural and social arena, a tendency known as 'technological determinism' (Williams, 1974) or 'technological reductionism' (Hesmondhalgh, 2002). Rather, technological change must be understood in relation to other contingent factors, and it must be recognised that there is a complex iterative path between technological advance and the successful implementation of these developments by organisations. Technological advance arises from the interplay between innovation, government policy, organisational behaviour and social influences. For example, Murdoch's controversial but successful launch of electronic newspaper systems in the UK in the 1980s, which paved the way for their wide-scale adoption by the industry, benefited not only from technological advance, but also from government objectives of stimulating the adoption of new technologies in the workplace and constraining trade unions which might act against such innovation (Marjoribanks, 2000). In his classic book *Diffusion of Innovations* Rogers (2003) highlights the role of sociological factors in technological adoption, particularly people's perception of value and fear of risks.

Technological advance can also involve the combination of a number of independent inventions. Drucker (1985) provides a number of media industry examples of this. To return to the newspaper industry, the independent mass market newspaper emerged as a result of two technological advances: the telegraph and high speed printing. These allowed James Gordon Bennett, founder of the *New York Herald*, to produce a paper at a fraction of the usual costs. However, his model did not exploit the potential of mass advertising as a source of revenue that allows editorial independence. This was added 20 years later by Joseph Pulitzer, Adolf Achs and William Randolph Hearst, who created the modern newspaper chain. In the case of news magazines, World War I created an appetite for national and international news. Henry Luce realised that a publication to satisfy this would have to be national rather than local since otherwise there would not be enough readers or advertisers. He also saw that it would need to be weekly rather than daily since there was not enough news of interest to a large public. These factors dictated the editorial format of *Time*, the first news magazine

'Organisational technology'

Fostering technological advance is a government goal in many countries because new technologies are source of economic growth. The path from technological discovery to economic growth runs through organisations: new technologies require an organisational response, an effective organisational response, if they are to realise their potential.

These issues underlie the substantial attention management researchers have paid to technology. A strand of this theory, one which is of considerable relevance to strategy in the media industry, is known as 'organisational technology'. It concerns the interrelationship between technology, organisations and innovation. The field itself has a long pedigree with roots stretching back to Marx and Schumpeter (1934, 1942), both of whom viewed new technology as an underlying driver of organisational and political dynamics and therefore a critical determinant of societal and institutional outcomes. But while long established and carrying significant implications, it is also a fragmented field (Tushman and Nelson, 1990). This perhaps explains why, despite its potential import, it has not featured strongly in industry discussions about recent technological upheavals.

Dominant designs and technology transitions

According to organisational technology researchers, the technological evolution of industries follows a cyclical pattern where long periods of relatively minor change are punctuated by rare instances of technological discontinuity which disrupt entire product classes and require a response from virtually all companies in a sector (Abernathy and Utterback, 1978; Tushman and Anderson, 1986; Tushman and Smith, 2002).

These periods are confusing, uncertain and expensive for firms involved. They trigger a period of ferment where rival new technologies compete intensively between themselves and with the existing technological regime (Henderson and Clark, 1990). They are also of tremendous strategic significance, because they close with the emergence of a 'dominant design' (Tushman and Smith, 2002). This normally synthesizes aspects of prior technological innovations and provides a basis for standardisation that allows scale economies to be established (Utterback, 1994).

The dominant design has a profound impact on subsequent technological advance, the industry and the structure of competition. Its emergence represents a 'technology transition'. Once it has been established other paths of product innovation are in the main abandoned and competitors must adopt the standard or risk exclusion (Abernathy and Utterback, 1978; Tushman and Anderson, 1986; Tushman and Smith, 2002). It is followed by a period of incremental as well as architectural technological innovation (for a discussion of these terms, see below p. 133).

An alternative name for this cycle, by which organisations in a sector evolve through periods of stability during which incremental changes occur that are punctuated by irregularly occurring discontinuous transformations has also been termed the punctuated-equilibrium model (Gersick, 1991). But, either way, technologies gradually evolve through a clearly distinguishable life cycle, starting with an early fluid state characterised by relatively easy entry opportunities, moving to a highly rigid one where entry is more complex and expensive.

Theories of organisational technology view technological development as an important growth driver, spurring them to enter new markets and revitalise existing products and services (Tushman and Nelson, 1990; Nelson, 1995). However, that process of development is messy, unpredictable and interactive, with causal relationships flowing in both directions: technical change affects organisations, institutions and society, while organisations, their markets, and society, influence the path of technological advance (Tushman and Nelson, 1990).

A technology that has been enthroned as the 'dominant design' is not automatically the best one on offer – a point Apple fans will readily concur with.

Nor does the firm which pioneers a dominant design automatically retain control of it. Indeed, history shows again and again that technological superiority does not automatically bring market success. Scholars have offered a number of explanations for the triumph of inferior solutions, ranging from a combination of an early lead in the market and a dynamic of increasing returns, to adoption (Arthur, 1994), a superior match with consumers' needs as expressed in terms of the best 'bundle' of features (Utterback, 1994), or non-technological, 'socio-political' dynamics (Tushman and Rosenkopf, 1992). However, to bring discussion down to a pragmatic level for managers within organisations affected, an important common implication from this theoretical research is that the outcome of technology-based competition is always hard to predict and can have surprisingly little to do with the respective quality of the competing technologies on offer.

Encyclopaedia Britannica

This case is a rare example of a media product, a category killing, brand leader media product, being more or less wiped out within a few years as a result of the introduction of a new distribution technology. Over 200 years old, *Encyclopaedia Britannica* was the oldest continuously published reference work in the English language, one of the strongest and best-known brands in publishing, and a staple of the 'family library' (which ideally contained the Bible, a dictionary and an encyclopaedia). Its multi-volume sets cost around $1,500–$2,000 and were sold via door-to-door salespeople, who were legendary at persuading parents that the *Encyclopaedia Britannica* was essential if children were to grow up to be well educated. In terms of content, *Encyclopaedia Britannica* aimed for the best, and had a long-standing tradition of inviting text contributions from leading scientists and theorists of the time.

In the mid-1980s when CD-Rom technology emerged, *Encyclopaedia Britannica* was approached to licence its content for CD-Rom delivery. The company doubted the potential of CD-Rom technology, and was reluctant to cannibalise its printed version by launching a digital one. It chose to remain a book product, also turning down a joint venture approach from Microsoft, which went on to develop its own product *Encarta* (that later became the best-selling CD-Rom encyclopaedia in the world). *Encyclopaedia Britannica's* market collapsed. Between 1990 and 1995 it lost 50 per cent of its revenues.

Encyclopaedias on CD-Rom were then selling for $50 (with the majority of sales through computer retailers) but were also frequently given away free. Production costs were about $1.50 per copy against $200, being the cost of printing, binding and distributing a set of encyclopaedias in book form (although CD version production costs rose as the amount of multi-media content increased). *Encyclopaedia Britannica* belatedly responded to digital developments and launched a CD-Rom product (but priced at $1,000).

Encyclopaedia Britannica clearly misdiagnosed CD-Rom technology, in particular its disruptive potential, but it did not ignore technological advance. Indeed it engaged seriously, intelligently and speedily with various electronic formats. In 1981 they licensed their content to Lexis-Nexis, in 1983 they developed educational software programs with Apple, in 1985 they acquired Designware and Eduware to design and develop entertainment and education software, purchased the American Learning Corporation which provided specialised learning instruction using audio-visual equipment, acquired Blue Chip Software, and acquired a 75 per cent stake in *Encyclopaedia Britannica* Educational Corporation, a supplier of films and educational materials to elementary and secondary schools. In August 1988 they partnered with Educational Systems Corp to build an electronic version of *Compton's Encyclopaedia*, a networked CD-Rom for elementary and secondary schools.

In March 1989 *Compton's Multimedia Encyclopaedia* was launched. In 1991 a MS Windows version was produced, later that year a second version was release and in 1992 a CD-I version. In August 1992 an electronic index to Britannica was released (but without electronic access to the contents). Microsoft's *Encarta* was launched in 1993, in the same year Compton's was sold to the Tribune Company, and a CD-Rom containing the entire text of *Encyclopaedia Britannica* in searchable format was released, and a few months later this was distributed electronically to universities and some libraries over the Internet. A CD-Rom for consumer use was released in 1994, only a year after Microsoft's *Encarta*. This concern led to channel conflict, whereby existing sales forces and intermediaries fought hard against a new distribution channel that appeared to threaten their business. In July 1995 they offered free trial access to the Internet site. A year later *Encyclopaedia Britannica* was sold for $135 million. At this point sales had dropped 83 per cent since 1990. A new strategic goal was developed to leverage the brand into the electronic age. Over the next few years expanded and enhanced CD-Rom versions were produced at lower prices, as well as online versions which were initially subscription-based and later free.

This case offers many different insights and by extension shows the benefit of analysis using different diagnostic tools. It shows how the strategic value of content as a strategic resource can be undermined by technological advance. If we look at the first stage of the reference book transformation, from book form to CD-Rom, *Encyclopaedia Britannica*'s extraordinary content and brand position suggested it would be the logical player to dominate the multimedia encyclopaedia market. But this position actually went to Microsoft because multimedia encyclopaedias required a different set of competencies, not least software skills. *Encyclopaedia Britannica*'s content was indeed initially a liability, since in 1993 it was too big for CD-Rom and the company could not therefore launch a quick response to *Encarta*.

The case also demonstrates the utility of value chain analysis. This shows that the shift from print to CD-Rom altered every stage of *Encyclopaedia Britannica*'s value chain and by extension its competence profile (see Figure 6.2).

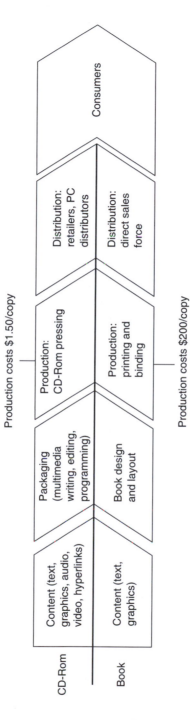

Figure 6.2 Value chain analysis of the impact of the CD-Rom on *Encyclopaedia Britannica*'s competence profile

Encyclopaedia Britannica's existing competencies in book design, printing, binding and in door-to-door marketing became irrelevant and indeed liabilities in that they represented high fixed costs that new entrants did not have to contend with, and the employees involved in these areas were understandably reluctant to accept new business directions. (For the sales force a drop in selling price meant an unwelcome drop in sales commissions.) In their place came a new set of skills that were required – multimedia text development, software programming, CD production and the development of a distribution capability based around the PC industry.

Untangling types of technological change

The messy and unpredictable impact of technological change results in part from difficulties in identifying differences in types of change and understanding their various implications. The nomenclature in this area is particularly confusing. Technological change can be radical, disruptive, discontinuous, and more. Some view these terms as distinct categories carrying precise meanings, others as interchangeable terms, and these semantic issues impede scientific understanding and managerial application (Tushman and Smith, 2002).

Clarification can be achieved by applying a typology that classifies technological change according to two dimensions: proximity to the current technological trajectory; and proximity to the existing customer/market segment (Abernathy and Clark, cited in Tushman and Smith, 2002).

Incremental innovations

During non-transition phases, when an industry is in equilibrium, technological change involves the ongoing adaptation and improvement of existing technologies. These incremental innovations extend the technologies currently used and usually involve alterations to either processes or materials, so creating improvements in products and increased customer satisfaction (Hill and Rothaermel, 2003). An example for the media industry would be the shift from manual to electric typewriters or improvements in types of paper used for publishing. Incremental innovations are so termed because they build upon the established knowledge base and current technological capabilities, and thus the organisational response required involves extending existing core capabilities and engaging in continuous improvement of production processes.

Architectural innovations

These involve often relatively simple technological or process innovations in the subsystems and/or linking mechanisms that allow existing products to be modified and directed at new markets (smaller cheaper copier machines or laser printers would be typical examples). Although they represent unspectacular technological advances, such developments have the potential to transform a product class or fundamentally change a business (Henderson and Clark, 1990). Their challenge lies in their deceptive simplicity, since there is a risk that incumbents 'mis-label' these as incremental rather than architectural changes, and miss their potential to undermine existing competencies and knowledge. Organisations may fail to realise they need to restructure their organisations, seek new markets, or alter their production processes (Henderson and Clark, 1990). Personal video recorders, which allow television viewers to record programmes and also to blend out advertising, are an example of an architectural innovation. They do not represent spectacular technological advances (VCRs have been around since the 1980s), but because they are often bundled with on-demand television services, they have accelerated the decline of the commercial free-to-air television model, by reducing advertising income and speeding the shift to interactive television.

Discontinuous innovations

These are 'transformational' developments that represent a break with existing systems and processes because they 'sweep away much ... existing investment in technical skills and knowledge, designs, production technique, plant, and equipment' (Utterback, 1994: 200), bringing 'discontinuous change to a core subsystem causing cascading changes in other subsystems and linking mechanisms' (Tushman and Murmann, 1998). They involve methods and materials that are novel to incumbents and are derived either from an entirely different knowledge base or from the recombination of parts of the incumbents' established knowledge base with a new stream of knowledge (Freeman and Soete, 1997; Hill and Rothaermel, 2003). These developments are dangerous for incumbents because they are 'competence destroying' (Tushman and Anderson, 1986). They make competencies which have hitherto been a source of competitive advantage obsolete and require firms to develop entirely new ones (Cohen and Levinthal, 1990).

The history of the print media industry is rife with examples of discontinuous innovation. The computerised newspaper production systems that emerged in the 1980s allowed newspaper pages to be assembled onscreen and transmitted electronically to printing plates. This made print workers' specialist competencies of setting hot metal linotype and composing text obsolete. Instead journalists were required to master desktop publishing skills (Marjoribanks in Cottle, 2003). The newspaper print unions in the UK mounted a powerful block to adopting this discontinuous innovation, until what proved to be an even more powerful element in the industry – Rupert Murdoch – decided to take on the unions and introduce the new technology, necessitating relocation to a new non-unionised workplace in Wapping in 1986 and leading to pitched battles between the police and striking print union members.

The launch of satellite television in Europe was also a discontinuous innovation, not simply because of the primary changes it brought – expanding distribution capacity and decoupling the cost and distance of transmission – but because it provoked a set of second order changes, relieving spectrum scarcity, 'de-legitimising' political interference in broadcasting markets, and weakening the philosophical foundations of public service broadcasters (Collins, 1998).

Disruptive innovations and the 'Innovators' Dilemma'

The dilemma is that the criteria managers use to make decisions that keep their present businesses healthy make it impossible for them to do the right thing for the future. What's best for your current business could ruin you for the long term. (Christensen cited in Hamm, 1999)

During the first Internet era, the adjective 'disruptive' used in connection with either 'technology' and 'innovation' became a catchphrase. This is probably due to the enormous resonance found by one concept in particular – Christensen's theory of incumbent failure in the face of what he terms 'disruptive innovation' (Bower and Christensen, 1996; Christensen and Bower, 1996; Christensen, 1997; Christensen and Overdorf, 2000; Christensen et al., 2002). A book on this theory became a bestseller, and the concepts in it a rallying point for managers of incumbent firms worried about the impact of the Internet on their businesses.

Disruptive innovations as Christensen defines them are disruptive to established market structures, but are not technologically disruptive. Indeed they often involve relatively simple technological developments, but these have the capacity to upset the structure of the markets and undermine the attractiveness of existing products. They 'disrupt' because they lead to new and often simpler product categories that incumbents may disregard because they fail to perceive their market appeal. However, once established in the market, over time these new products move upmarket and develop into serious challengers to the incumbent players' products. Because incumbents have failed to respond initially they cannot catch up on developments and unwittingly cede the market to new players.

Desktop publishing systems are an example of a disruptive innovation. The early versions could not match the output of traditional publishing systems with their high quality printing presses and skilled layout and design. Nonetheless, they lowered the cost of entry to the publishing business, allowing new institutions and individuals to enter the publishing field. As the market grew and economies of scale emerged, desktop publishing systems became more sophisticated and came to overtake traditional publishing systems. Digital on-demand printing threatens to take this process further.

Free newspapers also fit the classification of a disruptive innovation because although they cover a small number of topics, and rely on generic news agency feeds for their stories, they appeal to large numbers of readers, particularly the young readers that avoid traditional newspapers. At present, paid newspapers and free ones coexist, but there is a clear threat that eventually the free tabloids will move upmarket into the paid newspapers' domain.

Central to Christensen's work is the difference between 'sustaining' technologies and 'disruptive' ones. Sustaining technologies improve the performance of established products along dimensions that mainstream customers in major markets have traditionally prized. Disruptive technologies are technologies that, initially at least, offer little visible benefit to incumbents. They generate simpler, cheaper products that are inappropriate to the needs of an organisation's core customers, appealing instead to less sophisticated lower-margin niche markets. While these products often include new features, these interest only a minority of customers. Thus products based on disruptive technologies are in the main unattractive to incumbent players with established product-market offerings because they offer less financial and market potential than current ones. Over time, however, the ugly duckling grows into a swan. Applications of the disruptive technology become more sophisticated, the market appeal grows, and a new market is established, one which incumbents must now enter late and at considerable cost.

Consequences for organisations

These definitions show that all instances of technological innovation are not the same, and, critically, there are no universally applicable strategic or organisational responses. Different innovations affect different firms in different ways, and those tasked with finding a strategic response need to understand the nature of the innovation and its implications on the firm.

This presupposes, however, that firms will change. Often they do not, or change inadequately. The pattern by which dominant incumbents with strategically appropriate resources follow technological advances, but nonetheless fail to master the changes these advances bring, is well documented. Analysis of the largest US firms over a significant time shows that repeatedly some of the largest, best resourced and best managed firms decline and perhaps go out of business, to be superseded by smaller players or newcomers that exploit new technologies (Utterback, 1994). This is a critical point for the media industry. It is all too easy to deride the media majors for failing to respond adequately to new technologies, but the reality is that this is a well-established norm across all sectors. Examples of incumbents who do manage to extend their leadership positions across technology transitions are the exception rather than the rule.

Many researchers attribute this to the dilemma that the need to respond to innovation poses for established firms: the structures, routines, systems and processes that ensure survival in stable environments, coupled with the culture and self-identity that successful incumbents develop over time, can stifle attempts to respond to a changed environment (Tushman and O'Reilly, 1997;

Burgelman, 1983, 1994; Hannan and Freeman, 1984; Tushman and Anderson, 1986; Christensen and Tuttle, 1999; Christensen and Overdorf, 2000). This 'pathology of sustained success' (Tushman and Smith, 2002: 387) has been observed in a wide range of different national and industry contexts (Tushman and Nelson, 1990; Leonard-Barton, 1992; Prahalad and Hamel, 1994; Christensen, 1997).

That does not mean that newer and/or smaller firms are necessarily more entrepreneurial, but rather that larger ones are often hampered by inbuilt impediments in the form of the routines, systems and processes that all organisations develop over time to ensure predictability. These are not malign in themselves. But at the same time as they ensure reliability, reduce the risk of error, reduce costs and simplify decision-making, they also increase inertia.

Indeed, success in general is likely to increase inertia. This happens in the following way. Successful organisations normally seek to strengthen their position still further by extending their existing core competencies and making incremental improvements to their products and processes. However, when a technology transition occurs and a new dominant design emerges, the incumbent is required to dismantle some aspect of these structures, even if they are functioning well. This is counter-intuitive and normally hard to do – so the organisation is effectively trapped by its success (Tushman and Anderson, 1986; Tushman and Smith, 2002).

Drucker (1985) and Christensen (1997) both highlight how simply running a successful business can easily predispose it to fail in new markets, how, as Christensen puts it, 'doing the right thing' by existing markets can help leading companies to fail in new ones. Well-run companies focus on the needs of their best customers and invest in new technologies that promise to improve value for this group according to current understanding of their needs. Viewed against these criteria, investments in disruptive technologies make little sense. Why devote resources to products that are inferior to current ones? The result is that companies which listen to their best customers and identify new products that promise greater profitability and growth are rarely able to build a case for investing in a disruptive technology until it is 'too late' – that is until market leaders have established themselves.

Disruptive innovations therefore disrupt two elements of incumbents' activities. First, they disrupt incumbents' markets by introducing new segments and/or product categories (Tushman and Smith, 2002). Second, they disrupt the architecture of the incumbent firm, because the firm will need to revise its strategy, markets, product portfolio and business model. An organisation's ability to do this depends on its resources, processes, and, critically, values. (Christensen and Overdorf, 2000). Values are decisive because they determine how resources are allocated and thus which new activities will be supported by the organisation. At base, the innovator's dilemma is caused by a maladaptive resource allocation process that concentrates resource commitments on markets and products that match existing business priorities and ignores 'downmarket' customer groups or less sophisticated products (Christensen and Bower, 1996).

The media industry has a tendency to resist technological advances (Wolf, 1999; Picard, 2004). The US television networks' long-time decline described in Chapter 2 has been attributed to their failure to respond to cable television and VCRs (Auletta, 1991). Support for this argument can be drawn from the fact that the media organisations that were able to build sizeable businesses out of cable television were new. CNN was a start-up that exploited the potential of new technologies including satellites, cable technology, handicams and suitcase-sized satellite up-links. MTV was created when the Warner Amex Satellite Entertainment Company saw the potential of combining cable television with promotional music videos.

Avoiding inertia

Much attention has been focused on the issue of how incumbent organisations can overcome inertial pressures and innovate in response to changing technologies. It focuses on the central tension that exists in all successful organisations between the need to optimise current operations and boost productivity, and the need to be innovative and flexible. There are examples of incumbent media organisations that have managed to seize the potential offered by technological advance. One of the most unlikely is the UK's BBC, the world's oldest public service broadcaster, which was able to launch successful responses to both digital television and the Internet,[1] as the examples below show.

Freeview   Freeview is a digital terrestrial television service that was launched from the shell of a failed commercial venture – ITVDigital – in the UK in 2002, and which achieved a strong market resonance in a very short space of time. At time of launch the 'old' service had just 600,000 homes subscribed. By January 2005 Freeview had increased this figure to over 5 million.

Freeview was a three-way joint venture between the BBC, Crown Castle and BSkyB. Many aspects of the project were unlikely. First was the fact that the BBC and Sky had been rivals for decades. Second was the sheer speed with which the service launched, especially since this involved re-engineering the entire technological architecture and creating a new media brand in four months. Freeview's success reflects the expertise the BBC brought to the project – in solving technological problems, consumer marketing, branding and exploiting its network of industry contacts. But it also succeeded because it used an extremely well-managed combination of relatively mundane organisational elements – project management, teamwork, leadership and communication – to sidestep the inertial forces within the parent organisation.

BBC News Online   BBC News Online is another surprising example of the BBC launching a highly successful product for a new media platform. This was launched in November 1997 with the task of repackaging the BBC's extensive news coverage for the Internet and using this as the base for a public service news site. The site found immediate resonance with online users and reached its page impression target for 1998 after only three months. From its launch until January 2001 it achieved an average monthly growth rate of 7.3 per cent, leading all UK news competitors. Traffic to the combined News and Sport Online site increased significantly faster than the UK Internet market. By June 2002 it was one of the most popular content-only websites in the UK, one of the most visited non-portal websites outside the US, and a consistent winner of online journalism awards. This performance stood in stark contrast to that of larger commercial peers in the media industry, for example, Disney, Time Warner and Bertelsmann, all of whom were experiencing severe problems with their Internet initiatives.

From many perspectives this success is surprising. In pursuing this venture the BBC had to contend with a broad range of inertial factors present in the organisation. This included the fact that the BBC's finances were over-stretched, it was committed to maintaining a broad span of traditional media services, it was not allowed to use public funds for risky investments, all its content was in audio-visual formats, it had no Internet skills, its culture was focused on UK markets and traditional media, its management processes were centralised and complex, and it was under high levels of public scrutiny. Again, an idiosyncratic combination of relatively prosaic factors such as style of leadership, team composition, resource profile, cognitive assumptions and cultural influences allowed the BBC to sidestep many of the hurdles which might have doomed the project to failure. Particularly important was the fact that News Online occupied an independent organi-sational space – free from the constraints of the parent. It was able to define its product and to allocate resources as it saw fit. Because it was a small low-visibility unit in the midst of a larger, more complex one, it could depart from BBC traditions as necessary. This situation replicated the traditional advantages of start-up status.

Organisation structure and technological change

In both of the BBC cases mentioned above, autonomy granted to the projects was a central element in the new businesses' respective ability to launch their products successfully. Finding the appropriate organisational structure to accommodate new units tasked with responding to new technologies is a key theme in the organisational technology literature, with a number of different options being proposed.

Autonomy

Independence is central to these propositions. Autonomy has long been posi-tively correlated with innovation in broad terms. For example, Kanter (1992) speaks of the need for firms to develop 'entrepreneurial enclaves' where innovative new businesses can develop. Christensen argues that incumbents' initiatives that seek to capitalise on a disruptive technology will fail in most cases because the commercialisation of that technology will always require a business model different from that used by the firm, and it is difficult for an institution to manage two different business models within one organisation. The only way established firms can avoid this dynamic is to create a new organisational space where an existing company can develop a strong market position in a disruptive technology. This can be achieved in three ways. The first is to spin out an independent company capable of developing the necessary values and, by extension, processes. The second is to create a new organisational structure within the corporate boundaries in which new processes can be developed, and which is staffed by teams that are physically located together and individually charged with personal responsibility for the success of the project (this was the option used by the BBC for News Online). The third option is to acquire an organisation whose processes and values closely match the requirements of the new task (Christensen, 1997; Christensen and Overdorf, 2000).

Gilbert (2002) carried out comparative research of US newspapers' print and online operations. He found that newspapers that had granted their online sites autonomy were twice as innovative as those that had integrated operations and had 60 per cent higher penetration. The prime benefit of autonomy was mindset, or 'framing'. While parents tended to view online activities as a threat to established systems, processes and so on, the new ventures were able to view the Internet as opportunity and therefore avoided a syndrome known as 'threat rigidity'.

Combined structures

'Internal corporate venturing' is a term coined by Burgelman (1983) for the process by which diversified firms transform activities based on new technologies into new businesses that involve competencies not previously available to the mainstream business of the parent. He identifies the kernel of this issue as the 'fundamental paradox' between the 'chaos arising from the autonomous strategic behaviour necessary to initiate such businesses, and the administrative discipline that must be imposed at some point so the parent can take advantage of the new strategic thrust' (1983: 121).

For Tushman and O'Reilly (1997) organisations seeking to be incrementally innovative in the long run must be ambidextrous, that is combine 'explorative' and 'exploitative' units within a single organisational structure. The explorative units' task is to experiment with new technologies, products and services. They need to be small, decentralised and highly independent so that they can develop a climate that fosters risk-taking and fast response, and accommodates flexible product structures and work processes. These elements in turn foster entrepreneurial competencies. The exploitative units' role is to maximise the performance of existing products, driving out variation and maximising efficiency.

Integrating the different cultures, structures, processes, management teams and human resources of these two types of unit is the task of senior management. They must ensure that the strategic context, which determines corporate objective-setting and resource allocation, and the structural context (the mechanisms by which operational behaviour is kept in line with strategy) do not preclude autonomous strategic behaviour which falls outside current strategic goals. They must also show unwavering support for entrepreneurial activity, regardless of fluctuations in the parent's wider business. This in turn requires a 'flexibility and tolerance for ambiguity in … strategic vision' that allows 'experimentation and selection' (Burgelman, 1983: 1362).

An alternative structural recommendation for incumbents seeking to master technological turbulence is to combine organic and mechanistic structures. This, it is argued, is a key 'dynamic capability' required in 'high velocity' environments (Brown and Eisenhardt, 1998). The mechanism that will allow organisations to flex rapidly in response to technological discontinuities and resolve the contradictions inherent in the need for stability and change is the 'semi-structure'. These are strategic business units that are small enough to be agile but large enough to be efficient and achieve some level of critical mass (Eisenhardt and Brown, 1999). Semi-structures allow organisations to 'patch' – a corporate-level process that allows incumbents to 'remap dynamically' resources in response to changing market opportunities, by 'adding, splitting, transferring, exiting, or combining chunks of businesses' (Eisenhardt and Brown, 1999: 74). Over time, this pattern of 'small' realignments coalesces into an organisational routine, and, in retrospect, into a cohesive strategy, albeit an emergent one.

A number of processes are required to support patching. There must be clearly defined project priorities that are tightly tied to resource allocations, extensive communication, including cross-project communication, and unambiguous responsibilities. However design processes must allow products to develop iteratively and flexibly. The combination of these elements should be 'neither so rigid as to control the process nor so chaotic that the process falls apart' (Brown and Eisenhardt, 1997: 3).

BBC News Online could be classified as a semi-structure, and many of these processes were present. There was a clear, consistent articulation of realisable vision ('create a PSB news service for the Internet'). The project team was multidisciplinary and represented a variety of expertise and backgrounds. They had an open and intense communication style and met frequently, meaning ideas circulated fast. This, coupled with a good information base ('real-time' market data plus internal and external sources), allowed the development of 'collective intuition' and therefore a superior grasp of changing market dynamics. Freedom of implementation meant strategy implementation could march in step with the market.

Managing such dual organisational structures, whether permanent or temporary, is complex. Edgar Schein (Coutu, 2002) argues that despite the attractiveness of autonomy, some level of integration is necessary so that the individual and group learning achieved by the new venture can permeate the rest of the organisation – otherwise there is a risk that this becomes a case of 'uncoordinated learning'. Successful change initiatives often begin within small groups that are 'off the parent's radar screen'. News of their achievements then percolates first outwards and then upwards. However, when a group is really innovative and high profile the rest of the organisation can come to resent it. This brings the risk of 'autoimmune system rejection' whereby the rest of the organisation tries to subvert and even reject the new unit. Such situations require careful management on the part of the parent.

Conclusions

This chapter has discussed how even though it is not a very evident element of the industry's self-image, the media industry is rooted in technology, and its fate is intimately connected to the path of technological innovation. Strategy, the subject of this book, is in part about how an organisation orchestrates a response to a changing environment. Technological advance is a permanent aspect of that environment. This can be a force for good – a source of new products and services and therefore of economic growth, but at the same time it poses challenges. First, the existing media products and services tend to decline when innovative new ones find resonance with the market. Second, incumbents, even leading ones, may be unseated and also begin a slow process of decline. Third, the path by which new technologies find a market results from a complex interplay between policy, innovation, social influences and organisational response.

However, not all technological advance is the same, and one of the key messages in this chapter is that media firms, like their peers in other sectors, need to be able to differentiate between different types of innovation and orchestrate their strategic responses accordingly. Their ability to respond depends not only on the 'content' of their strategic response, but also on the strategy process employed. Specifically, as we have seen in this chapter, a number of relatively mundane organisational elements must be subtly conceived, tightly interlinked and well executed. Critical amongst these are furthering creativity and innovation, finding the correct structural option for the new venture tasked with responding to a new technology, and fostering the right culture, mindset and leadership. These topics have featured in this chapter's analysis, but are handled as stand-alone subjects in the following chapters.

Note

1 For full case studies of these examples see 'Digital terrestrial television in the UK: the BBC and the launch of Freeview'. ECCH Case Study Number 305-293-1, and 'When old dogs learn new tricks: the launch of BBC News Online', ECCH Case Study Number 303-119-1, both by Lucy Küng.

SEVEN

Creativity and Innovation

Ideas shape the course of history. (John Maynard Keynes)

This chapter explores one of the most important strategic issues for media firms – creativity. The links between this and the previous chapter are strong: innovation is implicit in all technological advance, and new technology is often an important driver of creative responses.

This chapter explores the role of creativity in media organisations, looking particularly at its strategic importance, and why that importance is increasing in the current environment. Like other chapters, it begins by reviewing theoretical understanding of this issue, that is, creativity in organisational settings. It looks at how this has developed over time, and at how creativity from this perspective is defined, in the process delineating the distinction between creativity and innovation, two terms that are frequently and erroneously used interchangeably.

Thereafter, the bulk of this chapter draws heavily on a single body of theory, socio-constructivist approaches to organisational creativity. These identify the sources of creative responses in individuals and institutions, and the aspects of the work context that ensure these are present. The reasons for focusing on this particular body of theory are first that is highly pertinent to the media field and provides enlightening insights into the reasons behind performance differences between media firms. Second, despite its significance it is not well known by scholars or managers. One of the purposes of this chapter is to rectify this by providing a media orientated overview of an important body of theory. Two case studies are used to underline the relevance of this theory for the media, HBO and Pixar.

Media firms must, however, be creative in a broader realm than simply the content they produce, and the chapter therefore also explores creativity in terms of systems and business models, and their strategic implications. This is supported by two examples, CNN and Freeview, the UK digital television platform that was introduced in the previous chapter.

Creativity and the media

Creativity is, of course, central to all organisations – a new idea is the uncircumventable first stage in all new organisational initiatives – whether involving products, processes or procedures (Amabile, 1988; Staw, 1990; Woodman et al., 1993), and these new products, processes and procedures are the cornerstone of an organisation's ability to adapt, grow and compete (Kanter, 1983, 1988; Porter, 1985; Van de Ven, 1986). It has been suggested that the creative class, professionals mainly engaged in innovation, design and problem-solving, makes up a third of the US work force (Florida and Goodnight, 2005).

Creativity is arguably even more important for media firms – they don't need the odd great idea, but rather an ongoing supply (Caves, 2000; Hesmondhalgh, 2002; Towse, 2000). Performance is strongly affected by the quality of content they create, with 'create' being the operative word. The act of content generation is the sector's fundamental activity and *raison d'être*, and thus the requirement for creativity is constant.

From an economic perspective, creativity is a critical strategic resource because of the nature of cultural goods. Because they can rarely be standardised on a long-term basis, and because customer demand is fickle, there is an incessant need for novelty: the higher the levels of product creativity, the higher the media firm's ability to satisfy this customer need, and the greater the potential for competitive advantage. This gives rise to the primacy of creativity as a strategic organisational resource, since 'without their employees coming up with ideas that can be turned into commercial, saleable commodities [media firms] are dead' (Scase, 2002: 8).

Inside the sector, creativity is so much part of the DNA of everyday activities that it is often hard to see at surface level. Researchers without empirical exposure to the sector can be surprised by the absence of roles or business units overtly tasked with 'innovation' or 'research and development', and wrongly conclude that the industry places surprisingly little emphasis on such an important factor. What they miss is that creativity is deeply embedded in many routine roles. And the need for creativity extends further than coming up with the original idea: decisions concerning how to develop the product, exploit technological features, find the right price, recruit the right talent, and promote the product to the industry and to consumers, all involve creativity.

The need for creativity – in all firms, not just media ones – is exacerbated when environments become more turbulent (Schumpeter, 1942; DeVanna and Tichy, 1990; Bartlett and Ghoshal, 1993; Bettis and Hitt, 1995; Ford and Gioia, 1995; Dutton et al., 1997; Hitt et al., 1998; Eisenhardt and Martin, 2000; Danneels, 2002), especially when that turbulence involves emerging technologies (Yoffie, 1997), as is currently the case with the media sector. Thus, while creativity has always been critical to the media industry, the current spate of technological changes under way has enlarged that need (Yoffie, 1997; Brown and Eisenhardt, 1998) to include activities concerned with the organisation's systems, processes and strategy. In a recent study of media majors' convergence strategies, Dennis, Wharley and Sheridan commented that:

> once associated with writers, producers and designers, creativity is now mentioned as an essential quality for managers and executives as well. Partly because some content producers are medium-centric and have little experience across platforms, business executives are increasingly asked to think creatively about integrating content, marketing strategies and audience data beyond decades old distribution channels as they seek new formats and communicative styles. Given the need for business models that exploit convergence, creativity is a critical skill set. (Dennis et al., 2006: 3a)

Although strategy theorists agree on the importance of creativity to organisations, overall, surprisingly little attention has been devoted to increasing understanding of its origins and influence on performance. This omission is reflected in science in general,[1] where for a variety of reasons the subject was long avoided, a tradition stretching back to Plato, who felt that creativity involved divine intervention and was therefore outside the scope of man's intervention. Popper concluded that research into creativity was irrelevant rather than unfeasible since creative inspiration is an irrational process and could not be accessed via scientific or systematic investigation. For management researchers, especially those of the positivist school, the inspirational component of creative acts made them hard to accommodate within rational management concepts.

Researching creativity

Despite these reservations, from the 1950s onwards a steady and growing stream of researchers has investigated the nature and causes of creativity, albeit not within the context of the media industry. In the period from 1950 to the 1980s there were two clear strands in this work: the first focused investigations on the creative individual, and the second on the creative process.

Investigations into gifted individuals were premised on the assumption that creativity was more or less determined at birth, that a few exceptional individuals are 'born creative'. This so-called 'person approach' looked at outstandingly creative individuals in the field of arts and science, often retrospectively through analysis of autobiographies, letters, journals and other first-person accounts, and sought to identify the cognitive processes and personality traits that might be predictive of creative performance (Barron and Harrington, 1981; Amabile, 1988, 1996; Deazin et al., 1999). A typical finding is Koestler's proposition that rather than being a random process, creativity results from the deliberate connection of two previously unconnected 'matrices of thought' (1964, cited in Amabile, 1996: 21). From a gifted individual's thought processes research shifted to the wider personality of creative individuals, that is to 'those patterns of traits that are characteristic of creative persons' (Guilford, 1950, cited in Amabile, 1996: 21), and an approach rooted in psychometric testing.

The second major strand in creativity research concerned the process by which creative products are generated, the so-called 'process/product approach to creativity'. This concentrates on the characteristics of processes that lead to creative outcomes (Amabile, 1988, 1996; Oldham and Cummings, 1996) and has now become the dominant approach to the field (Amabile, 1983; Woodman et al., 1993; Oldham and Cummings, 1996).

Context was seldom an explicitly addressed variable in these studies, although the majority of these were conducted in creative or intellectual settings such as schools and various types of cultural institutions (Ford, 1996). Over the years the research domain has broadened to include more prosaic institutional settings (Ford and Gioia, 1995) and from group and to pan-organisational environments – although investigations of small project groups have tended to dominate (Deazin et al., 1999).

However, an explicit focus on the influence of the work setting on creativity was absent until the 1980s when Amabile sensitised the research community to this omission and instituted a new branch of research (Staw, 1990; Ford and Gioia, 1995; Oldham and Cummings, 1996). This new research strand, also known as 'interactionist' or 'socio-constructivist' approaches, looks at how social influences and contextual factors influence creativity. Aspects previously stressed such as cognitive skills, personality traits and process issues, are not ignored but subsumed into a larger framework. The approach is more egalitarian than some: creativity is not restricted to the chosen few, rather it assumes that given the right task and circumstances most individuals are capable of certain levels of creativity. To that extent it is also positivist in that it assumes that changes in the environment can produce changes in levels of creativity – this has led to criticisms of functional-reductionism (Rousseau, 1985; Deazin et al., 1999).

This approach does, however, allow a coherent framework to be constructed concerning how strategic management can further creativity. It is therefore used to supply a backbone for the analysis and discussion in this chapter, since media organisations cannot rely on a scattershot approach to creativity but rather need a systematic strategy for building sustained creativity.

Defining creativity

This chapter discusses recent research looking at creativity in organizational settings, where the creative inputs are destined for commercial purposes.

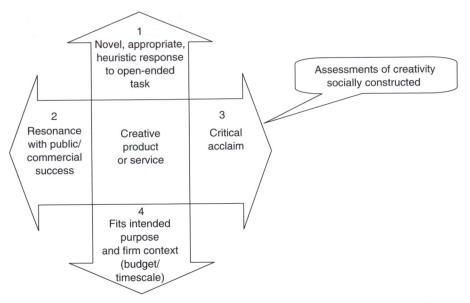

Figure 7.1 Defining criteria of creativity in organisational settings (adapted from Arnabile, 1983, 1988, 1986)

Lampel et al. (2000) note the challenges associated with establishing definitive definitions of quality for media products, arising from the fact that their consumption is a highly subjective experience.

Theories of organisational creativity do, however, provide a definition of creativity that is robust enough to be employed as a basis for research: 'A product or response will be judged as creative to the extent that (a) it is both a novel and appropriate, useful, correct or valuable response to the task at hand, and (b) the task is heuristic rather than algorithmic' (Amabile, 1996: 35). Drawing from this definition, four criteria can be identified to define creativity in a product or service:

1. It is original, novel or unique and solves a challenge that is open-ended, where there is no clear straightforward path to an acceptable outcome (in psychological terms an heuristic rather than an algorithmic response to a problem). The term 'path to a solution' is critical – with heuristic tasks it is part of the problem-solver's task to identify an appropriate solution, and identifying the nature and scope of the problem is a key aspect of the creative task (Amabile, 1983: 127). Novelty for commercial products that need to find a market, as opposed to those designed to meet purely artistic and cultural ends, does however need to be tempered. Originality is important, but commercial media products ideally blend familiar and novel elements (Lampel et al., 2000), and finding a synthesis of the two is a highly subjective process that depends on high levels of sector expertise (the importance of expertise for sustained creativity is discussed below).
2. It resonates with the public and/or finds commercial success, and by extension is useful, has value and/or brings benefits to others. An original product which pleases only those who created it, and perhaps a select group of industry experts, but which is not

perceived by potential users or customers as valuable and novel, cannot be termed a successful creative entity according to this body of theory.

3. It receives critical acclaim. Assessments of creativity are socially constructed, that is, there are no absolute criteria for judging whether a product is creative or not, subjective judgement is always involved. That subjective judgement derives from the social context and development of the particular field. It is therefore impossible to judge the creativity of a product without some knowledge of what else exists in a domain at a given time (Amabile, 1996: 38) – which means that creativity is linked with experience and expertise in a certain field. Thus definitions of creativity also include assessments from industry insiders and experts. A useful metric in this regard for the media industry is industry awards.

4. Finally, and here the organisational perspective comes to the fore, in order to be creative a product must help the organisation meet its strategic objectives and work within available budgets and timeframes.

Creativity versus innovation

Innovation and creativity are slippery concepts. Practitioners tend to use them interchangeably, and so do many researchers – see, for example, Drucker (1985) and Burns and Stalker (1961/1994). This does, however, confuse two different streams of scientific research with different scholarly associations, theoretical roots and areas of application.

Research into creativity is based, at root, on psychology. It focuses on the initial inspiration – the 'bright idea' – that leads to the creation of a new product or service. Innovation from this perspective is understood as the successful implementation of creative ideas in the shape of processes, products or services (Amabile, 1988, 1993; Woodman in Ford and Gioia, 1995; Oldham and Cummings, 1996).

Innovation is a broader concept. Innovation theory concerns the processes by which products are manufactured, the organisation structures and strategies that support this process, and the relationship between innovation and corporate performance (Utterback, 1994). Thus Janszen (2000: 8) defines innovation as 'the commercialization of something new'. Theories of innovation stem predominantly from the fields of engineering and technology management. These tend to subsume creativity under the umbrella term of innovation, viewing creativity as a subset of the broader domain of innovation, and innovation as a subset of an even broader construct of organisational change (Woodman et al. 1993). Innovation theory is closely linked to the study of entrepreneurship – thus Drucker (1985: 26) describes it as 'the specific instrument of entrepreneurship'.

Components of creativity

The successful introduction of new programs, products and services depends on a person or team having a good idea (the creative spark) and then being able to develop that idea further. Both stages of the creative process are strongly influenced by the social environment within organisations (Amabile et al., 1996). According to socio-constructivist approaches, three elements must be present in the social environment for creativity to occur and these are outlined below (these are discussed in detail in Amabile, 1983, 1988, 1993, 1996, 1998; Amabile et al., 1994, 1996, 2002, and the following text draws on these references unless otherwise indicated):

Creativity-relevant skills

The best way to have a good idea is to have lots of ideas. (Linus Pauling)

These refer to the ability to think creatively and generate different alternatives. Alternatives are necessary because individuals who have access to a variety of potentially relevant ideas are more likely to make the connections that can lead to creativity (Amabile et al., 1996). Creativity-relevant skills include:

- *Cognitive style.* This includes the ability to understand complexities, to break 'cognitive set' during problem solving, to keep options open as long as possible, to suspend judgement, to use 'wide' categories allowing relationships to be found between apparently diverse pieces of information, to remember accurately and to break out of 'performance scripts'. Bennis and Biederman (1997) point out that members of highly creative teams tend to enjoy this kind of problem-solving activity for its own sake.
- *Creativity heuristics.* This involves ways of approaching a problem that can lead to set-breaking and novel ideas. They can be highly idiosyncratic, but they should allow the exploration of new cognitive pathways.
- *Working style.* Creativity requires a working style that is far from popular preconceptions concerning the work style of 'creative individuals'. Rather than being chaotic and undisciplined, as popularly understood, creative teams need to combine a range of rather pragmatic abilities: to concentrate for long periods, to abandon unproductive searches or temporarily give up on stubborn problems, persistence, high energy levels, high levels of productivity, self-discipline, an ability to delay gratification, perseverance in the face of frustration, independent judgement, a tolerance for ambiguity, a willingness to take risks, and a high level of self-initiated, task-orientated striving for excellence.

Expertise

Termed by psychologists as 'domain-relevant skills', expertise represents a combination of knowledge of the existing facts and issues concerning a specific area, coupled with the experience necessary to be able to find feasible solutions to problems in that field. Expertise, unsurprisingly, arises from immersion and experience, and for that reason newcomers to an area who lack knowledge of prior work are unlikely to be able to come up with truly creative solutions.

Expertise in the media field tends to rest on tacit rather than codified knowledge (Lampel et al., 2000). It stems not from qualifications attained, as, say in the fields of engineering or finance, but from a combination of experience derived from exposure to the field and individual judgement and intuition.

Intrinsic motivation

The greatest pleasure that life has to offer is the satisfaction that flows from participating in a difficult and challenging undertaking. (Mihaly Csikszentmihalyi)

Intrinsic motivation, the final component of creativity listed here, is arguably the most important. It provides the cornerstone for this body of theory, which is also known as the 'intrinsic motivation theory of creativity'. Intrinsic motivation will be familiar to many as the state of 'flow'. It means being motivated to do something for its own sake, because the task in itself is pleasurable and rewarding, rather than because it provides a means to meet an extrinsic goal. Intrinsic motivation matters for creativity because when levels are high so too is cognitive flexibility and the ability to deal with complexity (McGraw, 1978), and individuals are more likely to take risks, explore new solutions and experiment. Intrinsic motivation explains why many talented and highly educated individuals are keen to work in the media industry and creative arts despite relatively low salaries: the state of flow is so gratifying that people will tolerate low pay (or no pay at all in the case of industry internships), and in extreme cases physical or psychological discomfort to achieve it, something that the media industry and cultural sector wittingly or unwittingly has long exploited.

By contrast external motivation – the motivation which results from external goals – can undermine creativity. External motivation is motivation that arises from sources outside of the task – evaluation, deadlines, rewards such as bonuses, competition – even a nagging parent in the case of children. It is important to note that extrinsic motivation does not preclude high quality output – rewards, bonuses, deadlines, even threats. It can give rise to good work, but it narrows the cognitive focus and precludes the path-breaking novel solutions that are the hallmark of true creativity. External motivation, especially financial rewards, has been found to 'crowd out' intrinsic motivation (Frey and Jegen, 2000) – as Drucker pointed out when he warned against 'bribing' knowledge workers with stock options (Drucker, 1985).

Factors in the work environment affecting intrinsic motivation

The idea that it is possible to 'organise' for creativity may seem like a contradiction in terms, but a prime contribution of this body of theory is to demonstrate that relatively prosaic planned changes in the work environment can have a direct effect on levels of intrinsic motivation, and therefore on creativity. Five aspects of the work environment have been identified as particularly influential (these are discussed in detail in Amabile, 1983, 1988, 1993, 1996, 1998; Amabile et al., 1994, 1996, 2002, and these sources are the prime references in the following sub-sections, unless otherwise indicated)

Encouragement	• Creativity needs explicit encouragement • Real value of project must be clear
Autonomy	• Freedom concerning means but not ends • Autonomy concerning process fosters ownership and intrinsic motivation.

Resources
  – money
  – time
	• Resource slack reduces focus and discipline
	• Parsimony means creativity channelled into increasing budgets
	• Over-tight deadlines reduce scope for 'combinatorial play' and risk burnout

Challenge	• Project goals should be clear, stable and feasible • Too much challenge overwhelms and demotivates
Team composition	• Should represent diversity of perspectives and backgrounds

Figure 7.2   Contextual factors influencing levels of intrinsic motivation (adapted from Amabile, 1983, 1988, 1993, 1996, 1998; Amabile et al., 1994, 1996, 2002)

Encouragement

If creativity is required from staff then this needs to made clear. This involves more than paying lip service to the idea of creativity: it must be demonstrated through management action (how priorities are set, which projects are viewed as most important, what kinds of behaviours are rewarded, etc.) that creativity is central to current operations and future success. Creative contributions need to be publicly celebrated. Feedback on new ideas is also important. If these are disregarded or handled clumsily staff can feel that the interest in creativity is only cosmetic and experimentation will be discouraged. This is dangerous since high levels of creativity need high levels of experimentation. Attention must be paid to all suggestions, good or bad, and ideas that are unsuitable need to be evaluated constructively.

Challenge

> Creative people work for the love of a challenge. They crave the feeling of accomplishment that comes from cracking a riddle ... they want to do good work. (Florida and Goodnight, 2005: 127)

One exception to the rule that extrinsic motivators hinder creativity is the finding that creativity is enhanced by clearly defined overall project goals (Amabile and Gryskiewicz, 1989). Complex tasks that that are challenging, multi-faceted and non-routine increase intrinsic motivation (Amabile, 1988, Oldham and Cummings, 1996), but the degree of stretch needs to be calibrated carefully. Complex challenges need to be mobilising but not overwhelming, and there needs to be a good match with expertise and creative-thinking skills. Kanter (2006) describes how adjusting the creative challenge increased creativity at *Time* magazine. In 1992, when new CEO Don Logan took over, the magazine was poor at developing new titles. This was reversed by replacing a too-demanding requirement that new concepts should have immediate bestseller potential with a requirement that staff experiment with original ideas with long-term potential.

Autonomy

Autonomy featured prominently in the last chapter's discussions of how organisations can structure themselves to respond to technological advance. This chapter provides insights into why autonomy also fosters creativity.

As we saw in Chapter 2's examination of value chain changes in the sector, and as is reviewed in Chapter 9's analysis of structural developments, in the current climate there are tendencies for media organisations to seek to increase critical mass, improve cross-platform synergies, and boost economies of scale and scope through increasing centralisation and integration and tighter management overall. However, such moves can be detrimental to levels of creativity because they limit autonomy, and autonomy is central to intrinsic motivation and therefore creativity.

Autonomy is perhaps first among equals of the contextual factors required for high levels of intrinsic motivation, but like other contextual factors discussed here, the amount needs to be carefully gauged. Those engaged in creative projects need autonomy, particularly freedom from organisational constraints such as burdensome reporting requirements and non-essential obligations. There needs to be autonomy, too, concerning how the goal is to be achieved (process), but not concerning the nature of the goal itself, which should remain clear, constant and unambiguous. Autonomy concerning process fosters creativity because it heightens a sense of ownership, and therefore intrinsic motivation, and allows employees to approach problems in ways that make the most of their expertise.

The link between small group autonomy and creativity appears to be familiar to some of the largest players in the industry. News Corporation views small decentralised groups as critical for generating quality content within the context of a large global media conglomerate,[2] and the CEO, Rupert Murdoch, has spoken of the dilemma of striking a balance between encouraging independence but ensuring overall responsibility. He gives executives at local level the freedom to deal with problems as they arise, but will personally intervene in crisis situations (Coleridge, 1993, cited in Marjoribanks, 2000).

Bertelsmann has also long had the policy of encouraging autonomy in its strategic business units. Reinhard Mohn made decentralization the company's official policy in 1959 because he believed that managers of profit centres would thrive best with high levels of autonomy and the freedom to diversify and expand. The company departed from this strategy under Middlehof, CEO from 1998 to 2002, who felt the decentralised structure inhibited a coherent Internet strategy and slowed decision-making. He increased centralisation to heighten cross-unit synergies and created an Executive Council and Office of the Chairman. By mid-2001

Bertelsmann's Internet businesses were failing, the Napster experiment had yet to bear fruit and company incomes were being battered by a global advertising downturn. Middlehof's subsequent exit arose from a variety of reasons, including the fact that his attempts at centralisation had brought him into conflict with the corporate culture which valued business unit independence. Bertelsmann has since returned to its policy of decentralisation:

> The principle of decentralization is at the heart of Bertelsmann's management philosophy. It enables our employees to act with flexibility, responsibility, efficiency and entrepreneurial freedom. Our operating businesses are run by managers who act as entrepreneurs: they enjoy considerable independence and bear full responsibility for the performance of their companies. Our executives act not only in the best interests of their individual businesses, but are also obligated to the interests of the group as a whole.[3]

Resources

The critical resources are money and time, and, as with autonomy, the levels of both need to be carefully judged. They should be sufficient to allow the task to be achieved, but not over-generous since resource slack can reduce project focus and discipline (Nohria and Gulati, 1996). Conversely, if funding is meagre, creativity can be channelled into finding additional funds. To return to News Corporation, Fox Searchlight places a cap of $15 million on budgets for speciality movies because this creates a culture where greater risks are taken because the potential damage is limited.[4]

In terms of time as a resource, deadlines for creative projects need to be carefully judged. Despite the received wisdom that deadlines focus the mind and increase creativity, if these are too demanding and unrealistic staff will have no time to 'play' with concepts and solutions. This is important since creativity results from the formation of a large number of associations in the mind, followed by the selection of associations that are particularly interesting and useful. Time pressures tend to remove scope for such combinatorial play and bring the risk of burnout.

Team composition and function

While creativity is popularly supposed to result from solitary acts of inspiration, in organisational settings creative projects require the coordinated contributions of a team representing diversity in terms of perspective, expertise and background. The reason is that creative challenges are often epistemologically unsolvable by any one person and require input from a range of specialist disciplines and a broad palette of expertise. Homogeneous teams work against creativity since too much social cohesion can inhibit the exchange of ideas and diminish creativity. Team working practices need to be open to encourage the constructive challenging of ideas and shared commitment, which in time can allow the development of a strong sub-culture. Attention needs to be given to the team's communication skills. If these are inadequate expertise will not be shared as necessary, and nor will the tacit knowledge that emerges during the course of the project (Kanter, 2006).

This body of somewhat practical theory has been discussed in detail because it provides many insights into differences between the respective creative performances of media firms. In the following pages these concepts are applied to two cases, Home Box Office Original Programming Division and Pixar Animation Studios. The goals are to illustrate how these theories work in practice, and to demonstrate how, in organisations with a track record of high levels of creativity, the various contributory factors are both deeply embedded and interlinked in a systemic way that is hard for competitors to replicate.

Home Box Office Original Programming Division

HBO has shaped a creative environment which almost anyone would tell you is the best place to work in town. (Peter Chernin, President and COO News Corporation, *Financial Times*, 1 April 2003)

Home Box Office, or HBO for short, is a pay cable television network in the US. Founded by Time Inc. in 1972, as the name implies, HBO started life as a pay movie/special service cable operation in New York offering recent Hollywood films and occasional boxing matches. When the channel was launched original entertainment content did not extend far beyond one-hour stand-up comic specials, and the channel was noted for its frugal spending in comparison with network television (Shamsie, 2003).

However, from these inauspicious beginnings its original programming division has grown into an industry leader in creative original programming, responsible for a chain of critical and commercial hits including *The Sopranos*, *Sex and the City* and *Six Feet Under*. These are credited with increasing subscriptions to the point that in 2003 one-third of all US households subscribed to HBO or its sister channel, Cinemax.

Under the slogan 'It's not TV, its HBO' original programming is now central to HBO's strategic positioning. Programmes such as *The Sopranos, Sex and the City*, and *Six Feet Under* can be judged as creative according to the definition given earlier in this chapter. They are novel, since HBO's trademark is its ability to disregard the elements judged pre-requisites of commercial successes by other broadcast networks, such as likeable characters or clear underlying premises (Shamsie, 2003), and yet be successful. Second, in terms of commercial success, HBO is one of the most profitable television companies in the US. In 2002 its earnings before interest, tax, depreciation and amortisation were $847m on revenues of just over $3bn, making it one of the most successful parts of AOL Time Warner,[5] with HBO joint ventures reaching 16 million subscribers in over 50 countries.[6] The season finale of *The Sopranos* beat all other broadcast networks for the time period in total viewers.[7] Third, HBO also enjoys substantial critical acclaim. It won 24 Emmys in the 2002 Primetime Emmy Awards competition, tying with NBC for the most awards, and seven Golden Globe awards in 2003, more than any other network.

HBO's series have been nominated for twice as many Golden Globe awards as those of any of the broadcast networks.[8] Senior executives in competing organisations view the network as leading the way in creative programming.[9] The products of HBO's original programming division therefore meet the defining criteria for creativity.

In terms of the core components required for creativity in organisational settings, two elements are particularly noteworthy. The first is sector expertise. Senior executives synthesise deep knowledge of entertainment content in the widest sense, that is, script writing, plot, character, dialogue, and so on, and also of how the business of cable television functions, particularly audience behaviour and business models. Further expertise comes from the freelance creative staff. Here a virtuous circle comes into play: the critical praise received by HBO programmes attracts high calibre writers who want to be involved in HBO programmes. Their high calibre skills contribute to the ongoing creative quality of the channel's output, which in turn leads to commercial and critical success, continuing to attract high-quality creative freelancers.

The contextual factors conducive to intrinsic motivation are also present in the HBO work setting. First, in terms of creative challenge, at HBO creativity is intrinsic to its strategic vision, and its core mandate, its strategic positioning, is 'to be good and different' (Shamsie, 2003: 63). Its advertising strapline is 'It's not TV, it's HBO'. The company seeks to ensure that staff have the scope to realise this goal, particularly ensuring they have the space to concentrate on the creative task. In the works of Alan Ball, screenwriter of *Six Feet Under*, 'there's less levels of bureaucracy to dig through ... To make a good show on HBO is almost easier work. You're living and dying by what you believe in, and you're not being nibbled to death by ducks' (cited in Shamsie, 2003: 64).

In terms of autonomy, although part of the Time Warner empire HBO enjoys high levels of independence, being physically and operationally removed from the conglomerate's other TV activities. Its policy is to give its staff scope for creativity within a tightly controlled operation – writers have high levels of artistic freedom, but must seek to create series that will garner critical acclaim and approval with the viewing public. HBO's business model also contributes to creative autonomy, since cable subscription funding means it is less reliant on fast ratings success and less burdened by regulation than the mainstream networks.

With regard to resources, HBO is adequately funded but finances are not over-abundant: it invests around $400 million annually in programming, around a quarter less than its network competitors. However the fact that this funding comes from subscription fees means that its income is relatively secure and not too sensitive to dips in the overall economy (which affect media advertising spend disproportionately). In terms of time, HBO's deadlines allow staff to play with concepts: it is unique in the industry for offering writers a five-year contract, with the explicit goal of providing creative stability and the psychological freedom to take risks.

Pixar Animation Studios

[T]he most reliable creative force in Hollywood. (Kenneth Turan in the *Los Angeles Times*, cited in *Slate*, 5 June 2003)

Pixar Animation Studios Ltd was founded in 1986 when Steve Jobs, co-founder and chairman of Apple Computer, Inc. used his private funds to purchase the computer development of Lucasfilm for $10 million and incorporated it as an independent company of which he became Chairman and Chief Executive Officer. His goal was to create a major movie studio that would combine computer-generated animation technology with creative talent to create full-length animated films that would appeal to audiences of all ages.

By the end of 1986, the company had developed a computer that processed 3D graphics at a speed of 40 million instructions per second. Pixar's technical and creative teams collaborated to develop three core-proprietary systems: the animation software system (used in modelling, animating and lighting); the production software system (used in the scheduling, coordinating and tracking of computer animation projects); and RenderMan (used to apply textures and colours to the 3D objects).

The first decade was a struggle financially. Revenues came mainly from sales of its software[10] and film activities were focused primarily on commercials for the advertising industry – it was producing up to 15 a year in the early 1990s.[11] It did, however, start producing highly acclaimed short films, such as *Luxo Jnr* (1986) and *Tin Toy* (1988), which was the first computer-animated film to win an Academy Award. These provided a foundation for its first major success, *Toy Story*, which was released in 1995 and was the world's first full-length 3D animated feature film and the first full-length computer animated film to win an Academy Award. Since then the studio has had a solid procession of box office hits.

In 1991 Pixar signed an agreement with Disney covering three movies whereby Pixar would create the screenplays and Disney would control the marketing and licensing. Disney would fund and distribute the films, which would be released under Walt Disney Pictures, and Pixar would share a portion of the profits towards the development costs. Disney also retained merchandising rights and the rights to develop sequels. After the success of the first film, *Toy Story*, where Disney retained 90 per cent of the profits, the deal was renegotiated. According to the revised arrangement both partners shared profits equally, once a distribution fee of 12 per cent had been deducted, and Pixar agreed to increase the number of joint movies to five.

Following the success of *Finding Nemo*, Pixar wanted to renegotiate again. Disney refused and relations soured to a point where the partnership ended in January 2004. However, after Michael Eisner left Disney in 2005 the relationship was rebuilt, and in 2006 Disney bought Pixar outright for $7.4 billion. Jobs joined the Disney board and John Lasseter, Pixar's Creative Director, became Disney's Chief Creative Officer.

Pixar's output in the period prior to its acquisition by Disney meets all the defining criteria for creative products. In terms of uniqueness, Pixar films were novel, not only in their content, but because they re-energised and expanded the animated film genre, allowing it to 'lead the computer animation industry, both technically and aesthetically',[12] in the process inventing a niche that proved very difficult for competitors to duplicate. They abandoned hand-drawn animation in favour of digital techniques, but used these to create extraordinary levels of texture and sensory detail – the matted wet rat fur in *Ratatouille*, for example.

Creativity was apparent also in the notion fundamental to its business model, that animated films could be made sophisticated enough to appeal to adults as well as children and therefore to work for both markets simultaneously. This contributed to the commercial success of their output. Pixar's first release, *Toy Story*, was the highest grossing film of the year, making over $362 million worldwide, and since then the studio has developed an unheard of succession of box office hits. With the exception of *Cars* (interestingly the first film to be released after the Disney marriage), each has broken box office records. The worldwide grosses for each film are as follows: *Toy Story* (1995) $362 million, *A Bug's Life* (1998) $363 million, *Toy Story 2* (1999) $485 million, *Monsters, Inc.* (2001) $525 million, *Finding Nemo* (2003) $865 million, *The Incredibles* (2004) $631 (the worldwide gross for *Cars* (2006), as of March 2007, was $455 million).

In terms of the third criterion, critical acclaim, Pixar has received countless industry accolades. *Tin Toy* (1988), was the first computer-animated short to win an Academy Award and *Toy Story* was the first computer-animated feature film to win an Academy Award. By 2003 the studio had won 15 Academy Awards, primarily for technical innovations. The fourth criterion concerns a product's fit with organisational requirements: all of Pixar's films have been developed on schedule and to relatively modest budgets.

To turn to the core components of creativity, Pixar's quotas of expertise and intrinsic motivation are substantial. Its technological expertise is renowned, and centres on RenderMan, a programing language that allows the disparate parts of the 3D production process to connect and communicate. This is available commercially and has become an industry standard, as have a batch of associated programs covering other aspects of the computer-animation process that it has developed and marketed. Its mastery of the artistic skills involved in animated film making is also widely respected, as are its narrative skills in the field of storytelling, script writing, portrayal of characters and storyboarding. The practice of using short films as a public interim milestone in its search to extend its artistic and technological expertise is an important structural element in this regard.

Levels of intrinsic motivation are also high – many working in the company share a passion for the animated film that started in childhood. In terms of creative-thinking skills, Pixar also lays emphasis on team brainstorming, a process it terms 'catalytic collaboration'.

If we turn to the contextual factors that boost intrinsic motivation, we see, first, that in terms of encouragement and challenge, Pixar seeks to further staff's existing love of the medium by enthusing them about the products in hand. The studio has shunned the 'hit model'. Instead, all energies are focused on a small number of films. In order to keep the creative challenge manageable, creatives are encouraged to break larger tasks down into creative steps (another factor behind its tradition of using short films as an opportunity to experiment with new concepts and techniques).

In terms of autonomy, it is an explicit goal at Pixar to foster a sense of creative ownership at team level. In terms of resources, financial resources are adequate but not over-generous. Deadlines are kept as reasonable as is feasible – efforts are made not to over-extend staff and to prevent burnout. Finally, teamwork is the basic building block of Pixar's modus operandi. It seeks to promote 'unfettered group invention' and stresses that its films are the product of groups, rather than key individuals.

Creativity and the business model

If we look at the two examples in this chapter, Home Box Office and Pixar, while the respective funding bases differ, their business models were similar in that they provided a degree of protection from market forces. HBO was subscription financed, which meant it had the luxury of being able to build audiences slowly in step with word-of-mouth publicity as people acclimatised to the novelty of their products. Pixar had a co-financing deal with Disney. This meant more freedom to incubate ideas, experiment and take creative risks. This dynamic, incidentally, also contributes to the BBC's track record in comedy. Licence fee funding allowed it to persevere with programmes such as *Fawlty Towers* and *Monty Python* – which ultimately proved to be lucrative long-term products – despite the fact that audiences were initially sceptical.

Thus this business model, or more accurately business models that provide a degree of cushioning from market forces, appears to be positively correlated with creativity. This is an area where more research is needed, but a likely mechanism might be that such arrangements create a level of psychological security that encourages playfulness and combinatorial play, a greater focus on product that is not diluted with hard-line management issues, and the freedom to incubate ideas and allow audiences to build slowly.

Creativity, systems and strategy

It is easy to restrict the search for creativity in the media industry to the realm of content, but creativity is also required in the broader set of activities concerned with how organisations mount a response to their strategic environment. Novel new ideas are needed to enable media firms to grow, adapt and compete. As we have seen, the media industry has been subject to a continuous stream of fundamental changes to the technologies used to develop and deliver products – ranging from new platforms such as cable, satellite and the Internet to the digital downloading and sharing of media files. This creates a fundamental ongoing need for renewal in terms of systems, process and strategy, irrespective of the need to develop new media products. Organisations that master these challenges can establish powerful bases of strategic advantage, as two examples from the broadcasting sector demonstrate.

CNN

CNN during the first 16 years of its life (from its founding in 1986 to its takeover by Time Warner in 1996) offers many examples of creativity in terms of systems and strategy. CNN's concept has been so widely adopted by the industry that it is hard now to view it as exceptional, but it as extremely novel when it first emerged.

The idea behind CNN was to set up a channel that concentrated only on news, and broadcast that news round the clock. The news would be global, and would be live. CNN would try to cover news as it happened, rather than report after the fact. A central element of this was to create 'a role in the process for the viewers'. This would be achieved by avoiding the groomed approach of the US networks in favour of open sets within newsrooms, and a presenting style that would create a sense of immediacy, authenticity, and of stories evolving as viewers watched. Overcoming industry cynicism this unconventional approach held real attraction for viewers and revitalised what had become a stale genre – so much so that two decades later the CNN style has become a standard for news delivery worldwide.

The core product can therefore be categorised as creative. But creativity was also evident in the systems and processes that supported the content proposition. The concept of CNN was designed to exploit a number of simultaneous technological advances – cable television, communications satellites, suitcase-size satellite uplinks and handy cams – in order to reinvent the way news is produced and delivered. A number of highly innovative processes were introduced in order to implement this strategy against a background of extremely limited resources – both in terms of time and money. The most famous example is probably the invention of the video journalist or VJ. The VJ is a 'one-man television band' that is capable of covering a story without the expense of a full film crew, shooting video as well as reporting, and then editing the material too. Like many of Ted Turner inventions, this concept has now been adopted by broadcasters all over the world. Similar organisational creativity can be found in CNN's network of broadcast affiliates all over the world. The traditional affiliate relationship is one-way from the channel or network, to the affiliate, and most news organisations pride themselves on the exclusivity of their content. CNN revisited this approach by establishing a reciprocal network of 600 television stations worldwide which both received news feeds from CNN, but also fed local footage back to CNN. This was initially a pragmatic solution to the need to offer cover global coverage without adequate resources, but it became a strategic asset in that it enabled CNN to build a global presence quickly, defray the cost of its own newsgathering, and provided footage of breaking events all over the world far more quickly than its competitors could get news crews on the scene.

Freeview

The Freeview case was introduced in the previous chapter where the various organisational elements that allowed the BBC to launch a complicated digital television product quickly and successfully were introduced. This chapter will extend the case by looking at the role of creativity in the venture.

Freeview is an unusual media product – a brand rather than a channel or broadcaster. It offers a number of digital services – television, radio and interactive content – and is managed and marketed as a joint venture between the BBC, Crown Castle and BSkyB. But many other external organisations are also involved in the service – supplying programming, managing multiplexes (MUX), running transmitters, producing set-top boxes, selling boxes, upgrading aerials, and so on. Its value system is almost an archetypical example of how in the complex converging media world the sequential value chains are being usurped by complex value-creating webs of interdependent actors (see Figure 7.3).

Many aspects of the Freeview project are surprising. Sky and the BBC had long been rivals. The project was launched extremely fast: work began in late 2001; the bid was submitted to the UK regulators in May 2002; the licence was awarded in early July; and the service went live on 30 October of the same year. This speed was achieved against a background of immense complexity, ranging from the restrictions inherent in the BBC's operating mandate, the legacy systems and customers inherited from a failed predecessor (ITVDigital), the competition between the BBC and Sky in other areas, to the necessity of gaining government approval at all stages.

The concept itself was original. The initial spark can be credited to Greg Dyke, the then Director General of the BBC, who realised that the real demand for the new channels that digital television could deliver would be from viewers who had become accustomed to free-to-air broadcasting and were therefore unlikely ever to pay for digital television. From this insight arose the customer concept for Freeview – that it should be free. This broke with the then norms governing digital television in Europe, where digital television was synonymous with pay-per-view. Freeview customers would need only buy a set-top box and plug this into their existing analogue television and thereafter there would be no further charges.[13] Further, the box would be priced as low as possible (initial prices were around £99 and soon fell to less than half that figure).

Creative insights also guided the technological aspects of the product. ITVDigital had failed in large part because the technology didn't work – it was famously reported that if a viewer opened a fridge door at home the signal broke up. The Freeview consortium had made explicit undertakings in return

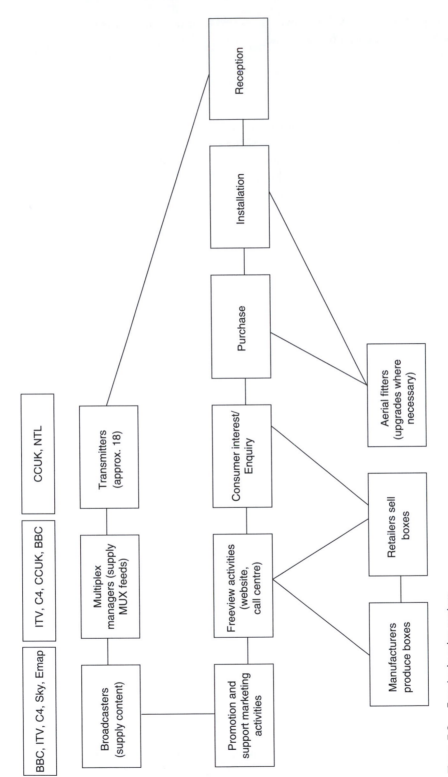

Figure 7.3 Freeview's value system

for receiving its broadcasting licences that these technical failings would be solved before the service was launched. To do this the consortium realised that the overall number of channels needed to be reduced, thus making the signal more robust and reliable. This was a 'frame-breaking' realisation, since until that point it had been assumed that digital television meant, per se, a plethora of channels: ITVDigital had packed as many channels as it could onto its multiplexes and the result was that the signal degraded easily. This realisation was closely linked to a marketing insight that customers might not want hundreds more channels preferring 'a little more', rather than 'lots more' television. A further insight was that power at 30 of the 80 transmitters needed to be increased, thus increasing the range of the signals, and thus the service's coverage – something that is easy to conclude but extremely complex to do. These two fundamental adjustments to the technology of the system were to ultimately mean re-engineering the entire technological architecture.

Creativity in terms of organisational systems was also evident in the leadership of the project. The formula was in part a pragmatic response to the extremely tight deadline, and in part a function of the complexity of the project. Freeview's leadership was collaborative – in effect a 'leadership relay' by which 'teams' of leaders worked together to run different aspects of the project during different stages of the project's life and where any individual who demonstrably had a necessary skill at an appropriate level was drafted into the leadership team.

Conclusions

This chapter links closely to the previous chapter on technological change. However, it differs in its approach to all previous chapters. So far the book has looked primarily at the strategic environment – particularly at the individual sectors that make up the media industries and the technological influences that are shaping their development. This chapter is one of the first that focuses on the impact of the strategic context on the internal organisation of the media firm, on the link between strategy and management in the media. It is also unusual among the other chapters in this book in that it focuses mainly on one particular stream of theory, socio-constructivist approaches to organisational creativity, while previous chapters have in the main covered a far broader theoretical terrain. The reason for this lies primarily in its high relevance for the field. Sustained creativity is one of the prime drivers of above average performance in the sector, and the need for creativity is enlarged when environments become unstable. This body of theory provides insights into how levels of creativity may be improved.

A key message is that creativity can be improved, not through expensive interventions by consultants and creativity experts, but by the carefully judged handling of relatively mundane aspects of projects – aspects such as deadlines, financial resources, team composition and goal-setting. Two aspects of this are interesting. The first is the sustained performance outcomes that can result when these elements are well and coherently managed, and by extension the scope for optimisation that probably exists in the majority of media organisations. The second is how some findings from this body of theory undercut received wisdom in the media industry. To take the hit model, this proposes that market success is contingent in large part on the amount invested in creative talent and processes – that higher budgets mean higher audiences. However, this framework shows that creative projects do not benefit from unlimited resources – and may perhaps even be harmed. The companies analysed in the case studies here all spent around 30 per cent less than their peers but achieved far greater creative and commercial success. Picking up on a theme raised in the previous one, this chapter also provides additional evidence of the importance of autonomy for creative teams, something which is clearly at odds with the strategic emphasis being placed on consolidation and cross-platform integration by many of the larger players in the industry at present (this issue is discussed in Chapter 9).

This chapter extends this core body of theory to explore the role of creativity in the wider organisation – in structures, processes and systems. This latter stream of work is in its infancy and much more work needs to be done in this field. It is, however, clear that not only do aspects of the creative project environment need to be carefully thought out and integrated, but they need to harmonise with wider systems, strategies, processes and business models. More intimate understanding of these systems and their interrelationships will contribute fruitful insights into how media firms can improve both creativity and performance.

Notes

1 For an overview of the development of creativity research see Amabile, 1996.
2 President and COO Peter Chernin speaking at Booz Allen Hamilton Gotham Media Breakfast 2003 www.boozallen.com/capabilities/Industries/industries_article/659265.
3 www.bertelsmann.com/bertelsmann_corp/wms41/bm/index.php?ci=356&language=2, accessed 30.06.07.
4 Ibid.
5 *Financial Times*, 1 April 2003: 8.
6 www.aoltimewarner.com/companies.
7 www.aoltweurope.com/en/companies/hbo_print.html.
8 'How to manage a dream factory'. *The Economist* Special Report on The Entertainment Industry. 18 January, 2003: 68.
9 'TV outside the box: U.K. broadcast executives ponder why U.S. programs beat theirs for creativity'. *Wall Street Journal*, Europe. 26 August 2002: A7.
10 www. Fortune.com. Posted 1 February 2003.
11 www. CGI/Who's Who 2002/Pixar.
12 *Animation World Magazine*, Isssue 3.8, November 1998. www.awm.com/mag/issue 3.8.
13 Although there was an option of buying a new integrated digital TV or IDTV, the majority of customers, however, opted for the set-top box.

EIGHT

Cognition, Culture and Strategy

Reality is an illusion, albeit a very persistent one. (Albert Einstein)

This chapter is concerned with the interpretive school of strategy and its application to the media industries. As discussed in the introduction to this second part of the book, the interpretative school of strategy views organisations from the point-of-view of those living in them, with a focus on how they construe meaning out of events and phenomena, and the implications this has for organisational outcomes. It looks at the implicit and unconscious aspects of organisational life, mindset, beliefs, values and emotions, which have a tremendous influence on strategic behaviour, but because they are highly subjective, operate outside conscious awareness, are hard to address, and tend to get overlooked in strategic activities.

This chapter explores two interpretative phenomena in particular: cognitions, that is the explicit beliefs and assumptions held by individuals in an organisation; and cultural assumptions, that is the collective unconscious beliefs that are present in all organisations. For each it explains the core concept and its origin, explores its role in the strategy process, and discusses how this plays out in the media industries.

Interpretative elements such as cognitions and cultural assumptions are subtle phenomena that do not make much sense outside their context and do not lend themselves to brief description. Therefore this chapter, in the main, draws on extended examples of cognitive and cultural beliefs within the BBC and their role in the success of a strategic initiative that was introduced in Chapter 5, BBC News Online.

Cognition

Your beliefs are cause maps that you impose on the world, after which you 'see' what you have already imposed. (Karl Weick)

The cognitive school of strategy draws on psychology, particularly cognitive psychology; indeed Morgan (1986) uses the metaphor 'organisations as brains' as a collective term for work in this field. The role of cognitive elements and interpretive processes within organisations is an area of scholarship that has expanded dramatically over the last decade (Isabella, 1990) but is still emergent (Huff, 1997), diffuse (Mintzberg et al. 1998) and hampered by confused terminology (Milliken, 1990).

Rational and interpretative approaches to strategy are complementary. While the former focus on exogenous changes and the content of the strategies developed to respond to these, the latter focus on the processes by which these changes are perceived and understood, and the outcomes of these processes.

Cognitive approaches to organisations (an important constituent of post-modern organisation theory)[1] are premised on the assumption that individual behaviour is guided by sets of governing beliefs. These develop through a range of sense-making processes, and affect how we perceive and interpret information about our environment. Cognitive approaches are therefore constructivist in that they assume, as Kant and Hume put it, that what exists is a product of what is thought: there is no objective measurable reality; rather we each construct our own realities based on our individual interactions, experiences, perceptions, needs, and so on. Organisations, by extension, are open social systems that interpret their environment according to the cognitive frameworks of individuals in the organisation (Abelson, 1976; Fiske and Taylor, 1991).

Weick's (1995) notion of 'sensemaking' is central to cognitive organisational theory. Sensemaking concerns the process by which an organisation takes in ambiguous and complex information from the environment, processes it, and then constructs meaning to guide decision-making. Processing involves activities such as defining, prioritising, constructing frameworks, highlighting significant factors, and interpreting. Thus organisations develop 'abstract representations' of knowledge path-dependently as individuals interact with their environments, build mental models, and use these to interpret future interactions. Thus sensemaking is retrospective (Weick, 1995): 'the past shapes the template for understanding the future' (Bogner and Barr, 2000).

Simon's (1955) concept of bounded rationality is another key component of cognition theory as applied to organisations (Gavetti and Levinthal, 2000). This concerns the fact that human information processing capabilities are too limited to fully comprehend the world in its entirety, or even every facet of ambiguous and complex issues. We therefore reduce uncertainty and complexity by applying inferential heuristics – or rules of thumb – based on analysing previous experience. These simplify decision-making by providing shortcuts but they also impoverish it, by limiting the amount of information we process and the number of options we consider. Thus our thought processes are rational, but to a limited extent that is, they are 'boundedly rational' (Simon, 1957; March and Simon, 1958).

Cognition and strategic change

In recent decades, recognition of cognition's influence on strategy has grown (Tversky and Kahneman, 1986; Fiol and Huff, 1992; Walsh, 1995; Mintzberg et al., 2003). Thus Burgelman (1983: 1350) has defined strategy as 'a shared frame of reference for the strategic actors in the organization [providing] the basis for corporate objective setting in terms of business portfolio and resource allocation', and Gioia and Chittipeddi (1991: 433) define strategic change as 'an attempt to change current modes of cognition and action to enable the organisation to take advantage of important opportunities or to cope with consequential environmental threats'.

Thus, while rational models of strategy assume that it is possible to analyse the environment objectively, interpretative approaches suppose that our understanding is more likely to be plausible than accurate (Weick, 1995). The data available is extensive but incomplete and often conflicting (Lawrence and Lorsch, 1967; Daft and Weick, 1984; Johnson, 1992). The heuristics we employ reduce ambiguity and complexity, but also oversimplify and introduce inaccuracies (Barr et al., 1992) and systematic errors (Tversky and Kahneman, 1986). They encourage us to focus on particular aspects of an issue, overlooking others (Hall, 1984), favour information that supports existing assumptions (Mintzberg et al., 1998), see causal relationships between variables that may simply be correlated (Makridakis, 1990) and limit the range of solutions considered (Cyert and March, 1963).

The greater the environmental instability, the greater the likelihood that cognitive structures will introduce inflexibility and flawed judgement (Meyer, 1982; Kanter, 1983; Wiersema and Bantel, 1992). Old beliefs die hard and can inhibit an organisation's ability to respond to environmental change (Tushman and Romanelli, 1985; Gersick, 1991; Drucker, 1994). The result can be organisational decline (Hedberg and Jonsson, 1977; Hall, 1984).

Cognition often surfaces in connection with problems faced by sectors of the media in coping with environmental change. It has been repeatedly suggested that cognitions arising from a different strategic environment and business model, or its 'legacy mindset' as the press described it, led the music industry to perceive the Internet primarily as a threat rather than as an opportunity for business growth (Downes and Mui, 1998; Ghosh, 1998; Hamel and Sampler, 1998; Kelly, 1997, Evans and Wurster, 2000; Foresight, 2000; Neilson et al., 2000). The movie industry also persists with a steadfast belief that big budgets and saturation advertising assure big audiences despite mounting evidence that this assumption is a major cause of the industry's current difficulties (De Vany and Walls, 1999). The newspaper industry's 'institutional memory' and belief that 'we have always done it that way and always will' has been blamed for the industry's reluctance to consider new models or processes to improve operations (Price, 2006).

Cognitive structures

Terminology in this field is confused. A number of different types of knowledge structures have been identified, although many of these concepts overlap, and they are frequently used interchangeably.

Cognitive maps – a widely used term for some kind of mental structure by which equivocal information in the environment is organised so that organisation members can make sense of it (Weick, 1995).

Schemas or schemata – as first defined by Bartlett (1932) and Piaget (1952) these are understood as knowledge systems comprising ideas, conclusions and presumptions, etc., which have emerged over time on the basis of experience. They allow information connected to a specific subject to be organised in hierarchical levels, and therefore speed assessments of events, likely consequences and appropriate responses. They allow disparate information to be organised and ambiguous data to be assessed quickly. However, information which cannot be accommodated into the schema can be ignored, meaning that they can be inaccurate representations of the world. The term schema can be used to denote individual or collective knowledge systems.

Mental models (or causal maps) – are understood as deeply ingrained assumptions, overt and covert, that capture the relationship between different factors and which develop through interacting with a complex environment. They influence how the world is understood and what action is taken.

Paradigms – this concept has achieved common management currency to denote an over-arching set of beliefs, or 'conventional wisdom' about the nature of the world, usually in the context of an industry. A classic use in this sense is Kuhn's (1970) theory that 'shared beliefs' and 'conventional wisdom' constitute a dominant paradigm that governs any particular science at any particular point in time by serving as a means of defining and managing the world and providing a basis for action.

Frames – are understood as 'underlying structures of belief, perception and appreciation through which subsequent interpretation is filtered' (Schön and Rein, 1994: 23).

Media industry cognitions during the Internet era

For the established media industries, the dramatic growth of the Internet gave rise to an entirely new environment for strategising and organising. It led to an intriguing example of the emergence of a new set of cognitions that were adopted by a strategic group, which represented a significant departure from those held hitherto. For example, it was widely held that the Internet represented the future of the mass media and that traditional media firms must enter the field or risk marginalisation. Thus, 'The TV model is no longer relevant; ... all becomes a variation on the Internet theme' (Adam Singer, Chairman of Flextech, 1998).[2]

Another pervasive conviction concerned the primacy of first-mover advantages. This, coupled with a sense that incumbency brought inherent disadvantages, meant organisations must not only change, but change fast.

> In the year 2000, the key word is velocity. This involves quick business trans-actions, quick and efficient information flow, and an aggressive strategy. Media companies have to deal with new organisations ... They play the game with new rules: be first or pay. (Thomas Middelhof, CEO Bertelsmann, 1999).[3]

Belief in first-mover advantages, coupled with an assumption that 'market share now means profits later', led to an Internet 'land-grab': frenetic investment in Internet businesses and in building online brands. This, in turn, reflected an assumption that in a confused media environment brands would be heuristics that guided consumers, and in a further incarnation of the first-mover advantage belief, it was also assumed there was only space for one brand online in each category.

These cognitions cumulatively resulted in some painfully unsuccessful strategic initiatives. Bertelsmann developed or acquired a range of Internet businesses (primarily in e-commerce), and even rescued the controversial downloading service Napster from bankruptcy, intending to restart it as an online music subscription service. Overall its Internet strategy was not successful. The Direct Group, where these businesses were housed, sustained $123million in Internet start-up losses in the second half of 2001,[4] and lost a further $125 million in the first half of 2002. Internet activities were folded back into the core businesses, and CEO Middelhof left in July 2002.

Disney was an early believer in the Internet, launching consumer websites ESPN.com and Disney.com in 1995 and establishing ABC.com in 1999. In 1998 it took a majority stake in Infoseek.com which was followed by outright purchase in 1999. All these Internet properties were then consolidated into a single portal, the umbrella-site Go.com. Go.com failed to meet its potential and was closed in 2001 at a cost of $862 million.[5]

Time Warner was also an Internet pioneer. In 1994 it created Pathfinder.com, an umbrella-site designed to consolidate all its content sides. This was never successful and closed in 2001. The lack of Internet presence, and the corresponding pressure from the financial markets, led Time Warner to merge with AOL in 2000, with the goal of creating a hybrid old and new media firm that could sell media products across as many platforms as possible. This also did not succeed. In 2002 a $45 billion goodwill write-down led to the largest corporate loss ever of $98.7 billion.[6]

Cognition and innovation

Innovation, almost by definition, requires an organisation to challenge existing assumptions. Much attention has been focused on this relationship, particularly on the mechanisms by which organisational cognitions hinder new ideas. In their research into 'architectural innovations' (apparently minor improvements in technological products that do not concern the components of a product but rather its 'architecture', that is, the knowledge embedded in the structure and information processing procedures) Henderson and Clark (1990) describe how 'old [mental] frameworks' hinder such innovations because:

> incumbents may not realise that an innovation is architectural because the information is screened out by the information channels and communication channels that embody old architectural knowledge ... the effect is analogous to the tendency of individuals to continue to rely on beliefs about the world that a rational evaluation of new information should lead them to discard ... organizations facing threats may continue to rely on their old frameworks. (Henderson and Clark, 1990: 17)

Christensen and Overdorf (2000) contend that the failure of many incumbents to seize the potential of disruptive innovation stems in large part from shared cognitions:

> The larger and more complex a company becomes, the more important it is for senior managers to train employees throughout the organization to make independent decisions about priorities that are consistent with the strategic direction and the business model of the company. A key metric of good management, in fact, is whether such clear, consistent values have permeated the organization. But consistent, broadly understood values also define what an organisation cannot do. (cited in Day and Schoemaker, 2000: 69)

Cognition and BBC News Online

Cognitive elements played a dynamic role in the establishment and subsequent success of BBC News Online: on the one hand they ensured that the initiative was positively received and on the other they meant low levels of interference from the rest of the organisation. Cognition can be identified at different levels of the organisation.

The Director General's cognitions

To start at the very top of the organisation, the Directior General of the BBC, John Birt, initiated and drove (from a distance) the development of News Online in response to a very specific cognitive frame. In the planning phase Birt had visited both Silicon Valley and CNN. His pre-existing conviction about the important national role played by public service broadcasting in general and the BBC in particular, coupled with his own background as newsman and head of BBC News and Current Affairs, led him to conclude (first) that the Internet would develop into a third mass broadcasting medium, after radio and television, (second) that in order to maintain its rightful position as the national media leader the BBC must ensure it not only masters the medium, but guides the British public to gain mastery also, and (third), that a news service should be a prominent aspect of the BBC's Internet activities.

Birt's construction was not self-evident. The majority of his peers running large media organisations (particularly those in the US) had far more alarmist views, seeing the Internet as an alternative rather than a complementary media platform, one that would, on one hand, destroy existing revenue-generating media products (the 'cannibalisation' threat), and, on the other, allow new-to-the-world products and markets to emerge, ones which incumbent media firms would be badly positioned to develop by virtue of the inertial elements they were riddled with. Further, the BBC's mandate from the government ruled out investments in risky new areas, which in 1996 the Internet certainly was. Birt, however, framed the Internet as a step forward into a digital future which was necessary in order to preserve and extend the BBC's historic role. This framing of the Internet as a threat (to the BBC's global position) and an opportunity (to expand and cement its international role) harmonised with the BBC's sense of identity and shared commitment to preserving the Reithian heritage and the dominance of its news services. This ensured a bedrock of passive support for the venture, despite the BBC's historically anchored and somewhat technophobic culture. Without Birt's cognitions it is unlikely that BBC News Online would ever have come into existence.

News Division Cognitions

Cognitions also influenced how the new venture was perceived by the BBC's News Division – which had one of the strongest occupational cultures at the BBC. First was a shared conviction that new platforms are dangerous because they can allow new competitors into the field. This belief was a product of history. The two most recent new mass media platforms – cable TV in the US and satellite TV in Europe – had each provided an entry opportunity for new players who were to develop into strong competitors: CNN had developed a dominant position in 24-hour news due to its early recognition of the potential of cable, and BskyB had created a monopoly in satellite television, including a strong international news presence, through a series of bold strategic moves in the 1980s and 1990s. Thus when the Internet emerged BBC News was clear that it needed to launch a convincing response.

A further theory in use was, in the words of a member of the team, that 'if you wanted to be a hero, you did great television … in an organisation like the BBC, the stars were people who were stars on television … [News Online] was a nerdy thing that didn't really matter'. This meant that while the news division accepted that a credible Internet presence was necessary, it was also not particularly interested in how this was achieved. News Online was free to 'get on with it', unhindered by interference from the rest of the organisation. This belief was buttressed by another one, a belief that 'piratical' new ventures operating outside the system were a model that could bring success and prestige for the News division, a conclusion derived from memories of a successful programme *Newsnight* which had been developed in such a way 10 years earlier.

From cognition to culture

The boundary between cognition and culture is blurred. Many researchers bundle cognitive and cultural phenomena together. Johnson (1987) for example defines strategy as the product of the ideologies (cognitive maps) held by individuals or groups in an organisation which are preserved in the symbols, rituals and myths of the organisational culture. DiMaggio and Powell (1983) refer to an organisation's cognitive 'pillar' which entails the taken-for-granted beliefs and values that are imposed on, or internalised by, social actors.

However, while both the cognitive and cultural schools draw on the same basic premise – that problem-solving and adaptive behaviour is driven by a set of governing beliefs – there are important differences. In cognitive theory, beliefs and assumptions are accessible at surface level and therefore far easier to address. Cultural assumptions are deeper, being unconscious beliefs that are much harder to access and change.

Culture

The impact of culture on strategic outcomes is now widely acknowledged – culture is an oft-cited culprit when organisations experience difficulties implementing strategies. But while its existence is widely accepted the concept itself remains vague, and while cognition is often viewed as a strategic issue, culture falls into a no man's land between organisation and strategy.

There is no shortage of examples of culture's impact on strategic initiatives in the media. The difficulties experienced by the Sony BMG partnership and the AOL Time Warner merger have both been ascribed in part to cultural differences. The strong and complacent culture of newspaper journalism has been blamed for that sector's inability to seize the potential of the Internet (Meyer, 2004). More broadly, the newspaper sector's culture of prizing consistency has been identified as a factor behind its resistance to change (Picard, 2003).

Management attention turned to culture in the 1980s when researchers proposed that if an 'appropriate' culture (a combination of values, norms and behaviours) is compatible with the strategy of an organisation, performance improvements will result (see, for example, Pascale and Athos, 1981; Peters and

Waterman, 1982). The assumed relationship between culture and corporate success was straightforward: good performance resulted when culture and strategy were in harmony, and management's task was to ensure that culture was brought into line with strategic initiatives.

As the 1990s progressed, the intricacies and challenges involved in reconciling culture and strategy became evident. Culture was far more than an organisational variable that could be manipulated, engineered or harnessed: indeed, when culture and strategy were in opposition, it appeared that culture normally won out. The term culture came to stand as a metaphor that 'encodes an enormous variety of meanings and messages into economical and emotionally powerful forms' (Bolman and Deal, 1991: 250) that should be the starting place for strategy (Hampden-Turner, 1990).

The essence of an organisation's culture is contained in an underlying paradigm of commonly held unconscious assumptions. These affect how the environment is perceived by members of an organisation, and how they react to the strategies designed in response. The assumptions are a quintessential and often unacknowledged driver of strategic actions. All other things being equal, provided the cultural assumptions and the strategies are appropriate to the environment, the organisation is likely to experience success. That success will reinforce the 'rightness' of cultural assumptions.

But a strong culture forged through success can also become a liability in that gives rise to a rigidity that impedes the ability to adapt. The mechanism is as follows. Cultural assumptions about the correct responses to the problems of internal integration and external adaptation are formed through organisational success. Continued success validates these further and they are passed on to new members as the 'correct' way to feel and act. In this way an organisation's culture is perpetuated. Yet should the competitive environment change markedly, members of the organisation must change their core assumptions substantially, but such changes are hard to make (Schein, 1992). Revising basic assumptions means altering some of our deepest cognitive structures. This destabilises our cognitive world, releasing large quantities of anxiety (Schein, cited in Coutu, 2002). Many employees would rather hold on to existing cultural beliefs than experience such anxiety.

Defining culture

One of the most precise definitions of this rather ethereal entity comes from Schein, who defines culture as a pattern of basic assumptions shared by a group of organisation members that were learned as it solved problems of external adaptation and internal integration and that are taught to new members of that group as the correct way to respond to such problems (Schein, 1992). Culture is therefore the accumulated learning shared by a group that has been acquired as it deals with its external environment and internal growth. This process gives rise to a set of tacit assumptions about how things do and should function, which determine perceptions, thoughts and feelings and function as short-cuts to decision-making.

The founder of the culture plays a disproportionate role in shaping its subsequent development (Bolman and Deal, 1991; Kotter and Heskett, 1992; Schein, 1992), and building and shaping an organisation's culture is 'the unique and essential function of leadership' (Schein, 1992: 212). Leaders employ a number of 'culture-embedding mechanisms', including what they pay attention to, measure and control, how they react to critical incidents and crises, the criteria by which they allocate resources, rewards and status, and the criteria by which they select, promote and 'ex-communicate' members (Schein, 1992: 231).

Culture and creativity

Since both culture and creativity involve internal drivers of action and have roots in the psychology of organisations, it could be expected that they would also be linked in theory. In fact this is not the case, except tangentially via research into the link between culture and overall firm performance. The fields' respective theoretical bases do however provide clues as to how these elements are linked, with the connection running through intrinsic motivation. Levels of intrinsic motivation are influenced by characteristics of the work setting, but the nature of the work setting is also influenced by the cultural influences present, since at its deepest level culture concerns the underlying belief structures which give purpose to the working life – 'the ... expressive social tissue around us that gives ... tasks meaning' (Pettigrew, 1979: 574). Thus a shared sense that a task has meaning will be embedded in the culture, and will manifest itself in elements such as the positiveness of the work climate, the strength of the team spirit, and the commitment to the task, which in turn contribute to intrinsic motivation and thence to creative achievement.

Layers of culture

For Schein (1992) culture has three distinct but interconnected layers. The top layer comprises 'artefacts' – behaviour, dress style, rituals, publications, stories, and so on. These are easy to access but hard to interpret without prior understanding of the deeper levels of culture. The second level comprises 'espoused values' – officially expressed strategies, goals and philosophies. This level of culture may appear to reveal a group's underlying beliefs but in reality represents how that group feels it should present itself publicly or would like to be seen. Espoused values can be used to check hypotheses about underlying assumptions but are not an accurate representation of them. 'Basic assumptions' are the third and deepest level of culture, and its essence. These are the unconscious, taken-for-granted beliefs, perceptions and feelings about the organisation and its environment which act as the ultimate source of values and drivers of actions, and which contain the key to a culture, and the tools by which the other levels – espoused values and artifacts – can be interpreted.

Assumptions take the form of an interrelated belief system or paradigm. According to Schein it is because they are not an assortment of beliefs, but an interconnected system, that they have so much power. To decipher a culture a researcher must understand not only the assumptions, but the interrelationships between them.

Uncovering and deciphering an organisations's culture is a challenging proposition. Because the underlying assumptions at the heart of a culture operate outside conscious awareness, they are not accessible at the surface attitudinal level – even though many attempts are made to research culture using survey instruments (Schein classifies such tools as artefacts). This makes researching culture complicated. Studies require prolonged access to the organisation to allow opportunities for observation.

Types of culture

Although organisations are often reflexively assumed to possess a single corporate culture, in any given organisational setting a range of sub-cultures will also be present. Members of an organisation will share a common culture, but will also share assumptions with individuals that have similar professional or personal circumstances or experiences. These cultural pluralities mean an organisation's culture is multifaceted and increase the potential for cultural tension. For example, members of staff at a movie studio will share assumptions common to the film industry, assumptions common to their studio, but also assumptions common to their particular profession. These sub-cultural distinctions can give rise to conflict, for example, between the 'technical creatives' – the photographers, lighting engineers and cameramen who are involved with the 'nuts and bolts' aspects of content creation – and the 'talent' – the actors, directors and writers (Wolff, 1998: 127). Some of the most common sub-cultural groupings are:

Inter-organisational cultures (sub-cultures)   Inter-organisational cultures arise among groups of individuals who share a particular hierarchical level, gender or ethnic subgroup, or who work in a particular department. In the BBC News Online case discussed below, the BBC News division has a strong inter-organisational subculture which exerted a powerful influence on the acceptance of the strategic initiative.

Professional cultures   Professional cultures are shared by individuals with a common profession or industrial background. For example, computer programmers in Silicon Valley share a number of common cultural assumptions that influence behaviour and motivation: 'for a programmer, worse than owning worthless options is the humiliation of having built great software that still

sits in some dark closet, never having been implemented .... "going dark"'
(Bronson, 1999: 108).

Much research into culture in the media industry has concentrated on the
culture of journalism and its implications for newspaper management (see Fee,
and Sylvie and Moon both in Achtenhagen, 2007). The American Society of
Newspaper editors (cited in Picard, 2006) identified a number of fundamental cultural values shared by newspaper journalists including fairness and
balance, editorial judgement, integrity, diversity, and community leadership
and involvement. Georgiou (1996) describes how journalists' culture interacts
with strategic change initiatives:

> commitment to the organisation is both an emotional and a calculative one. In the case of
> journalists, while the calculative one ... is important, the emotional attachment ('I believe
> in what we do') can be very strong. This high level of commitment means that anything that
> is perceived as diminishing a journalist's ability to 'do the job' is likely to face fierce resis-
> tance. Conversely, anything that demonstrably makes the job 'easier' is likely to be
> adopted quickly. (Georgiou, 1996)

Industry cultures

> the beauty of Silicon Valley is that the culture and the structure reinforce each other. Do not
> regard it as some sort of economic machine, where various raw materials are poured in at
> one end and firms such as Apple and Cisco roll out at the other, but rather as a form of
> ecosystem that breeds companies: without the right soil and the right climate, nothing will
> grow. (The Economist, 1997)

An industry culture is a value orientation common to those working in a certain
industry. The success of Silicon Valley has been ascribed to the unique combination of its culture and structure (Saxenian, 1994). This is an industry
environment where the speed of technological development mandates high
levels of adaptability and flexibility, achieved in part through high levels of collaboration and outsourcing, giving rise to loose network structures (Saxenian,
1994). The sector's structure comprises clusters of highly entrepreneurial organisations which are flatter and more egalitarian than is the norm for US industry.
This reflects the fact that many employees are shareholders but is also a means
of ensuring that there is cross-functional interaction at all levels. Structure and
culture together have created a micro economy that can adapt fast: as existing
companies die, new ones emerge allowing capital, ideas and people to be reallo-
cated, a phenomenon termed 'flexible recycling' (Bahrami and Evans, 1995).

The media industry's shared culture is described in very different terms.
Frequently cited are its anti-commercial overtones, reflecting a shared belief that
media businesses are 'different', in fact, in many respects not really businesses at all:

> the people who work in and own and manage businesses, newspapers, broadcasting sta-
> tions, etc, are terribly in love with those businesses and have a devotion to reinvestment
> and to expanding that often doesn't defy economics but has little to do with economics.
> (Savill and Studley, 1999: p.)

This assumption derives in part from the creative imperative of content creation. But it also reflects a deeply rooted belief that content should not simply entertain but also fulfil important societal and political functions, ranging from enriching the life of consumers to promoting democracy and furthering social cohesion. This has two strategic implications; first, it creates a sense of 'higher purpose' which is an important motivator in traditional media organisations, and second, it can create an antipathy towards goals that are viewed as overtly commercial or managerial in orientation.

Culture and strategic change at BBC News Online

In the case of BBC News Online, cultural elements played dynamic and positive role in the venture's success (Küng, 2005). This is surprising – the culture of the BBC might have been expected to resist this type of project for a number of reasons, not least its commitment to existing core media platforms, to the UK as its core market (while the Internet is essentially a 'stateless' medium), and to traditional broadcast media skills.

Pan-BBC cultural assumptions   Cultural assumptions were active at three levels. To start with the pan-BBC organisational culture – while in some respects this was conservative and backward-looking, with a deep emotional commitment to serving UK licence fee payers with traditional media products, there was also a belief that the BBC must remain the dominant media player in the UK, and that its primary duty was to meet the needs of all licence fee payers, whatever the medium (Küng-Shankleman, 2000). This created broad acceptance of Internet involvement and reduced potential resentment of the resources News Online was consuming. The sense of duty towards serving licence fee payers in a fragmenting society led the site to focus on feedback, community-building, ease of use and absolute reliability.

Professional cultural assumptions   The professional cultural assumptions shared by the journalists, particularly their mission to provide the best news service possible, provided a surprising match with the capabilities of the Internet and this, in turn, led to high levels of motivation, engagement and creativity.

The intrinsic functionalities of the Internet – unlimited space and the possibility to combine text, graphics and video – meant stories could be handled in greater depth and richness. The fact that stories remained accessible for long periods and that readers could respond to them, all fed directly into the core desires of BBC news journalists: to provide the highest quality news possible – where 'quality' encompasses not only speed and accuracy, but depth of analysis, compelling delivery and so on – and also to influence public opinion and have their voice heard. Therefore the Internet allowed news journalists to do their job better. As a result, rather than the antipathy which might have been expected from traditional news journalists schooled in 'old media', there was a surprisingly high level of enthusiasm for the news potential of the Internet. This, in turn, led to the quick and animated adoption of the new technology.

Unit sub-cultural assumptions   The venture also developed a strong sub-culture, which, while rooted in the cultures of the BBC, its News division and the occupational sub-culture of journalism, nonetheless displayed a number of independent characteristics.

'Sense of urgency'. The venture had got off to a false start under an inaugural manager who had left relatively quickly. It was also a pet project of the Director General that was running behind schedule. This created a sense of urgency, which was probably heightened by the general pressure for speed endemic to the Internet era.

'Can-do spirit'. The leader of the venture, Bob Eggington, was an isolationist and fought hard to keep the unit free from the cloying tendrils of BBC bureaucracy to ensure that it was free to find its own momentum and respond to a changing environment as necessary. It also gave rise to a proactive approach to problem-solving.

'Frontier mentality'. News Online, a unit working independently from the rest of the organisation on a new technological platform hardly recognised by that organisation, appeared to be fired up by a strong sense of adventure which motivated it to explore and exploit the potential of the new medium and contributed to the creativity present in the unit. This was expressed through metaphors such as 'wild west' and 'pirates'.

'Countercultural tendencies'. There was also a subversive element to the News Online sub-culture. While they were clearly part of the BBC and drew on the organisation's traditional strength in newsgathering, there was also a shared assumption that they were to some extent operating outside the routines and procedures imposed on the rest of the BBC. This assumption was indicated by the use of metaphors such as 'parasites', 'pirates' and 'under the radar'.

The net result was a context with a plethora of intrinsic motivators that was also a psychologically safe environment where staff could experiment, and was characterised by a strong team spirit and positive feedback. Within this context it is important to consider that this was not only a new project working in a new medium, but also that the majority of staff were also new to the BBC, and it is far easier to achieve a new culture with new populations of people.

Conclusions

This chapter focuses on issues central to the adaptive school of strategy, cognition and culture. Both concern the influence of shared assumptions on organisational outcomes, and both have common roots in psychology and an acknowledged impact on strategic issues. But interpretative approaches to strategy represent a relatively recent wing of strategic theory – one that has expanded rapidly in recent years, but which still lacks the cohesion and clarity of, say, the rationalist field. This chapter has tried to build understanding of interpretative approaches by discussing the underlying theories and analysing the role of interpretative phenomena in the media industry. A central argument of this book is that this body of theory is potentially highly relevant to the media industry and can complement the insights that have been generated through the application of positivist models. But we are still at the early stages of exploring how this area of theory relates to the media. Much more research is needed into how interpretative elements affect strategic behaviour in the sector, and this in turn, as discussed in the book's conclusions, will require an increase the amount of primary research conducted within media organisations.

Notes

1 For a discussion see Bergquist (1993).
2 Cited in the UK Government's Culture, Media and Sport Committee's *Fourth Report on The Multi-media Revolution*. 6 May 1998: xiii.
3 Citation from speech 'Content and Customers – The Kingdoms of Media Business in the Digital Era', at mcm Forum Customer Perspectives in the Age of Information. St Gallen, Switzerland.
4 *Wall Street Journal Europe*, 21 July 2002.
5 *Walt Disney Company Financial Statement*, 2001
6 *Television*, July/August 2002.

NINE

Organisational Structure

We aren't really a television producer at all anymore. We are a content provider for multiple platforms. (John de Mol, former head of Endemol, cited in Moran with Malbon, 2006: 85).

As the media industry evolves rapidly, so too do the structures of the organisations that provide the architecture for the sector. This is an intriguing development but how does it relate to strategy, the subject of this book? The link is that the structure of an organisation is both an expression of, and extension to, its strategy. Miles et al. (1997) describe an organisation's form as 'the logic shaping a firm's strategy, structure and management processes into an effective whole'. Strategy involves responding to changes in the environment. As the environment changes, strategies alter and existing organisational forms become less capable of meeting the demands placed on them, forcing organisations to experiment with new ways of orchestrating processes and coordinating resources.

This is certainly true for the media industry, where changes in the strategic environment have led to profound the alterations in the sectoral value chains discussed in Chapter 2. The newly constellated value chains, in some cases value systems, have simultaneously eroded the rationale for existing organisational structures and encouraged the development of alternative ones.

The result is a complex picture in which a number of distinct trends, ranging from mergers and divestitures, alliances and joint ventures, to networks of collaboration, spin-offs and start-ups are all evident. Interestingly, these trends are far from mutually exclusive, as is evidenced by some of the largest media organisations where vertical integration and divestiture can be taking place simultaneously.

The goal of this chapter is to explore these developments and analyse how they relate both to each other and to the wider topic of strategy, as well as to understand their implications for the management task. It begins by reviewing the 'generic' drivers of changes in structure that apply to organisations in all sectors – the emergence of new coordination technologies and of a new type of employee, the knowledge worker. It then reviews, primarily from a chronological perspective, the changes taking place in the organisation structures in the media sector and the reasons for these changes.

From industrial age to information age organisations

Social and organisational theorists have suggested that since the 1970s traditional vertically integrated large corporations are ceasing to be the default structural model for organisations, with looser structures of inter-firm alliances emerging as the alternative (Miles and Snow 1986; Castells, 1996; Hesmondhalgh, 2002).

A key driver of this change was identified by a Nobel Prize-winning economist, Ronald Coase, whose work predated the Internet by over 50 years, but who was often employed to explain its dramatic effect on the firm structure. Coase (1937) identified the concept of transaction costs and suggested that one underlying objective of an organisation is to reduce these. 'Coase's Law' dictates that an organisation will expand to the point where the costs of organizing an extra transaction within the firm become equal to the costs of carrying out the same transaction through exchange in the open market. Thus, when it is cheaper to conduct transactions internally, organisations carry out more activities in-house, and firms grow larger. When it is cheaper to conduct transactions externally in the open market, firms will outsource more to external suppliers, thus stay small or shrink.

For much of the industrial age the communication and coordination technologies available – the train, the car, the telephone and the mainframe computer – meant that communication was far slower and more cumbersome than is today. It made sense to conduct transactions internally, thereby improving scale and scope economies. The structure of 'industrial age' organisations reflects this situation: they were large, stable, hierarchical entities with centralised common functions coordinated by an administrative bureaucracy (Malone, 2004).

New information and coordination technologies, particularly the Internet, have speeded communication and improved the efficiency of firms and markets, and therefore reduced transaction costs inside and outside firms. In this context external transactions become more advantageous and there is less value in centralised bureaucracy and decision-making. Thus the benefits of large, complex, hierarchical organisations decrease and in fast-moving sectors become potentially strategically disadvantageous. This led some to conclude that the Internet would cause organisations to reduce in size, with an accompanying shift from hierarchical governance structures to market exchange – the 'Law of Diminishing Firms' (see, for example, Evans and Wurster, 2000).

A parallel phenomenon that affected organisation structure is the emergence of the 'knowledge worker' (Drucker, 1985). These employ intellectual rather than physical skills and their output is conceptual rather than the concrete. Knowledge workers are viewed as central to value creation in developed economies. They are not considered best suited to hierarchical organisations, partly because knowledge creation requires interaction and knowledge exchange, something that formalised or rigid structures often preclude, and also because they tend to value self-direction. The confluence of the knowledge worker and digitalised networked communications that offered the potential to reduce transaction costs were expected together to spur the emergence of 'Information Age' organisations (Malone, 2004). These institutions would allow information to be shared instantly and inexpensively amongst small geographically dispersed units. As we shall see, these did not emerge exactly as anticipated in the media industry, but elements of the concept can certainly be found in the sector.

Broadcasting industry as microcosm

The changes in organisations in the broadcasting industry demonstrate the link between a changing environment and changing organisational forms particularly clearly. Historically, the emergence of mass media products saw the parallel emergence of a typical organisational structure to house their production. This was similar to the organisations that orchestrated the production of most industrialised products, where high fixed costs (in the media field this included items such as printing presses, delivery vans, newsprint, broadcasting transmission infrastructure, etc.) meant it was only through producing products in large quantities or for large audiences that the scale economies could be achieved to sell them at mass market prices.

These organisations were centrally coordinated and vertically integrated with a high degree of functional specialism. They controlled all stages in the media value chain from origination to delivery to the consumers. This 'integrated factory' structure became the default model for European public service broadcasters. It meant that they made the bulk of their programmes themselves in their own studios, assembled these into a schedule and transmitted this over a national network over which they had control.

Technological advances in distribution and production and market liberalisation have together contributed to an explosion of new channels and other media offers that has eroded the rationale for this model. Vertical integration is increasingly unfeasible in a digital context where the range of distribution options, reception devices, content categories and market segments make 'going it alone' neither practical nor affordable. This has led to the disintermediation of value chains in the broadcasting sector discussed in Chapter 2, which in turn created entry opportunities. These have often been seized by new players, since start-ups enjoy the speed and flexibility needed to capture first mover advantages, and are less inert because they have a lower investment – psychological or physical – in existing business practices. The result is that new breeds of organisation have emerged with different structures, processes and business models, and over the years many such start-ups have matured into established players.

The 1980s saw the emergence of cable television broadcasters, companies such as MTV, CNN and HBO. The 'publisher-broadcaster' model emerged at around the same time and has since become a popular model for cable and satellite broadcasters. This describes organisations that package and transmit broadcasting commissioned from outside suppliers. The model is popular because it allows organisations to offer a broad span of programming and respond quickly to consumer tastes, at a much lower fixed cost base than integrated factory producers.

In his review of the growth of the television format industry, Moran (with Malbon, 2006) notes that the intersection of new technologies for transmission and reception, new forms of financing, and new forms of content in the 1990s accelerated the shift from oligopolistic television systems based on scarcity to one of abundance or even saturation in terms of new technologies, channels and programming. A direct consequence has been declines in audience numbers, so much so that hit shows, no matter how successful, can seldom attain the reach common in previous decades. Falling audiences have meant lower budgets, which in turn reduced demand for more expensive types of prime time programming such as drama and current affairs. These changes have, however, increased demand for other types of content – particularly content involving the adaptation, transfer and recycling of narratives from one type of platform, or geographic market to another – and thus in the multi-channel television system there is an abundance of particular genres of content at the expense of others.

This situation has given rise to one of the most notable developments in the television industry in recent years, the growth of the international television format industry. Companies such as Endemol (the Dutch originator and producer of *Big Brother*) and Freemantle (the UK creator of the *Pop Idol* format) have become major players in the television industry. Their appeal, like that of the hit model, is straightforward. Adapting materials that have succeeded in other markets or formats offers a degree of security in a highly competitive market, plus having invested in developing a product or brand it makes sense to derive as much value from this as possible. And programme concepts can deliver unmatched audiences in a competitive digital environment: in 2002 the first part of the *American Idol* final attracted 20.4 million US viewers, making it the most watched show on the Fox TV network that year (Moran, with Malbon, 2006). In addition to bringing large audiences, formats also confer other advantages, particularly the fact that they allow purchasers to produce programming that qualifies as 'local', but which applies concepts developed by leading creative talent that have been tested and refined in other markets.

These format producers combine a number of different structural characteristics. While on an entirely smaller scale than the media conglomerates they are both vertically integrated and transnational. They own a large catalogue for formats outright but also have numerous joint venture arrangements and production offices across the world.

Mergers – the emergence of the conglomerates

Media firms have been joining forces at a faster pace then ever before. They have been involved in takeovers, mergers, and other strategic deals and alliances, not only with rivals in the same business sector, but also with firms involved in other areas now seen as complementary. (Doyle, 2002a: 4)

Ironically, while theorists were predicting the end of the hierarchically organised conglomerate an opposing trend could be observed in the largest organisations in the media sector – a wave of mergers and acquisitions that gave rise to one of the most newsworthy structural changes in the media industry in recent decades (the other being the temporary mushrooming of dotcom Internet ventures) – the growth of the global media conglomerate.

The vogue for mergers grew in strength during the 1980s and peaked around 1998 when the media sector took third place in the US mergers and acquisitions league tables. The first merger wave meant that by the mid-1990s a 'super-league' of media industry giants had been established, plus a second tier of several dozen large players (Picard, 1996; Albarran and Moellinger, 2002). Thus Disney was created from a merger between Disney, Capital Cities and ABC (1996). Viacom emerged from a coming together of Paramount Communications (1994), Blockbuster Entertainment Group (1995) and CBS (1999).[1] Bertelsmann grew significantly when it acquired Doubleday (1986) and Random House (1998). News Corporation took control of Metromedia (Fox TV) (1986), then 20th Century Fox Film Studios (1995). Vivendi was created when it merged with Seagram in 2000 creating Vivendi Universal. Time Warner was created from a merger between Time Inc. and Warner Communications (1989) and the acquisition of Turner Broadcasting System (1996). It was acquired itself by AOL (2000).

These developments drew intense media attention and regulatory scrutiny: the union between America Online and Time Warner was the largest merger to date in US business history. They created a cadre of large complex integrated multidivisional global conglomerates with activities spanning several areas of converging industries. This represented a profound restructuring of the sector: none of these organisations had existed in that form as recently as 20 years ago (Eisenmann and Bower, 2000). By 2000, nearly all ranked among the largest 200 non-financial firms in the world (McChesney, 2004), and all exhibited strong similarities in terms of revenues, market capitalisation (with the exception of AOL Time Warner) strategic goals, and corporate objectives (Albarran and Moellinger, 2002).

The 'urge to merge' arose in part from the prosaic fact that for large companies organic growth alone can seldom meet the growth expectations of the financial markets or maintain strategic advantage. But a range of other factors also contributed:

1. Globalisation allowed the integration of previously national markets into larger transnational ones (Doyle, 2002a; McChesney, 2004). This was partly a reflection of a broader trend for organisations to develop, source and market products to exploit competitive advantages internationally, but also the result of market liberalisation arising from the relaxation of regulatory barriers concerning the commercial exploitation of media.
2. Technological change, particularly the Internet and digitalisation, created opportunities for media firms to move into new fields and compensate for actual or anticipated decline in core businesses. The Internet and digitalisation together allow different forms of media to be converted into a common format and to be moved rapidly around the globe. In conjunction with globalisation, these developments increased the opportunities for, and attractions of, consolidation: there were more platforms for media content, formats for content to be 'repurposed' into, and markets in which products could be sold. This in turn increased the potential for economies of scale and scope and made global media organisations both feasible and financially attractive for the first time (McChesney, 2004).
3. The development of global capital infrastructures and the internationalisation of financial institutions provided a source of finance for large media firms to both expand and become more global (Picard, 2004). The market liberalisation and advances in communications technology, which had enlarged potential markets and allowed the provision of media content in a faster more efficient manner, meant media industries became more attractive for capital investment (Chan-Olmsted in Picard, 2004).
4. Sizable consolidated firms offer increased potential for economies of scale and scope, leverage and synergy. Economies of scale are a fundamental characteristic of mass media products: because they have high first copy costs and low marginal costs they are expensive to produce but cheap to reproduce and distribute. This means once a product has been created and a distribution system established it makes sense to push as many copies of that product as possible through that system. Consolidation also increases economies of scope because concentrated media organisations can spread their costs over larger audiences, with cost per consumer falling as the audience grows (Doyle, 2002a). The new conglomerates were global and they could make better use of their resources by straddling wider product and geographic markets. This was important to US media firms, as demand in the US for media products such as broadcast and cable television became saturated (McChesney in Cottle, 2003) and lifestyle differences between different national markets became less significant (Chan-Olmsted in Picard, 2004). Consolidation also increases the potential for leverage and synergy creating more opportunities for content repurposing, promotional synergies and cross-media advertising packages
6. Large diversified media firms benefit from increased control and reduced exposure to risk. Not only are they more cushioned against problems in particular sectors (Doyle, 2002a), but as the media industry consolidated, relying on other players to supply activities in the value chain became a risk (McChesney, 2004).Vertical expansion ensures access to essential and scarce resources and inputs (content) or outlets (distribution platforms), preventing upstream or downstream players from extracting excessive profits. Conglomerates can also establish monopoly access to either of these, and in terms of content, access to exclusive content assets was a significant driver of merger activity.

Having accepting the widely held cognition that in a converged media world, 'content will be king', media companies needed to find new sources of attractive content with which to expand their range of products or markets. Media organisations that were strong in content assets sought to divesify by acquiring organisations that offered additional distribution capacity – for example cinema chains and television stations.

Clearly, any particular merger will result from a particular combination of these drivers. The fusion of Time Warner and AOL, for example, represented a solution to different problems the two partners were facing at that time. AOL needed quality branded media content to meet its broadband aspirations (which it acquired in the form of Warner Bros music, TBC, HBO and Time Inc. magazines) and would also benefit from the global promotion platform Time Warner's products would provide, which in turn would allow it to reduce advertising spending. Time Warner needed a strong Internet presence, not least to satisfy shareholders and the financial markets, because its own Internet strategy had failed.

Impact of the conglomerates

Many were concerned about the potential impact of these massive media organisations. It was feared they would constitute a global oligopoly and prevent new players from entering the sector (see, for example, McChesney, 2004), and that their appetite for dependable ratings and advertising revenues would create pressures to homogenise products with a concentration on those appealing either to the largest markets or those segments with the highest disposable income.

In terms of the homogenisation of products, the result of concentration appears to be neither clear-cut nor wholly negative. It has been suggested that large media organisations are better placed than smaller ones to innovate and therefore media concentration may well increase pluralism (Doyle, 2002a). There is evidence that the unpredictability and hit driven nature of the sector are stimulating creativity and diversity, despite consolidated ownership (Davis and Scase, 2000). (This may also reflect the largest conglomerates' understanding of the role of autonomy in creative organisations, discussed in Chapter 7). This, coupled with the need to serve fragmenting audiences, would appear to be countering the risk of mass standardised products.

Mergers are also notoriously difficult to make work. The AOL Time Warner marriage in 2000 had led, by 2002, to the largest corporate debt in US history, $98 billion. A wide range of problems prevented the fusion from bringing its anticipated benefits, with poor post-merger integration a central cause. In fact, overall, the global media conglomerates have struggled to realise their potential advantages and this has led some to question whether the conglomerates are becoming too large and complex to operate effectively. North American players are experiencing problems building truly global operations while Bertelsmann, the only European contender, after a period when its centre of gravity seemed to be shifting more and more to the US, appears to be returning to its European roots.

The potential for improved economies of scale and scope has been badly damaged by the collapse of long-standing mass media business models arising for example from falling newspaper sales and network television audiences, the gradual growth of online advertising and the illegal downloading of music tracks. Indeed, these developments call into question the assumption that consolidation and increased size bring strategic advantage (Gershon in Albarran et al., 2005). Intriguingly, the conglomerates are increasingly describing the benefits of size not aggressively but defensively, that is, not in terms of critical mass and market dominance, but in terms of positioning the organisation for all eventualities in an environment where uncertainty is high and existing business models are under threat.

Consolidation does also not preclude the need to develop additionally a wide range of temporary relationships with other organisations. Even the largest players have found that partnerships in local markets and adjoining sectors are inevitable. In a comparative analysis of the strategic style and orientation of the six largest media conglomerates, Sjurts (2005) found that the simultaneous presence of diversification strategies and cooperation between conglomerates has led to complex co-opetition arrangements where partners in one setting are competitors in another. Strategies for market dominance are diluted by the need for glocalisation also. The strategic imperative of a broad span of national markets means conglomerates cannot afford to neglect local tastes, thus contradictory trends can be observed where activities are simultaneously generic and customised for local tastes (Castells in Castells and Cardoso, 2006).

That having been said, the merger activity that died down as a result of the dotcom crash reasserted itself from the mid-2000s. These structural changes, however, present a mixed picture featuring both divestiture and acquisition. While some media companies are still seeking to accumulate critical mass and broaden their span of activities through wholly-controlled operations, others are streamlining their businesses, shedding non-core assets (with many divested businesses being acquired by the private equity community).[2] For example, in 2005 Paramount acquired Dreamworks SKG, a straight acquisition. Walt Disney acquired Pixar, but sold the ABC radio stations and network. News Corporation acquired the 18 per cent stake of Fox Entertainment that it did not own, but Clear Channel Communication divested its entertainment unit. In a hybrid move, Viacom split itself into two publicly traded units, Viacom and CBS.

Established media organisations and the Internet

A particular structural issue that the media faced at the close of the 1990s concerned the location of their Internet businesses. This issue received almost obsessive attention during the dotcom era due to a prevailing assumption that the inbuilt conservatism of the traditional media would kill off the innovation required for Internet businesses.

The intrinsic tension between entrepreneurial new activities and mature old ones is well explored in the literature on adaptive approaches to strategy and discussed in Chapter 6 (on technological change) and Chapter 7 (on creativity and innovation). As we saw in these chapters, the standard theoretical recommendation is that new ventures tasked with radically new strategic departures need autonomy. In practice the established media firms displayed considerable similarity in their organisational arrangements for Internet activities, involving a three-stage cycle of integration, autonomy and re-integration.

Early experiments with the Internet were in the main conducted within existing 'old' media divisions. This was because at that point the new media products were seen as experimental extensions of existing old media ones. However, early success with these products and the explosive growth of the Internet sector as a whole led to the establishment of independent new media divisions. It was assumed these would increase the number and diversity of new media activities, allow expertise to flourish in 'hothouse' environments, and, because they stood outside of the parent's legacy systems and bureaucracy, would be able to respond to market opportunities more quickly. Stand-alone units would also be much easier to spin-off, creating 'web currency' to fund further Internet-related acquisitions. The final stage in the cycle occurred after the implosion of the dotcom sector. This saw new media divisions reintegrated into the parent organisations, for example News International disbanded its News Networks division, and Bertelsmann integrated its Internet activities back into the corporate centre. This was due to the changed context. The collapse of the Internet economy meant spin-offs were no longer financially attractive, and it was necessary to rein in costs, especially since revenues were still largely absent. In addition there were tensions between the core and the new media divisions over shared customers, resources and revenues. These were costing management time and causing delays in market entry.

An alternative third stage for the new Internet business (very popular during the dotcom boom) was the spin-off (it was even said that the business model of the Internet was the IPO). This involved the divestiture of high-growth units to benefit both the parent and the spun-off organisation. In this context the parent capitalised on the higher valuations for the Internet businesses and also reduced risk, since the Internet companies consumed significant amounts of capital and often incurred large losses. The parent also gained capital for further Internet acquisitions and if the spin-off succeeded it often reflected positively on the parent's stock. For the spin-off it provided the freedom to operate entrepreneurially and allowed it to offer stock options which were then essential to attract and retain talent. Bertelsmann employed this strategy twice, spinning off Pixelpark in 1999 and Lycos in 2000.

Start-ups

New firms are favoured by policy makers for their positive impact on innovation and job creation, economic growth and competitiveness (Baumol, 1993; Turner, 1997). Start-ups have a long tradition in the media, partly due to the fragmentation of value chains, and partly because of the scope for surprise hits from 'unknowns' to achieve significant market success. It was feared that consolidation in the media industry would deter new entrants because they could not match the economies of scale and market penetration of the largest players. Ironically, however, mergers to some extent prompted the formation of new business as employees who had been let go and had fewer job options in a consolidating sector chose to start up independently rather than abandon their specialist field.

Alliances

Strategic alliances are normally understood as cooperative arrangements between two or more potentially competitive firms, but the term can encompass a variety of inter-organisational arrangements ranging from strategic link ups between major players (for example the Sony–BMG joint venture, which is discussed below), to short-term partnerships (such as the BBC's fleeting link up with Yahoo! to supply Internet news content for mobile devices) and cross-border alliances.

The motivations behind such partnerships are equally diverse. They include gaining access to specific competencies, talent or technologies, the desire to speed up entry to new markets, the need to reduce the risks of new products or services, and to reduce entry barriers by acquiring strong brands or improving scale economies, or to defray the cost of content investments. Alliances can also serve as a precursor to a full-blown acquisition or merger.

Alliances have long been a tool for strategic growth in the media industry (Chan-Olmsted, 2006). The globalisation of the television industry since the mid-1980s has been achieved largely through a multitude of small-scale cross-border collaborations involving financing, production, distribution and programme format deals. Convergence has increased levels of alliance activity (Chan-Olmsted and Kang, 2003; Fang and Chan-Olmsted, 2003). As value chains have expanded, fragmented and unbundled and as distribution options and end-devices multiplied it has become increasingly difficult for media firms to cover all stages and keep all strategic options open. Some of the largest players responded to these uncertainties through acquisition, but the majority also became active in alliances and joint ventures (Chan-Olmsted in Picard, 2004). These were particularly favoured as a method of entering the Internet, broadband or wireless markets (Chan-Olmsted and Kang 2003; Fang and Chan-Olmsted, 2003). Many alliances are between actors in the media industry but there are also numerous examples of inter-organisational ventures between players in converging sectors (for example CBS's project to distribute old episodes of television programmes via Google). Thus the trend towards alliances in the media sector arising from the emergence of the Internet can be viewed as furthering the process of convergence between this and the neighbouring industries of telecoms, information technology and consumer electronics.

While the logic behind an alliance may be straightforward, implementation is often fraught with difficulties. The 50/50 joint venture between Sony's recorded music business and that of Bertelsmann was conceived as a response to falling sales and the growth of digital downloading. The alliance did yield cost savings but these were counterbalanced by legal costs and accounting charges associated with the deal, as well as disagreements over leadership, cultural tensions, and partners' differing performance.

From alliances to networks

Where many alliances are created, network structures emerge. Notionally networks are open adaptive structures of 'interconnected nodes' that evolve as new nodes are added and existing ones disappear in response to the requirements of the environment.

Interest in networks from a number of perspectives has grown in recent decades. As discussed earlier in this chapter, information scientists predicted that the impact of global digital networks on firm transaction costs would cause large complex hierarchically governed structures to gave way to constellations of smaller flexible ones operating on principles of market exchange. Economists and political scientists became interested in the superior performance and competitiveness of economies characterised by networked clusters of organisations, especially those in the information and communication technologies (Castells in Castells and Cardoso, 2006), often citing the Silicon Valley model discussed in the previous chapter, as an example.

Networks became a dominant topic in the study of organisational structure during the 1980s (Fenton and Pettigrew in Pettigrew and Fenton, 2000). They were viewed as bringing benefits in complex uncertain environments, in terms of flexibility, increased scope, access to resources, capabilities, technologies and markets, and a safety net for uncertain exploratory projects. Castells (Castells and Cardoso, 2006: 8) predicted that the increasing importance of information technology and knowledge, and the opportunities for increased effectiveness and cost efficiency provided by network structures, would mean that while the firm might persist as the legal entity and unit for the accumulation of capital, the business network would emerge as the operational unit. This would benefit small and mid-sized organisations who could maintain autonomy and flexibility while having access to the critical mass necessary to compete. Doubts have however been raised about the likelihood of a wholesale shift to network structures (Pettigrew and Fenton in Pettigrew and Fenton, 2000).

Nohria and Ghoshal (1997) found scant empirical evidence of such a development.

Networks in the media industry

For the media industry, the network is not a new structure. Hollywood has displayed network features since the 1950s when the large-scale industrial film 'factories' that had dominated the industry between the 1920s and 1940s, and which had controlled the entire value chain from actors to projectionists, began to break up. In their place came relatively stable networks made up of producers, directors, actors, screenwriters and other industry specialists who were involved in persistent patterns of contracting (Christopherson and Storper, 1989).

But in recent years the network structure has become more prevalent. If the media merger was the defining structural option for the 1980s and 1990s, the network may well be that for the new Millennium. Chan-Olmsted (in Albarran et al., 2006) attributes an increase in networks in the media industries to the public good aspects of media content, the industry's need to respond to audience preferences and technological changes, and the symbiotic relationship between content and conduit. Hesmondhalgh (2002) notes that the launch of digital television in Europe required various difficult and complex technologies to be combined, plus significant resources to subsidise installation to a point of achieving a critical mass of subscribers large enough to attract advertisers and to support the necessary infrastructure. This in turn mandated a complex network of companies working together spanning the telecoms, cable, computer and media sectors.

News Corporation has also been described as a loose global network (Coleridge, 1993; Louw, 2001) with Murdoch at the centre, the various regional and sectoral businesses operating autonomously in their markets, and resources flowing as necessary between these nodes. Although network structures in the media tend to span sector boundaries. Thus Disney, cited in the 1990s as a prime example of the synergistic media conglomerate (Slywotsky and Morrison, 1997), could also be described as the hub of a complex network structure involving a major partnership with Pixar and associated alliances with a wide range of strategic partners, ranging from consumer goods organisations such as Mattel, Nestlé, IBM, Coke and McDonald's to industry specialists such as Industrial Light & Magic (see Figure 9.1).

Network elements can also be found in the UK television industry. The traditional structure was that a handful of large vertically integrated organizations produced programmes in-house for terrestrial broadcast channels. Between the 1980s and 1990s this structure changed fundamentally, largely as a result of the 1990 Broadcasting Act, which imposed quotas on the BBC and ITV to source at least 25 per cent of their programming from independent producers

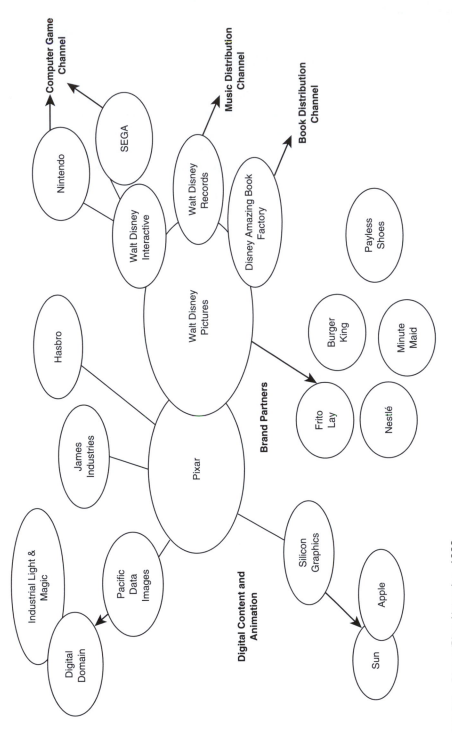

Figure 9.1 Disney/Pixar Network c. 1999

by 1993, coupled with an increasing global trade in television programming and programme formats. This led to the emergence of the 'publisher-broadcaster' model discussed earlier in this chapter. Thus the architecture of the sector shifted from a handful of monolithic 'integrated factory' producers controlling all stages of a traditionally organised value chain, to a 'multi-network value chain', where a 'primary network' of freelance creative labour and facilities joins with a 'secondary programme production network' of independent producers who work on a project basis. The output of their efforts is bought by publisher-broadcasters who are at the centre of these organisational networks (Starkey et al., 2000).

Project-based organizations

The structures discussed in this chapter have moved progressively from stable arrangements to increasingly fluid ones. Even more temporary than alliances and networks are the ad hoc structures based on inter-organisational and inter-personal relationships that revolve around one-off projects (although these can also evolve into serial project relationships).

In the media industries, project-based structures are primarily a response to the individual nature of many media products, just as the conglomerate structure is a response to the economies of scale that characterise mass media products and the continual need for short-run or unique products (Manning, 2005). While they sound transitory in the extreme, they can paradoxically constitute stable sectors of the economy. Temporary enterprises have been central to the US film industry for decades (DeFillippi and Arthur, 1998), and the UK film industry has been described as entirely project-based (Davenport, 2006). Such structures provide flexibility and stability, specialisation and innovation (Christopherson and Storper, 1989). They allow a continual adaptation of activities, a constant reconstitution of creative elements. They integrate different types of knowledge and skills, and reduce costs, while at the same time reducing the risks and uncertainties intrinsic to novel products (Davenport, 2006). A hybrid form spanning the project organisation and the network is the 'latent organization' (Starkey et al., 2000: 229), 'groupings of individuals that persist through time and are periodically drawn together for recurrent projects by network brokers who either buy in programmes for publisher-broadcasters or draw together those artists and technicians who actually produce them'.

Strategically, flexible organisation forms like these bring potential benefits in terms of increased creativity and improved performance. Davis and Scase (2000) argue their popularity also stems from the particular requirements of creative individuals in the media, which can preclude traditional hierarchical management structures. Media professionals have specialised skills, high levels of general education, and use sophisticated developed social processes to interact and achieve project goals. They therefore require the freedom to exercise independent judgement in how they solve problems, undertake tasks and achieve strategic goals.

Conclusions

The changes to organisational forms in the media industry over past decades underline the link between the environment, strategy and structure. Indeed the sector's recent history can be traced through these developments: the decline of the centralised integrated factory model in response to a multi-channel digital environment and deregulation; the wave of mergers in response to the opportunities and threats of convergence and the need to recycle and maximise the returns from increasing investment in content; the dotcom start-ups and spin-offs in response to the emergence of the Internet and skyrocketing valuations of Internet business shares and; the growth of fluid and temporary forms in response to globalisation glocalisation and ever more complex value chain constellations. The painful results of some of these organisational transitions and adaptations suggest that in deciding strategic courses of actions, managers might need to reflect carefully on the structural ramifications of their chosen course of action, and pay heed to the importance of organisational factors, particularly culture, in deciding their outcomes.

While a chronological development can be traced, this picture is muddied because the various new structural changes taking place are not mutually exclusive. Apparently conflicting trends – each bringing different strategic benefits – are observable. These include consolidation and integration, alliance and partnership activity, and a growth in fluid and temporary structures. As discussed in Chapter 11, the challenge for media organisation is to accommodate these equally compelling organisational imperatives and continue to function as cohesive and coherent organisations.

Consolidation and increased vertical integration create opportunities for improved economies of scale and scope, despite the fragmentation of audiences and the increased complexity of distribution options. Thus while the appeal of M&A activity as a route to growth has lessened, it still persists, as speculation about the fate of the UK's ITV and Disney's purchase of Pixar shows. Partnership activity allows for increased speed and agility and faster adaptation to environmental opportunities, and under this banner comes a range of structural options moving from formal long-term joint ventures, through networks of alliances, to project-based organisations and what have been termed 'latent organisations'. This suggests that the popularity of flexible and fluid organisational forms will continue to grow (although the scope and speed of growth of this phenomenon is not clear and research that provided definitive data would be welcome).

Alliance- and project-based organisational forms are characterised by weak corporate boundaries, high levels of autonomous decision-making and a need for good communication. Strategically important competencies and knowledge may be located at the periphery of the organisation or outside it (that is, with a partner) and by extension decision-making may be devolved to the fringes of the organisation, beyond the direct authority of the corporate centre. Power is more broadly distributed throughout the organisation and formal structures and hierarchies are weakened. Such contexts place specific demands on the leaders of media organisations, and these are explored in the next chapter.

Notes

1 Viacom split into two companies – Viacom and the CBS Corporation – in January 2006.
2 Price Waterhouse Cooper's *Insights Entertainment and Media: Analysis and Trends on US M&A Activity*, 2006.

TEN

Leadership

Either lead, follow or get out of the way. (Sign on Ted Turner's desk, pictured in *Fortune*, 5 January 1987)

The leaders of media organisations have always commanded intense scrutiny from regulators, policy makers and the press. This is due in part to the potential of the medium: control of media content confers considerable opportunities to influence public opinion, build personal profile, and gain access to politicians (Rupert Murdoch's 2006 annual conference in California was reputedly attended by Tony Blair, Bill Clinton, Arnold Schwarzenegger, Al Gore and Shimon Peres). The industry also has a tradition of flamboyant leaders, from the press barons of the early twentieth century such as Hearst, Beaverbrook, Northcliffe and Rothermere to the moguls controlling global empires today, such as Murdoch and Jobs. But while the business press has devoted much attention to these individuals, the subject of leadership in the media industry has received far less attention from media management scholars making it 'arguably the single most neglected area of research and theory development in the field of media management' (Mierzjewska and Hollifield in Albarran et al., 2006).

This chapter explores leadership in the media industry and its influence on strategy. It reviews theoretical approaches to the subject of leadership and the strands within this body of research that are most frequently applied to the media sector. A number of cases are brought into this discussion which both contextualise the theory, and provide insights into the specific requirements of leadership in the media sector. This chapter therefore straddles adaptive approaches to strategy – in that it reviews leaders' role in shaping and implementing strategy – as well as interpretative ones – from the perspective of reviewing how leaders employ the organisation's social architecture to implement strategy.

What is leadership?

The study of leadership can be traced back to the ancient Greeks. Research from a management rather than an historical perspective began in earnest in the 1920s and in the ensuing years leadership has been investigated from many different theoretical standpoints using an enormous variety of different methodological approaches.

As research has progressed, perspectives have shifted. Universal recipes that assume there is 'one best way' to lead have been buttressed by contingent orientations that stress the context-dependent nature of the leadership task. A tight instrumental focus on traits, skills and styles has been broadened to involve the interactive processes between leaders and those led. A narrow leader-centric focus on the leader's abilities and attributes has evolved into integrated conceptual frameworks encompassing relationships and the strategic context. Objectivist approaches that see leadership as an absolute and measurable entity have been challenged by subjectivist ones which view leadership as something constructed through social interaction.

The result is an extensive body of theory, but one lacking commonly-accepted definitions and riven by methodological divisions. Debate persists concerning fundamental issues, such as what leadership is (Bass, 1990; Yukl, 2002; Northouse, 2004). For example, does leadership reside in a set of qualities or characteristics belonging to those acting as leaders (Jago, 1982), or in a social influence process, which seeks to get a group of individuals to move towards a specific objective (Jago, 1982; Kotter, 1988; Northouse, 2004)? Consensus is also lacking on where leadership is to be found. Some researchers view the terms of manager and leader as interchangeable (Conger, 1999), the assumption being that authority inevitably involves a degree of leadership. Others, for example transformational theorists, assume leaders are senior figures involved in strategic decision taking. Trait theories classify anyone with responsibility for achieving a given task that involves a group of individuals as a leader, especially if that individual has the specific competencies required or an influence over the situation.

Trait approaches – born to be a leader

Also known as 'great person approaches', trait approaches represent some of the earliest systematic research into leadership. In vogue from the early 1900s to the 1940s, trait approaches view leadership as residing in a set of definable, measurable inborn traits that are possessed by a 'natural leaders' (Jago, 1982), which range from physical characteristics such as height, to aspects of personality and temperament, motivation, needs and values. Researchers sought to identify the traits that were linked positively with successful leaders and often turned to historical figures such as Napoleon or Gandhi for their data. The assumption was that once the 'right' traits had been identified, potential leaders could be identified by screening for these (Jago, 1982). Trait approaches held great intuitive appeal, but despite extensive research a definitive list of leadership traits never emerged (Jago, 1982).

Risk-taking and media leadership

He gambled. [Jobs] put $50 or $60 million into Pixar. The gamble paid off. (Young and Simon, 2005: 247)

The business literature often stresses media leaders' entrepreneurial abilities. In addition to Steve Jobs, Joseph Pulitzer, William Randolph Hearst, Ted Turner, Rupert Murdoch and Robert Maxwell have all been described in these terms.

From the perspective of leadership theory, an entrepreneurial leader is understood as one that is closely attuned to environmental change, who employs a visceral mixture of intuition and experience to interpret this, and whose strategic behaviour involves hunting out opportunities in the environment and making bold resource commitments in response to that change (Mintzberg et al., 1998). This definition is close to that of the media mogul. Thus Tunstall and Palmer define such an individual as someone who:

owns and operates major media companies, who takes entrepreneurial risks ... who largely built up his own media empire: ... [the] entrepreneurial element can include the launching of new media enterprises, ... but often consists of largely buying up, and taking over, existing media companies. (1998: 105)

A facility with risk is common to both the concept of the entrepreneurial leader and of the media mogul. McClelland (1961) introduces a valuable distinction between 'gambling' and 'calculating', suggesting that successful entrepreneurial leaders take highly calculated risks rather than make gambles. Strategic risk-taking also features in biographical accounts of many media leaders. For example Murdoch and Turner are both credited with a facility with risk, and in both cases it is implied that this is an inborn trait rather than acquired skill. Both individuals have reportedly gambled since childhood (Bibb, 1993; Shawcross, 1994; Auletta, 2004) and built their empires by defying convention and taking risks. Thus it has been said that 'no one else bets the farm quite like Murdoch' (Gibson, 2007), 'the most gifted opportunist in the media' (Pooley, 2007), and Turner has been described as a 'risk-taking opportunist' (Bibb, 1933: 416). Murdoch has a propensity for placing large bets on particular categories of content that stretches back at least three decades. For example in the 1960s he broke a gentleman's agreement among Australian television executives not to pay more than $6,000 an hour for acquired programming and agreed to pay $1 million a year for everything that ABC produced or distributed for the next five years (Shawcross: 1994: 89–90).

Skills approaches – leadership can be learned

Trait approaches are absolute: they assume there is one best way to lead and that depends on a set of immutable predispositions. Skills approaches are more egalitarian, seeing leadership as residing in a combination of skills which can be acquired through experiences such as training programmes, career progression, mentoring and so on (Northouse, 2004). Thus leadership is within the gift of many, rather than a few.

Research in this field seeks to identify the learnable skills, knowledge, behaviours and competencies that underlie effective leadership (Jago, 1982; Mumford et al., 2000; Northouse, 2004). Katz, who carried out much initial work in the field, identified three core categories (Katz, 1955). The first is technical skills. This is the ability 'to work with things' and includes analytical skills as well as expertise in domain-appropriate tools and techniques (although these are judged to be more important for lower level leadership). The second is human skill. This is the ability to work effectively with colleagues at all levels, being sensitive to their perspectives, needs and motivations, and being able to create a climate of trust. The third is conceptual skill – the ability to work with abstract ideas and hypothetical notions (Northouse, 2004).

During the 1990s the concept of skills was broadened into 'capabilities', understood as the 'knowledge and skills that make effective leadership possible' (Mumford et al., 2000: 12). As research progressed, the cognitive skills of solving problems and constructing solutions became a focus. These require a facility with abstract and hypothetical ideas that allows a leader to identify complex relationships and predict future events from current trends (Yukl, 2002), and find solutions to new, unusual and ill-defined problems (Mumford et al., 2000; Northouse, 2004).

Finding appropriate solutions to such problems becomes more difficult as environments become turbulent. As we saw in Chapter 8, the risk of cognitive rigidity and erroneous conclusions increases in step with environmental instability. Leaders must not only become more structured and vigilant in environmental scanning and problem solving (Ancona, 1990), but also capable of challenging and updating their operating assumptions. Schein (1992) terms this learning leadership. Learning can take place in two 'modes'. In first-order, or single loop learning, this arises through repeated exposure to similar types of problems. The type of knowledge that arises is advantageous in stable contexts, especially if other players are new to an issue and do not possess it, but it can be a liability in turbulent ones since it reduces the likelihood of recognising a need for change (Weick, 1979). In unstable contexts double loop, or second-order, learning can be required. This involves questioning the governing norms, unlearning prior assumptions and developing new heuristics (Tushman and Anderson, 1986) and is a central to improving the organisation's ability to adapt (Virany et al., 1992).

It can be argued that single loop learning aided Michael Eisner during his first decade at Disney, and that weaknesses in double loop learning contributed to his downfall in the second. During his first decade, when the media industry was relatively stable, he applied the formula that had brought him success in his previous role at Paramount (and indeed the position of CEO at Disney): keep budgets low, eschew expensive stars, control all aspects of the organisation closely, grow internally where possible, and stick to the areas you know well (Stewart, 2005: 80). However, 10 years on the context had changed. Digitalisation and the Internet had taken hold, convergence was under way and blockbuster strategies were entrenched. The assumptions that had served Eisner so well previously were no longer appropriate. Big budgets were unavoidable if Disney movies were to compete with other major studios. The new business areas that were emerging as a result of convergence were far outside the traditional media realm and made alliance or acquisition a smarter strategy than internal growth. Eisner was not comfortable with this, and, for example, rejected a proposal to buy a minority interest in Yahoo!, choosing instead to merge its own Internet assets into a new portal, Go!, a decision that ultimately cost over $1 billion on paper (Stewart, 2005). The Pixar joint venture is a notable exception to the 'grow businesses internally' rule. This accounted for 45 per cent of the Disney film studio's operating income between 1998 and 2001, but was reputedly instigated by Katzenberg, not Eisner (Young and Simon, 2005).

Leadership skills in the media

There is a slim body of research into leadership skills required in the media sector. Sanchez-Tabernero (in Küng, 2006) identifies the ability to 'build great teams'. This involves a long-term orientation, an ability to motivate, strong beliefs, and an understanding of consumer tastes. While not addressing the media industry specifically, Burns and Stalkers' (1961/1994: 102) research into environments that further innovation identifies two leadership skills: to grasp the changing dynamics of the strategic environment, particularly technological ones, and recalibrate the internal organisation in step; and to 'define the work situation, displaying ... the commitments, effort, and self-involvement ... the individual ... should attempt to meet'.

The ability to see business opportunities in turbulent environments surfaces frequently in analyses of successful media leaders. In her research into the establishment of the UK pay television platform BSkyB, Spar highlights Murdoch's skill at designing business models that exploit multiple uncertainties – in that case advances in satellite and encryption technologies, a regulatory vacuum arising from the confluence of domestic and EU broadcasting regulation, and the UK government desire to increase competition in UK broadcasting:

again and again, the same pattern unfolded: Sky would recognise how some emerging technology could enable the firm either to leap through a regulatory barrier or consolidate a competitive foothold. Then Sky's managers would move to grasp this technology, develop it, create whatever standard might be necessary, and thus control its usage by any other parties. This was how Murdoch had first used satellite technologies to circumvent the otherwise solid net of British regulation: this was how Sky operated throughout the next decade. (Spar, 2001: 156)

when Sky Broadcasting first burst onto the British scene, it simultaneously circumvented one set of rules and established another. Officially ... Sky was not transmitting under British jurisdiction: it was beaming from Luxembourg and subject only to that country's minimal set of rules. And even on the ground, where Sky was subject to British law, the novelty of Sky's practices made it very difficult to lodge legal complaints against it. Was Sky a monopolist? It's hard to say. Did it behave anti-competitively? Hard again. It was a classic case of creative anarchy, with technology opening spaces and creating markets that defied existing regulation. (Spar, 2001: 183–4)

Ted Turner has been described as (someone who 'sees the obvious before most people do ... And after he sees it, it becomes obvious to everyone' (Wallace and Marer, 1991). In Turner's case 'the obvious' was the potential created by combining a number of technological advances – satellite distribution, cable television, handicams, small satellite up-links – with a government agenda to boost cable television and the broadcast networks' scaling back of news coverage. CNN started when he created the world's first satellite superstation by placing the signal of his small local Atlanta station on the newly launched RCE satellite which distributed the signal to cable systems around the country, thus acquiring a domestic audience of millions and viewers in Canada and Mexico.

Style approaches

In the late 1940s, 1950s and 1960s dissatisfaction with trait approaches led researchers to focus on leadership style, that is on leadership behaviour and its impact on others (Stogdill, 1974; Jago, 1982; Yukl, 2002). The first empirical studies were conducted at Ohio State University in the late 1940s. Two dimensions of leadership were identified: consideration – the degree of two-way communication and consultation, mutual trust, respect and warmth a leader exhibits towards his followers; and 'initiating structure' – the degree to which a leader organises relationships between group members and establishes channels of communication and methods of establishing the group's task. These dimensions were used to identify the optimal leadership style. Research suggested that an effective leader developed good rapport and two-way communication, and took an active role in planning and directing group activities. Subsequent research by the University of Michigan identified two critical dimensions of leadership style – employee-centred (concern for people) and job-centred (concern for production). In the mid-1980s Blake and Mouton used these dimensions as the basis for a diagnostic tool for managers, the 'managerial grid', which identified five different leadership archetypes.

Leadership styles in the media

Research into leadership skills in the media makes some prescriptive recommendations concerning leadership style. These follow a general line that consensus-based approaches are more appropriate than hierarchical authoritarian ones because creative employees resent being told what to do (Davis and Scase, 2000), will not accept unquestioningly directions from above (Lavine and Wackman, 1988), and when working as news journalists need editorial freedom and protection from managerial or owner influence (Curran and Seaton, 1981). Aris and Bughin (2005) propose two leadership styles for media organisations: an inspirational, charismatic, hands-on-style; and a performance-orientated, structured style, involving systematic setting of strategic corporate and individual goals.

Transformational leadership

A major recent concept in leadership theory is 'transformational leadership'. The origins of this are credited to political sociologist Burns (1978) who identified a leader who changes organisations elementally – transforms them – by evoking followers' intrinsic motivation and harnessing this to realise performance outcomes that exceed expectations. The focus on intrinsic motivation distinguishes transformational from 'transactional' leadership, where followers act in a certain way in return for specified extrinsic rewards (Conger, 1989).

The transformational leader's levers to transform an organization are elements in the social architecture of the organisation, plus a number of specific behaviours (Conger, 1989; Senge, 1990; Bass and Avolio, 1994; Bass and Steidlmeier, 1999). A key lever is a new vision. This should encourage individuals to question assumptions that might hold back the change process, find new solutions to existing problems, and select new courses of action (Senge, 1990). The leader's charisma, termed idealised influence in this body of theory, builds emotional commitment to the vision, by engaging followers' higher order needs and encouraging them to transcend self-interest in order to reach new the goals (Bass, 1985; Kotter, 1996; Hitt et al., 1998). The transformational leader changes the cultural assumptions also (Morgan, 1986; Sackmann, 1991; Schein, 1992), employing a number of mechanisms to embed new ones. Critical are which issues a leader pays attention to, his or her reactions to critical events, resource allocation criteria, plus which individuals are promoted and which 'ex-communicated' (Schein, 1992).

Other tools include providing coaching, mentoring and growth opportunities to followers and skilled communication: Mintzberg and Westley (1992) note that transformational leaders often have a strong facility for language, particularly symbolism and metaphor.

Charismatic leadership

His remarkable charisma ... that drew people to him even when they knew he might attack at any moment, created a degree of loyalty few executives ever match. (A colleague describing Steve Jobs, cited in Young and Simon, 2005: 201)

Charismatic leadership is a close cousin of transformational leadership (Hunt and Conger, 1999). This form of leadership occurs when a leader employs personal magnetism to evoke followers' trust and to influence them to act in certain ways in the pursuit of specific goals (Bass, 1985; Conger, 1989, 1999; Conger and Kanungo, 1998; Yukl, 2002). Like transformational approaches, charismatic leadership is understood as collective, processual and also as attributional – that is, it exists in the perceptions of others – and has been found to improve employee satisfaction, motivation, and performance (Yukl, 1999).

As with transformational approaches, vision is a central tool of charismatic leadership. A definition of a visionary is someone with an inner vision that is not supported by external facts. A prime example is Steve Jobs, whose vision to build 'insanely great' machines that will 'make a dent in the world' swept away rational objections. An Apple employee describes how: 'We really believed in what we were doing. The key thing is that we weren't in it for the money. We were out to change the world' (Trip Hawkins cited in Young and Simon, 2005: 62).

A vision should appeal to followers' higher order needs and link with their own values and ideals. As evident in the quote above, this engenders emotional commitment and encourages group members to cooperate to achieve their collective task (House, 1977; Conger, 1999; Yukl, 2002). The vision will often represent a marked departure from what has gone before, but not be so dramatic that followers might reject it, and it should resonate with follower disenchantment with current conditions. To embed the vision the charismatic leader models the behaviours, norms and values followers should adopt. He or she may also act unconventionally – making self-sacrifices or taking personal risks for example – to underline the importance of the changes that need to be made.

The distinction between transformational and charismatic leadership is not easy to establish. The fields certainly overlap. Conger (1999) sees charismatic leadership as an offshoot of transformational leadership now of almost equal stature. Certainly, charisma is central to transformational leadership; however, Bass (in Yukl, 1999) argues that a leader can be charismatic without being transformational. It is suggested that the emotional component on the part of leaders and followers distinguishes charismatic leadership as particularly concerning the compelling nature of the vision and the way it is communicated (Conger and Kanugo, 1998).

Further, while transformational leadership is normally understood as a positive concept, charismatic leadership has a shadow side – as can be inferred from the quote about Steve Jobs above. Howell (in Conger, 1999) describes it as running a spectrum from leaders who empower and develop their followers, to authoritarian and narcissistic ones who use their power for personal gains. Conger (1999) argues that a charismatic leader may well possess elements of both poles.

The success of charismatic leadership is affected by context (Bryman et al., 1996). While charismatic leaders improve employee satisfaction, motivation and performance, they can also underestimate threats in the organisational environment, screen out negative information, be overly self-confident and have an inflated sense of their own importance (Yukl, 1999). A charismatic leader's strategy may fail if implemented either too early or too late in a strategic initiative (Conger and Kanugo, 1998).

Transformational or charismatic? Greg Dyke at the BBC

Greg Dyke's tenure as Director General of the BBC (2000–2003) has many hallmarks of transformational leadership and arguably of charismatic leadership also. In 2002 he launched an ambitious initiative, 'Making it Happen', which was designed to transform the BBC into the most creative organisation in the world within five years and redress the damage that had been done to the social fabric of the organisation by his predecessor. The underlying rationale was that raising levels of creativity and providing better service to audiences would ensure the BBC's survival as a publicly funded broadcaster in a multi-channel, multimedia environment.

'Making it Happen' was a 'do-it-yourself' intervention designed to harness the energy, commitment and ideas of the BBC's thousands of staff (Spindler and van den Brul, 2006–7). This was to counteract the 'change fatigue' felt by many that had resulted from a massive strategic initiative introduced by the previous DG, John Birt. Known as 'Producer Choice', this had involved establishing an internal market between 'producers' and 'broadcasters' and involved a complete and complex restructuring of the entire organisation and its processes. In addition to never entirely succeeding (steps to dismantle it began within two years of its introducution) this project was viewed as the brainchild of management consultants and senior managers and never 'penetrated the heartland editorial areas of the BBC' (Spindler and van den Brul, 2006–7).

Dyke employed a number of strategies to build commitment for his initiative. First was a series of 'Just Imagine' brainstorming workshops. Ten thousand staff participated and contributed over 25,000 suggestions about the BBC's challenges and how these might be overcome. A handful of the best ideas were implemented very publicly within weeks to demonstrate that staff involvement was valued. Dyke also abandoned the formal and organised communication style of his predecessor. All staff were on first name terms, meeting documentation was reduced to a minimum and yellow 'referee' cards stating 'Cut the Crap, Make it Happen' were distributed to staff who were expected to bring these out if they saw good ideas were being rejected or that bureaucracy was surfacing.

In January 2003 Dyke published a new set of BBC values and stressed these should become the bedrock of the new culture. In the same month proposals from the staff teams tasked with investigating how the BBC could realise its new goals were consolidated into a BBC-wide change plan with five main sections: Providing Great Leadership; Making the BBC a Great Place to Work; Getting Closer to our Audiences; Inspiring Creativity Everywhere; and Working as One BBC. In total this made up over 40 separate initiatives, many of them involving radical changes to the status quo. These were presented to staff through 'The Big Conversation', a live, televised, interactive BBC-wide conversation involving 17,000 staff at over 400 meetings.

These activities did lead to significant change in the organisation. Internal research two years into the process (March 2004) showed that 62 per cent of staff felt 'Making it Happen' would make a real difference to the BBC, 22 per cent were actively championing change; 58 per cent felt valued by the organisation (up 28 per cent on 2001) and 50 per cent felt management behaviour was consistent with BBC values (up 18 per cent on 2001).

The means by which Dyke achieved these improvements do fit the tenets of transformational leadership theory (Kanter, 2004). He harnessed staff members' intrinsic motivation and altered aspects of the BBC's social fabric to achieve fundamental change. His vision encouraged staff to rethink their assumptions, find new solutions to the BBC's problems, and change day-to-day behaviour, and capitalised on both the resentment caused by Producer Choice, and nostalgia about the familiar historic goals of the BBC – serving the nation with the highest standard of programming. He succeeded in shifting the culture, making it more creative and open to change, and through his personal style – approachability, informality, directness, communicativeness – modelled the behaviours he wanted staff to emulate.

There are signs of charismatic leadership also. Dyke's autobiography shows how crucial emotions were to the initiative. He personally was extremely involved, and he sought to ensure staff were too: 'The real point about Making it Happen was that I engaged people's emotions, not just their brains. Culture change is above all an emotional experience, not an intellectual one' (Dyke, 2004: 215).

Dykes's charismatic style ran into problems when the context shifted, also conforming to theory. In 2003 a BBC radio reporter claimed on air that the UK Government had made a false claim in an intelligence dossier. The government was outraged yet the BBC's response was somewhat half-hearted, with Dyke in particular misjudging the seriousness of the situation, which was perhaps influenced by his personal disapproval of UK involvement in the Iraq

War. A crisis in the relationship between the two institutions ensued which escalated when the weapons expert who had briefed the BBC committed suicide. In 2004 the Hutton Enquiry was tasked with investigating these events and found fault with the BBC's management, editorial systems – and by implication with Dyke's delegated leadership style – and both Dyke and the BBC Chairman resigned. This series of events suggests that Dyke's desire to speed up decision-making and make the organisation's output more compelling may have led him to oversimplify or shortcut procedures to ensure editorial quality, and that over-confidence may have led him to underestimate the situation and be over-confident of his ability to solve it.

The crisis also shows the depth of the emotional bond that had been formed between the DG and staff. Dyke's resignation brought thousands of employees into the street in protest and a full-page newspaper advert was taken in his support. At the BBC Governor's Private Session at which Dyke resigned, the BBC's HR Director spoke of Dyke's 'huge personal impact on the BBC' and described how his 'emotional connection with staff at all levels was very different from the previous management regime'.[1]

Leading for creativity

An important aspect of strategic leadership in the media relates to the connection between leadership and creativity. This issue is under-explored, although broad suggestions have been made for organisations that need creativity, for example that hierarchical, paternalistic management styles limit creativity, and inclusive ones that distribute creative decision-making throughout the organisation promote sustained creativity (Mauzy and Harriman, 2003).

For more insights into the mechanisms underlying this connection we can refer back to theories of organisational creativity. These identify three obvious links between leadership and organisational creativity. The first is intrinsic motivation. This is central to transformational and charismatic leadership theories, and also to creativity theories, although it confers different advantages: in creativity theory, intrinsic motivation catalyses expertise and creative-thinking skills in the pursuit of novel solutions; in leadership theories intrinsic motivation promotes followers' receptivity to higher order goals and suppresses self-interest.

The second link is vision. A leader's vision drives strategic action, especially when seeking to achieve transformational change. Vision is central to creativity also, since no new product or service can be created without a clear vision that is simple, achievable, but also stretching and inspiring. The 'right' vision will resonate with pre-existing intrinsic motivation and lay the seed for ultimate success by sparking both a creative response to the core concept, and a deeper-lying sense of commitment to its fundamental goals.

The third link involves establishing an environmental context conducive to creativity. This is addressed, albeit tangentially, in the 'initiating structure' dimension of leadership discussed in style approaches, where the leader is viewed as the architect of the work environment, dictating the nature of creative challenges, how resources are allocated, and establishing wider contextual elements such as structure, coordination mechanisms, culture, business processes and management. The provision of autonomy for teams required to be creative also features.

A fourth point of connection concerns emotions. Emotional commitment by the leader and emotional engagement on the part of followers are fundamental to transformational and charismatic leadership. Emotions – desire, enjoyment, interest[2] – are also present in the intrinsically motivated state, which is central to organisational creativity. The role of emotions in leadership has been acknowledged – Burns (1978) argued that the genius of Mao Tse Tung was his understanding of others' emotions – but is under-explored.

Leadership and creativity: Michael Eisner at Walt Disney

Eisner's two-decade tenure as Disney's CEO provides valuable insights into the interrelationships between a leader, his strategy and creative outcomes. In 1984 Disney was an 'all but dead duck', struggling to maintain its independence and no longer even classified by the industry as a studio. 'Team Disney' comprising Michael Eisner, as Chairman and CEO, Frank Wells as President and COO, and Jeffrey Katzenberg as head of the film studio were brought in to rescue the organisation. Between the mid-1980s and mid-1990s the Walt Disney Company (it was renamed in 1986) underwent a remarkable turnaround. In four years it became the number one ranked studio as existing areas such as animation were revitalised (*The Lion King*, released in 1994 had by 1995 become the second largest grossing film ever) and new businesses were developed (including publishing, retailing and baseball). By 1987 Disney was a vertically integrated conglomerate with an operating income that had jumped from $300 million to nearly $800 million.[3] It was one of the most valuable brands in the world and a case study on its tight internal management and aggressive exploitation of synergies was taught in MBA schools worldwide.[4]

Eisner ascribes much of the success to his formula for creative leadership (Wetlaufer, 2000). A central building block was the Monday staff meetings

> where people are not afraid to speak their minds and be irreverent ... an environment in which people feel safe to fail [and where] criticism for submitting a foolish idea is abolished.... We like to think we have fun here – we're loosey-goosey' [with a] 'freewheeling, spontaneous exchange of ideas', [but at the same time discussion is] 'brutally honest', which was 'confidence building'.

In terms of resources, creative staff had time to incubate ideas because green-light decisions were deliberately delayed. Autonomy was furthered because the long creative meetings were 'non-hierarchical – everybody becomes equal'. Eisner describes himself as 'a great believer in initiative and responsibility at every level'. He also supported diversity in creative teams because this was 'a great force towards creativity ... the more diverse the organisation, the more diverse the ideas that get expressed' (Stewart, 2005).

However, in 1994 things started to go wrong. Wells was killed in helicopter crash, Eisner underwent quadruple heart bypass surgery, and Katzenberg, having been denied Well's job, left to found Dreamworks SKG. In the ensuing years Dreamworks' and Pixar's animated films started to outperform Disney's. Live action films started to do poorly, and video and merchandising income fell, as did earnings and stock price. Disney's internet portal, Go.com, was closed in 2001 with an $800 million charge. Unsurprisingly, Eisner's reputation soured. In 2003 Roy Disney and Stanley Gold started a campaign to oust him, charging him with 'cultural decay'. A year later, Comcast launched a hostile bid, and negotiations concerning the renewal of the Pixar joint venture that had contributed so handsomely to Disney's profits fell apart. In March of that year 45 per cent of shareholders voted to withhold support for Eisner's re-election, Eisner subsequently announced his resignation.

Disney's poor financial performance was attributed in large part to Eisner's leadership, and criticism became widespread. For example, 'Eisner' it was said 'managed creative ventures, Steve [Jobs] created' (Young and Simon, 2005: 305). Eisner was accused of being 'such an oppressive force that creative talents felt muzzled' (Young and Simon, 2005: 311), and of 'extinguishing the company's creative spark'. Politics inside the Disney organisation were said to be 'cut-throat' (Stewart, 2005) and the focus on synergy led to 'endless iterations of existing properties'.[5] If these criticisms are correct (and they stem primarily from business journalists who conceivably sympathised with Disney's beleaguered creatives and were perhaps envious of Eisner's compensation package) they suggest that although Eisner did institute mechanisms to further creativity, other aspects of his management priorities undermined these.

Theories of organisation creativity provide hints to how this might have happened. In terms of the creative challenge, the profit-multiplier business model that was the engine behind Disney's stellar financial performance (Slywotsky and Morrison, 1997) had the unintended effect of limiting the creative challenge, with encouraging a concentration on consumer characters that fit existing merchandising categories. Further, since compensation levels were tied to synergies, there was contingent extrinsic motivation which theory suggests would have crowded out intrinsic motivation (Frey and Jegen, 2000).

The Monday staff meetings were described as follows by Michael Ovitz, a leading Hollywood agent and one-time friend, who was brought in as Eisner's second in command but sacked acrimoniously soon after:

> Although the focal point of [Eisner's] management of the company [was] extolling the free-wheeling, spontaneous exchange of ideas and the 'synergy' that he was so proud of, there was actually very little exchange of ideas. Most of the lunch was a stream of consciousness monologue by Eisner. No one disagreed with anything he said. (Stewart, 2005: 219)

Financial control was tight. For Eisner, 'discipline is also part of creativity', but he was perceived as 'rapacious, soul-less, and always looking for a quick buck'.[6] According to theory, a tight limit on financial resources restrict intrinsic motivation and circumscribes experimentation. Autonomy was compromised by Eisner's: 'centralised and controlling management style [which led]… managers [to] feel second guessed; [and] artists [afraid of] surrendering creative freedom' as well as Eisner's propensity to 'sweat the details'.[7]

Collaborative leadership in the media

Leadership is often reflexively assumed to be a singular activity: In fact, this is seldom the case. In practice, while one leader may hold ultimate authority, frequently leadership is distributed between individuals, classically in the traditional combinations of CEO and COO, or of Chairman and CEO. (Peace and Conger, 2003; Voogt, 2006).

The issue of collaborative leadership, of course, is addressed in the corporate governance literature, Within leadership theory there is an emerging stream of research into collaborative leadership structures. It has been acknowledged that the role of leader is not restricted to a formally-designated individual, that leaders and followers can swap positions, and that multiple leadership roles may exist in a single group, with each serving a different leadership function (Jago, 1982). Change initiatives that involve a number of leaders operating at different levels of a firm have been found to be more effective (Pettigrew and Whipp, 1991), and multiple leaders are often required to change the culture of organisations failing to adapt to a changed environment (Schein, 1992).

Distributed leadership (Ancona et al., 2007) is a hybrid model combining concepts from skills and transformational/charismatic approaches. This involves four capabilities: sensemaking (understanding the context); relating (listening actively, advocating a point of view, and connecting with others); visioning (the collaborative creation of common vision); and inventing (transforming a vision into a present-day reality). Since few individuals possess all four capabilities, most leaders will need to find others they can work with. As a result the leadership task will be dispersed. There is an interesting correlation between this model and the findings of research into leadership derailment discussed below. Both highlight the importance of a leader's ability to relate to others and use this as a basis for a leadership team, and be able to lead in dynamic and complex environments.

In the media industry collaborative leadership arrangements are common and there is anecdotal evidence that such models have a positive impact on performance. This makes intuitive sense, for all industries, not just the media ones. The increasing complexity of the business environment and the leadership task makes it unlikely that a single individual will encompass all the competencies necessary to master both external and internal environments. Pixar has always had collaborative leadership, with the task split between John Lasseter, Ed Catmull and Steve Jobs. In the early days Roy and Walt Disney shared the running of their studio: 'Roy was the guardian, the protector who allowed genius to flourish ... not only freeing Walt to make creative decisions, but running the business side of Disney with great skill' (Bennis and Biederman, 1997: 45).

Eisner's most successful period at Disney also featured collaborative leadership. He was Chairman and CEO, but was supported by Frank Wells, who handled the administrative and financial tasks, and was the 'filter and interpreter who turned Eisner's ideas into practical reality (Young and Simon, 2005: 204) leaving Eisner to run the creative side (Stewart, 2005), and also by Jeffrey Katzenberg who possessed great skills in crafting creative concepts (Young and Simon, 2005). Despite the fact that Eisner never sought to recreate this structure once he lost his two co-leaders, he has acknowledged the importance of shared leadership: 'the most successful movie studios and television networks have had at least two strong executives at the top, supporting and counterbalancing one another' (Eisner, cited in Stewart, 2005: 142).

The case of BBC News Online provides insights into how collaborative leadership brings positive results in creative contexts. This venture had a dual leadership structure whereby the two leaders contributed to creating an environment conducive to creativity in different but complementary ways. John Birt, the BBC's Director General, established pre-conditions by setting a creative goal that resonated with the BBC's self-perceptions, providing the resources and ensuring autonomy, and then stepped back and allowed the venture to operate autonomously. He never actually visited the operation, but followed its progress closely at second hand. Bob Eggington, project manager, realised Birt's vision on the ground and on a day-to-day basis, providing strategic clarity by shielding the venture from the bureaucracy of the parent and establishing a positive culture.

Andy Duncan, Chief Executive of the UK's Channel Four, ascribes the success of Freeview, a digital television platform in the UK that he helped lead, to collaborative leadership: 'The leaders of projects have to realise that they don't have to supply all the answers, the real trick of getting the best out of people is to accept that answers come from everyone.'[8]

Knowing when to go

The higher the position of the person making the mistake, the more interesting the fall, and the further the fall. (Eisner in a 1995 memo to Ovitz, cited in Young and Simon, 2005: 317)

Eisner's departure is one in a stream of awkward exits by leaders in the media industry that includes Gerald Levin, Thomas Middlehof, Jean-Marie Messier, Steve Case, Greg Dyke, Conrad Black, and, of course, Robert Maxwell. The ability to make a graceful exit might be described as the ultimate leadership skill. The issue of leadership departure has been exhaustively studied, but diversity in terms of research contexts, methodologies, basic definitions and research fields make it hard to draw general conclusions from this work for strategy in the media sector.

Some of the most insightful findings come from derailment studies conducted by the Centre for Creative Leadership in the 1970s and 1980s. These identified four main causes for general managers' exits (Van Velsor and Brittain Leslie, 1995) (and it is intriguing how many of these apply to the Eisner case). The first is problems with interpersonal relationships, often arising from a failure to transition from the task-based leadership approach required in previous roles to a relationship-based one needed for general management. Failure to meet business objectives because environmental conditions have become more dynamic and complex is the second reason, again this stems from failing to transition from one leadership context to another. Failure to build and lead a team is the third issue. This arises from difficulties in shifting from a task-orientated, assertive approach to a participative and relational one. The final hurdle concerns an inability to adapt to changes in the marketplace or the organisational culture.

Leaving a good successor is part of the exit task. The findings of research into leadership succession are contradictory (Virany et al., 1992), perhaps due to methodological problems concerned with measuring leader effects (Yukl, 2002). Executive succession is a powerful means of correcting misalignments between an organisation and its environment (Virany et al., 1992), and a change of leadership is often required in mature and potentially declining organisations (Schein, 1992). Failing firms have lower rates of succession than non-failing firms (Schwartz and Menon, 1985). Such failures can stem from incumbent leaders' difficulties in changing established patterns (Bettman and Weitz, 1983).

Entrepreneurs and founders (both are prevalent in the media sector) have particular difficulty in giving up what they have created: they may be consciously grooming successors, but unconsciously seeking to prevent powerful and competent people from taking over, or they may designate successors but prevent them from having enough responsibility to learn how to do the job (Schein, 1992). Recent events at News Corporation and Viacom suggest that Rupert Murdoch and Sumner Redstone may be experiencing conflicts in these areas.

Conclusions

Leadership in the media is an under-researched field. Leadership theory is extensive but, because it is disjointed, hard to apply systematically to the media. This chapter therefore needs to be viewed in the spirit of seeking to capture the current state of knowledge and giving impulses for further research.

It does however underline the close link between leadership and strategy, and the relevance of this interrelationship for the media industry. It also suggests that the media leadership role encompasses three different spheres: the outer, strategic environment which provides a starting point for strategy; the inner environment, the organisational eco-system comprising the many different organisational phenomena – particularly the interpretative ones – which must be brought into alignment if a strategy is to be implemented; and the internal relationship with the self – the ability to reflect and learn and to connect with others.

The examples in this chapter also underline the context dependent nature of the leadership task in the media. Eisner offers perhaps the cruellest example since he was in many ways a victim of his own success. During the first 10 years of his tenure his entrepreneurial, detail-driven leadership fitted excellently to the nature of the management challenge and harmonised with the abilities of his leadership colleagues, and allowed him to transform a failing collection of media assets into a highly successful and complex media conglomerate. However, his success in this changed the leadership challenge, at the same time that he lost his co-leaders. The organisation he created was too complex to be micro-managed, too diverse for a single management approach. His risk aversion and preference for internal growth were disadvantages in a converging industry where the blockbuster model was becoming the norm. The tight divisional coordination he championed maximised efficiency and return on investments but depressed creativity.

Finally, the chapter also shows that the task of leadership in the media sector contains many inherent paradoxes: the span of competencies and talents required is best served by multi-leader structures, yet these clearly complicate the decision-making process; the intricacies of the environment mandates that leaders develop heuristics to reduce complexity, but these can also limit strategic options when that environment changes too dramatically; the power, influence and responsibility make huge requirements in terms of self-knowledge and emotional maturity, yet individuals possessing such characteristics are unlikely to be able to stomach the temperamental, ego-driven, hard-nosed, power-hungry individuals that populate the sector. Paradoxes such as these are one of the subjects covered in the next chapter, which seeks to identify common themes and issues from the ideas presented in the book so far for researchers, students and practitioners.

Notes

1 Stephen Dando, Head of BBC for People, cited in the Minutes of BBC Governors' Private Session, 28 January, 2004 (www.bbc.co.uk/bbctrust/assets/files/pdf).

2 There are a number of categorisations of emotions. Those mentioned here come from Fridja's (1986) list of 10 basic emotions.

3 Increased profits stemmed from three main sources: raising admission prices at theme parks; greatly expanding the number of company-owned hotels; and distributing the animated classics on home video (Stewart, 2005)

4 Reavis, C., Knopp, C.-I. and Rapport, J. F., *Disney's "The Lion King" (A): The $2 Billion Movie*, Harvard Business School Case 9-899-041.

5   *Fortune*, 6 September 1999.
6   Roy Disney's Letter of Resignation from Board (http://www.usatoday.com/money/media/2003-12-01-disney-letter_x.htm)
7   *Fortune*, 6 September 1999.
8   Cited in L. Küng, *Digital Terrestrial Television in the UK: The BBC and the Launch of Freeview*, European Case Clearing House Case Study, Ref 305-293-1.

ELEVEN

Conclusions

The task of this concluding chapter is pattern recognition. Drawing on Part I's exploration of the changes taking place in the media industry's constituent sectors and their broader context, and Part II's examination of key facets of the strategic management task in the industry, it seeks to identify common themes surfacing in the strategic context, their common implications for strategic management in the media and the common impulses for future research in the emergent field of media management they supply.

Change – faster and more complex

The first common element affecting strategic management in the media industry concerns change, which is a sub-text of this entire book. The contours, sector trajectories and boundaries of the media industry are increasingly hard to make out due to the extraordinary level of change that has taken place over the last 30 years. The industry is truly in a state of flux as such factors as, deregulation, new technological options for producing, transmitting and consuming media content, increasing competition for leisure time, disposable income and customer attention, changing lifestyles and patterns of media use, and the erosion of mass audiences, have caused fundamental shifts to many aspects of the industry's constituent sectors.

The scope of the challenge this presents is significant. Toffler's (1970) change typology provides insights into why. First, the pace of change is accelerating – developments are following another with increasing rapidity. This is particularly evident in television. For decades major shifts occurred every decade or so: black and white television developed in the 1950s, colour television in the 1960s, the VCR and cable television in the 1970s and 1980s. However, since the 1990s the industry has had to contend with a series of changes that seem to follow each other with increasing rapidity, or occur at the same time. Second, the 'novelty ratio' is rising, meaning that the change underway involves unfamiliar or unprecedented elements. An example of novel change is social networking sites such as MySpace. These exploit content and delivery functionalities to develop categories of products that are entirely new, hard to classify and therefore hard for established organisations with established competencies and assumptions to respond to. Third, the change is diverse in that changes of different types are occurring simultaneously and therefore the range of possible outcomes is very wide, which complicates strategic decision processes. For example, strategic scenarios for the development of television need to take the combined influences of the Internet, broadband delivery systems, HDTV, personal video recorders, social networking sites and digitalisation into consideration.

The result is upheaval and uncertainty, an environment rife with developments that theorists would term discontinuous or transformational (DeVanna and Tichy, 1990; Kotter, 1990): existing structures are being destabilised and business models undermined, but a new industry ecology has yet to emerge.

This sounds bleakly challenging for media organisations, but historically viewed the media industries are surprisingly resilient. In the 1920s the music industry was almost destroyed by the advent of radio. The film industry hit crisis in the 1940s when television became a mass consumer product. The music industry is currently being buffeted by the combined impact of digital downloading and Internet file sharing. But these sectors are still in business, although they may have to adjust their business models and income expectations.

The scope, velocity and convoluted nature of environmental change have had a massive impact on content strategies. Content has always been supremely unpredictable. Demand is uncertain, success is random, and there are no guarantees about what products will capture the public's imagination. The traditional response, as discussed in Chapter 3, was the 'mud against the wall' formula: invest in high volumes of new products hoping some will spark random interest. Essentially, a portfolio of products – books, CDs, films, etc. – are made available on the market, and the media company then waits to see what sells.

An amalgamation of the factors discussed in this book, including digitalisation, globalisation, new distribution platforms, increasingly powerful agents and consolidation, have caused a new content strategy to emerge – the blockbuster or hit model. This involves an aggressive focus on the few products judged to have the best likelihood of success and has had widespread ramifications. Not only has the industry has become increasingly hit- and star-driven, but costs for talent and marketing have escalated. Deep pockets are needed to finance media products and a multi-platform infrastructure to ensure they reach their market, creating pressures for further consolidation. Creativity suffers as product development is increasingly market-driven and product diversity is reduced.

Reconciling dualities

The fact that a blockbuster strategy designed to produce best-selling creative products runs the risk of reducing the creativity that theoretically should be a vital to the success of those products is paradoxical – something organisational researchers term a duality. Dualities are situations where opposing priorities need to be balanced because even if they appear contradictory they are in fact complementary (Bahrami, 1992; Sanchez-Runde and Pettigrew, 2003). Reconciling these opposing forces represents a huge management challenge because as priorities they are equally valid.

Dualities are a second common recurring theme in this review of strategic management in the media. An obvious duality concerning media products, one that has been mentioned in this book but is also cited often by practitioners and scholars, is the tension between creative and business imperatives. Hirsch (1972) sees this as the fundamental driver of all strategic choices in the cultural industries. Lampel et al. (2000) identify a sub-facet of this 'ur-dilemma': that is, that in addition to reconciling artistic expression with business imperatives, media organisations need to create products that are novel but still recognisably belong to a specific category which means they are therefore likely to find a market.

The tension between artistic and commercial imperatives is a central force in many media organisations. But in the current environment arguments can be made for second 'core dilemma'. This relates to issues of strategy and organisation rather than content, and concerns reconciling the need to innovate *and* optimise, which is expressed in the need for diversity *and* harmonisation, for autonomy *and* centralisation.

Because audiences are fragmenting, demand is fickle and attention spans are shrinking, media firms need to be able to depart from standard product formats and experiment with new content concepts, perhaps addressing new market niches or using emerging technologies. As we have seen, this type of creative output flourishes in environments that offer autonomy, flexibility, creative freedom and the opportunity to develop independent sub-cultures, and where roles are loosely defined, reporting mechanisms relaxed and there is scope for experimentation.

However, generating great content requires more than a steady stream of great ideas. In the current globalised hit-driven environment, great content also requires high levels of investment and expertise, particularly in terms of marketing and distribution, to reach its potential. This in turn mandates critical mass and mastery of the complexities of cross-media product management. There needs to be the intelligent central coordination of media firms' substantial investments in existing content. Robust systems need to be in place to support and market the products, and ensure cross promotion is coordinated.

Creating an organisation that combines the free space for small groups to be creative, unencumbered by bureaucracy, with the resources and infrastructure needed to finance and support successful products represents a tremendous challenge. Failure to master this duality is implicated in some high profile leadership failures. Greg Dyke, while Director General of the BBC, made one pole of the spectrum his priority. He sought to make the BBC less bureaucratic and to reduce the hierarchical and rigid processes that had been introduced by his predecessor and which Dyke believed were limiting creativity and depressing morale. He strove to make the BBC more flexible, open and innovative, and emphasised the importance of imagination, involvement and personal empowerment. He was successful in this task – creativity and audience responsiveness increased and the workforce became markedly more enthused and committed. However, the internal control processes that are necessary in a publicly funded organisation with strong social interest obligations were weakened. The furore over the broadcaster's handling of the Iraq dossier affair highlighted how the BBC's internal management processes had loosened in the Dyke era and led to his resignation.

Conversely, while CEO of Disney, Michael Eisner laid an operational emphasis on the other end of the spectrum. He favoured tight internal coordination and process optimisation, and indeed was lauded for his synergistic management of Disney's content assets. But these systems squeezed out creativity leading to an unremitting series of box office failures. Disney was left an organisation that could exploit creativity but not engender it.

A further duality is particularly apparent in Chapter 8 on cognition and culture and concerns the tension that arises from needing to distil a set of operating precepts that allow the members of an organisation to meet strategic goals in a complex environment, and which will simplify decision making, reduce ambiguity, and introduce stability, against the fact that the ongoing nature of that organisation change means that even as they are learned they need to be challenged, revised and updated.

Implications for media management research

As discussed in Chapter 1, the unusual way in which the discipline of media management has developed, and the range of non-management researchers active in it, means that research has applied a wide range of theories from economics, political science, media studies, and mass communications and journalism, but fewer from the disciplines of management and organisation. Much attention is focused on exogenous changes (technology, regulation and consumption for example), and relatively little on internal firm dynamics and how these impinge on performance outcomes.

The research that does exist into strategy tends to employ models from the rational school. This has increased understanding, for example, of the structure and dynamics of firms and their changing environment and of the strategic resources that will lead to strategic advantage. A research priority for the future is to complement insights from the application of rationalist approaches with those applying models from the adaptive school (relevant for unstable environments), and from interpretative schools (which concern how the higher order aspects of firms influence performance).

In addition, there are streams of management research that are relevant but seldom applied to the media but should perhaps be – business history, for example, because of the opportunities it offers for capturing learning from the past and seeing retrospective patterns. Theories on the management of professional service firms might also be pertinent since they centre on the challenges of working with intellectual capital and a highly educated independently minded workforce.

Research methods

With these conclusions in mind, recommendations can be made for research methods. All stem from a central premise that researchers need to get 'inside the black box' of media firms and gain deeper insights into the phenomena that guide behaviour and strategic outcomes in the media industries.

First, a contextualist orientation, that is one that places research within a broader frame that includes the organisation's internal and external environments in the widest sense, and particularly social, political, technological and historical influences, is important. Further, because environments, organisations and strategies are constructed rather than natural objects, research needs to capture the perspective of the actors involved: we need to supplement studies on how structures and systems are materially changing, with studies that provide insights into how these developments are perceived by those involved.

Processual approaches, which do not assume a linear relationship between formulation and implementation, but rather seek to understand the multiplicity of non-rational elements that are called into play, would provide deeper understanding of how these changes take place. They can accommodate the intangible covert organisational elements that are so important to the performance of media firms.

Finally, pluralism is necessary because both the industry and the changes taking place in it are complex phenomena. Time and again, the examples in this book show that performance arises from constellations of factors – cognitions, unique strategic assets, creative insights, collaborative leadership and other idiosyncratic combinations of phenomena. Thus, the issues that influence strategy and performance in media firms are many and interwoven, and to investigate these we need integrative methodologies that incorporate different perspectives, that allow entities to be understood in their context, and the relationship between variables to be teased out and analysed. Multi-lens analysis, which involves applying a series of theoretical lenses to data, is an option since it allows cross-disciplinary and cross-paradigm interpretation and can accommodate the untidy, idiosyncratic and dynamic interrelatedness of organisations and their strategic activities.

So what should managers in the media do?

The subtitle of this book is 'From Theory to Practice'. So far practical advice has been interwoven with case analysis and theoretical review, as is the convention in academic texts. This final chapter will, however, break with academic convention and shift from the analytic to provide some normative guidance for managers in the media. The shift from descriptive to prescriptive is uncomfortable for any researcher alert to the myriad of contingency factors present in any situation. But management is an applied discipline and its theoretical constructs should have practical relevance.

This section of the book will attempt to build a bridge between theory and practice. The impetus for it came from a senior manager who asked a simple question: on the basis of this argumentation, what five things should managers in the media focus on to ensure they survive and succeed in the current environment? What are the rules for strategic management in the media? The following text will attempt to answer this.

Forget the 'mass'

It really is time to drop the mass market mentality or at least to redefine it. Mass markets are evaporating inexorably, be they for national newspapers or national television channels. Trying to maintain position by rebranding campaigns, redesigns and giveaways may provide an interim solution, but also run the risk of burning cash and diverting attention from the need to find a new way of doing business in an era without the types of mass audiences the current industry has grown up with.

But there is an important semantic distinction here: the end of the mass market does not mean the end of critical mass. Critical mass will still be achievable, but it will be constituted differently. National mass markets will continue, but they will be far smaller than they once were and than strategic assumptions have been hitherto built around. Mass markets of the size familiar in previous decades will coalesce less around portmanteau media offerings designed to provide something for everyone, and more around niches that are magnified through the potential of global digital electronic networks. They may gather around franchises (Harry Potter, Big Brother, James Bond) and talent (Madonna, P Diddy, the Rolling Stones), or slim national market segments that become substantial because they are available internationally. Thus American Internet users make up an average of 36 per cent of the online audience for British news websites, with a further 39 per cent coming from other overseas territories (Thurman, 2007).

Capitalising on these differently calibrated markets requires media organisations to change their mindset (see below). For example, to change perhaps the unit of analysis – to cease to think in terms of coherent channels, publishing lists, newspapers, but rather focus on the products or product genres, that is, to focus on narrow niches with large potential. This is the Endemol formula. It has spotlighted two genres of programming (reality television and quiz shows) that were long viewed as low in status and revenue-generating potential, and through a creative rethink of content and business model transformed them into high status and lucrative fields. Agents – a significant but under-explored element of the media industries that has grown dramatically over the past 20 years – have built a business around exploiting niches of one, creative talent.

Build expertise in managing technological change

Technological advances will continue to undermine established structures in the media industry. The sector is now firmly linked to those of IT, PC, consumer electronics and telecoms. These industries will continue to invest in R & D as the key to growth, and governments will also push innovation in these fields for the same reason. Even if the media industries are relatively passive about advancing technology, they will inevitably be swept along by advances in neighbouring sectors.

However, as we learned from the first Internet boom, this change is unlikely to occur at the breathless pace anticipated by consultants, pundits and those seeking to market the new products and services arising from these developments. Their more general prognoses will probably prove broadly correct, although developments will likely occur more slowly and more circuitously than anticipated. But this is, in some ways, an ideal change scenario for strategic planning: there will be substantial change but it will occur slowly, allowing organisations to ready themselves.

Adapting to changing technology will become a permanent facet of organisational life. Techniques for understanding such changes will need to be sophisticated. Media firms need to be discriminating. They need the capacity to judge how a new technology will affect them, and the extent to which they can build on what they have or must access new competencies and resources.

They must also make their organisations flexible and capable of adaptation. This may involve some combination of small project teams, response units who produce initial assessments of and/or responses to changes (see autonomy, below), backed up by mechanisms which transfer learning to the parent. These units would also function as culture change prompts – some of the newspapers that adapted best to the Internet used short stints on online operations as a means of 'converting' recalcitrant old school employees to the Internet world.

Learning is also central to adaptation. During a long career analysing organisations and their environment, Drucker consistently emphasised that trying to predict the future is pointless in an environment that is uncertain. Rather, companies must mine recent experiences in order to identify opportunities and threats, to establish how much of the existing 'rule book' has been rewritten, and translate that learning into action. Learning needs to be routinised to ensure it happens on a continual basis, and in an environment of increasing numbers of joint ventures, learning from new initiatives, internal or with partners, needs to be captured. The Centre for Creative Leadership's studies of executive derailment (Van Velsor and Brittain Leslie, 1995) judged the ability to learn as the most important single skill required in executives dealing with change and complexity. A news organisation, for example, needs to understand developments in citizen journalism and social networking sites, mobile content, interactive television, free newspapers and podcasting, to name but a few. It must be alert to their implications for personal news agendas, for the skills of journalism, for revenue streams and business models.

The ability to learn rests on being able to shift one's cognitive frame. Innovation in the media sector traditionally comes from smaller players who are assumed to be more creative (Davis and Scase, 2000) (although this widely held assumption might repay investigation). Certainly the organisations that master technological advance tend to be new players who may lack the advantages of brand, content assets and financial reserves, but are also unencumbered by the legacy hindrances of mindset. Some of the most creative new media organisations of the past decades – MTV, CNN, Endemol, YouTube – emerged from under-funded beginnings to create new categories of media businesses. Arguably their newness and outsider situation allowed them to frame change in terms of a business opportunity rather than in terms of potential damage to existing businesses. It is also noteworthy that the organisation that found a commercially successful answer to digital downloading in the music business was Apple, far from a start-up but which was still an outsider to the music industry, and therefore approached the problem with a different mindset.

Understand autonomy

Autonomy is another sub-theme in many of the issues discussed in this book. As discussed above, the media organisation needs to master the paradoxical demands of being able to reap the benefits of economies of scale and scope and cross platform synergies, and also provide small-scale autonomy to those tasked with creative projects.

The reason is that, for the media industry, autonomy appears to be first among equals of all the organisational elements that further creativity, as discussed in Chapter 7. The ability to synthesise autonomous small group creativity with the marketing and distribution capability of a large sophisticated organisation is a consistent trait that distinguishes strong performers in the field – Pixar, Home Box Office, BBC News, News Corporation and Bertelsmann. This means cutting bureaucratic sinews. As Jeremy Isaacs, Founding Chairman of Channel Four once put it, creative people need the space to be creative. But as the theory discussed earlier demonstrates, that autonomy needs to be carefully calibrated, and small groups operating autonomously still need to be well linked to the rest of the organisation to ensure knowledge and learning can be transferred and creative potential fully exploited.

Tap unexploited reserves of creativity

All media organisations need to be creative. And all media organisations – like any other institution – have reservoirs of unused creativity. The majority of creative individuals who have chosen to work in the media want to exercise their talents and will do so in the face of organisational obstacles. But an important element of managing creative organisations is not to strew unnecessary obstacles in the path of creativity. Before sending staff on creativity courses, firms could first examine the creative context in their organisation and see if this can be improved. Theories of organisational creativity show how just about any employees can be more creative given the right circumstances. Levels of ongoing creativity can be raised through the appropriate management of a range of subtle interdependencies spanning team tasks, job descriptions, feedback, performance metrics, control mechanisms, even business models.

However, and this is a point for researchers rather than managers, while these theories provide a promising foundation, more research is needed. They have project teams as their unit of analysis and 'generic' organisations as their context. More study is needed into the specificities of creativity in the media industries. How do the strong professional cultural identities shared, for example, by journalists, relate to intrinsic motivation and creativity? What leverage can they provide for strategic activities or how could they aid processes of environmental adaptation? How should units generating creative products interact with the larger organisation? How is autonomy to be balanced with internal coordination and control? How is intrinsic motivation, the cornerstone of creativity, connected to other aspects of the social architecture such as cognition and culture? The act of content creation involves emotional energy, emotional honesty and emotional risk? How do emotions relate to intrinsic motivation and creativity?

And if continued ongoing creativity is to be a real strategic goal, what does this mean for the wider strategy of an organisation? The sobering case of Eisner at Disney illustrates how a well-judged corporate strategy can improve overall performance while at the same time gradually killing off the very creativity it seeks to foster. How do creativity and the business model interact? The cases of the BBC, HBO and Pixar suggest a positive relationship between protection from market forces and levels of ongoing creativity. What mechanism is involved?

Reflect on how you lead

What's really needed is a clear sense of leadership. (Jeremy Paxman, McTaggart Lecture, MediaGuardian International Film Festival, 2007)

An explosion of media choice means mass market media products are fighting to maintain their market position. At the same time, regulation is more relaxed. The result is that media firms are chasing audiences and customers harder than they have ever had to and exploiting new income streams as aggressively as they can.

This has had implications for content. Many media firms appear to have concluded that in order to compete they must make complex content accessible and standard content more compelling. This can give rise to a range of distortions from over-simplification to inaccuracy. It can involve misleading the public in terms of how stories are covered or how footage is edited. It can mean pushing the boundaries of public taste in terms of topics covered.

It has also had implications for the business models employed. As audiences shrink, so too, do revenues. Yet costs, especially for talent and technology, are increasing. There is real pressure to maintain revenues, and this has encouraged broadcasters in particular to turn to new income sources. A decade ago this led to scandals surrounding product placement on television, today problems are surfacing around revenue streams from audience phone-ins.

It falls to the leaders of media firms to meet the conflicting demands of maintaining ethical standards in terms of content and business models, but at the same time guaranteeing audiences and keeping firms in business. They must balance the need for viewers and revenues against the need to serve the public interests, reconcile the search for mass markets with the need to act responsibly, and ensure that those creating content exercise good judgement. These are serious challenges: genies cannot be put back into bottles, taboos once broken cannot be repaired, and audience trust, once lost, is hard to win back.

Conclusions

These are interesting times for the media industry, and interesting times in which to be writing a book on strategic management in the sector. This volume has tried to keep two goals in mind: to present an appropriate and meaningful analysis of strategic concepts that are significant for the media industries, bearing in mind the enormous range of potential candidates, and to apply these using examples from the media industry in such a way that their relevance is evident.

The media industry is at an extraordinary point of transition. The mass paradigm is suffering from erosion, but the underlying structure is still intact. The media industry is inexorably drawing closer to the fields of telecommunications and information technology, but sector boundaries are still discernible, although new products, business models and new cultural forms are emerging.

This is a context that presents both enormous challenges and significant opportunities, for researchers and students in the media field as well as for those engaged in strategic activities in media organisations. The strategic concepts and examples covered in this book have been selected with this context in mind, and I hope they provide some assistance or enlightenment to anyone involved with strategic management in the media, whether from a theoretical or a practical standpoint.

Bibliography

Abelson, R.P. (1995). 'Attitude extremity', in R.E. Petty and J. Krosnick (eds), *Attitude Strength: Antecedents and Consequences*. New Jersey: Lawrence Erlbaum. pp. 25–42.

Abernathy, W.J. and Utterback, J.M. (1978). 'Patterns of innovation in technology', *Technology Review*, 80(7): 40–7.

Albarran, A.B. (1996). *Media Economics: Understanding Markets, Industries, and Concepts*. Iowa: Iowa State University Press.

Albarran, A.B. and Moellinger, T. (2002). 'The top six communication industry firms: structure, performance and strategy' in R.G. Picard (ed.), *Media Firms: Structures, Operations, and Performance*. New Jersey: Erlbaum. pp. 103–22.

Albarran, A.B., Chan-Olmsted, S.M. and Wirth, M.O. (2006). *Handbook of Media Management and Economics*. New Jersey: Lawrence Erlbaum Associates.

Aldrich, H.E. (1979). *Organizations and Environments*. Englewood Cliffs, NJ: Prentice Hall.

Alvesson, M. and Sköldberg, K. (2000). *Reflexive Methodology: New Vistas for Qualitative Research*. London: Sage.

Amabile T.M. (1983). *The Social Psychology of Creativity*. New York: Springer.

Amabile T.M. (1988). 'A model of creativity and innovation in organizations', in B.M. Shaw and L.L. Cummings (eds), *Research in Organizational Behaviour*, 10: 123–67. Greenwich, CT: JAI Press.

Amabile, T.M. (1993). 'Motivational synergy: toward new conceptualizations of intrinsic and extrinsic motivation in the workplace', *Human Resource Management Review*, 3(3): 185–201.

Amabile, T.M. (1996). *Creativity in Context*. Bolder, CO: Westview Press.

Amabile, T.M. (1998). 'How to kill creativity', *Harvard Business Review*, September: 77–87.

Amabile, T.M. and Gryskiewicz, N.D. (1989). 'The creative environment scales: the work environment inventory', *Creativity Research Journal*, 2: 231–54.

Amabile, T.M., Hadley, C.N. and Kramer, S.J. (2002). 'Creativity under the gun', *Harvard Business Review*, August: 52–61.

Amabile, T.M., Hill, K.G., Hennessey, B.A. and Tighe, E. (1994). 'The work preference inventory: assessing intrinsic and extrinsic motivational orientations', *Journal of Personality and Social Psychology*, 66: 950–67.

Amabile, T.M., Conti, R., Coon, H., Lazenby, J. and Herron, M. (1996). 'Assessing the work environment for creativity', *Academy of Management Journal*, 39(5): 1154–84.

Ancona, D. (1990). 'Top management teams: preparing for the revolution', in J. Carroll (ed.), *Applied Social Psychology and Organizational Settings*. New York: Erlbaum. p. 99.

Ancona, D., Malone, T., Orlikowski, W.J. and Senge, P. (2007). 'In praise of the incomplete leader', *Harvard Business Review*, February 2007: 92–100.

Anderson, C. (2006). *The Long Tail: How Endless Choice is Creating Unlimited Demand*. London: Random House.

Anonymous, (1998). 'Wheel of fortune', Survey of Technology and Entertainment, *The Economist*, November 21: 3–4.

Argyris, C. (1990). *Overcoming Organizational Defences: Facilitating Organizational Learning*. Boston: Allyn and Bacon.

Aris, A. and Bughin, J. (2005). *Managing Media Companies: Harnessing Creative Value*. Chichester: John Wiley and Sons.

Arthur, B. (1994). *Increasing Returns and Path Dependence in the Economy*. Chicago: University of Michigan Press.

Arthur, W.B. (1996). 'Increasing returns and the new world of business', *Harvard Business Review*, 74, July-August: 100–11.

Arthur Andersen (1998). *Net Results: Annual Report on the Communications, Media and Entertainment Industries*. London and New York: Arthur Andersen.

Auletta, K. (1991). *Three Blind Mice: How the TV Networks Lost their Way*. New York: Random House.

Auletta, K. (1997). *The Highwaymen: Warriors of the Information Superhighway*. New York: Random House.

Auletta, K. (2004). *Media Man: Ted Turner's Improbable Empire*. New York: Norton.

Bahrami, H. (1992). 'The emerging flexible organization: perspectives from Silicon Valley', *California Management Review*, Summer, 33–52.

Bahrami, H. and Evans, S. (1995). 'Flexible re-cycling and high-technology entrepreneurship', *California Management Review*, 37(3): 62–98.

Baistow, T. (1985). *Fourth-Rate Estate: An Anatomy of Fleet Street*. London: Comedia.

Bakker, P. (2002). 'Free daily newspapers – business models and strategies', *International Journal on Media Management*, 4(3): 180–6.

Baldwin, T.F., Stevens McVoy, D. and Steinfeld, C. (1996). *Convergence: Integrating Media, Information and Communication*. Thousand Oaks: Sage.

Barney, J.B. (1986). 'Organizational culture: can it be a source of sustained competitive advantage?', *Academy of Management Review*, 11: 656–65.

Barney, J.B. (1991). 'Firm resources and sustained competitive advantage', *Journal of Management*, 17(1): 99–120.

Barr, P.S., Stimpert, J.L. and Huff, A.S. (1992). 'Cognitive change, strategic action, and organizational renewal', *Strategic Management Journal*, 13: 15–36.

Barron, F.B. and Harringon, D.M. (1981). 'Creativity, intelligence, and personality', *Annual Review of Psychology*, 32: 439.

Bart, P. and Guber, P. (2003). *Shoot Out: Surviving Fame and (Mis)Fortune in Hollywood*. London: Faber and Faber.

Bartlett, F.E. (1932). *Remembering*. Cambridge: Cambridge University Press.

Bartlett, C.A. and Ghoshal, S. (1993). 'Beyond the M-form: toward a managerial theory of the firm', *Strategic Management Journal*, Winter Special Issue, 4: 23–46.

Barwise, P. and Hammond, K. (1998). *Media*. London: Phoenix.

Bass, B.M. (1985). *Leadership and Performance Beyond Expectations*. New York: Free Press.

Bass, B.M. (1990). *Bass and Stogdill's Handbook of Leadership: A Survey of Theory and Research*. New York: Free Press.

Bass, B.M. and Avolio, B.J. (1994). *Improving Organizational Effectiveness Through Transformational Leadership*. Thousand Oaks: Sage.

Bass, B.M. and Steidlmeier, P. (1999). 'Ethics, character, and authentic transformational leadership behavior', *Leadership Quarterly*, 10(2): 181–217.

Bateson, G. (1972). *Steps to an Ecology of the Mind*. New York: Ballantine Books.

Baumol, W.J. (1993). *Entrepreneurship, Management and the Structure of Payoffs*. Cambridge, MA: The MIT Press.

Bennis, W. and Biederman, P.W. (1997). *Organizing Genius*. London: Nicholas Brealey Publishing.

Bennis, W. and Nanus, B. (1985). *Leaders: The Strategies for Taking Charge*. New York: Harper and Row.

Berger, P. and Luckmann, T. (1966). *The Social Construction of Reality*. London: Penguin Books.

Bertelsmann Foundation European Institute for the Media (eds) (1995). *Television Requires Responsibility*. Volume 2 International Studies. Gütersloh: Bertelsmann Foundation Publishers.

Bettis, R.A. and Hitt, M.A. (1995). 'The new competitive landscape', *Strategic Management Journal*, 16: 7–19.

Bettman, J.R. and Weitz, B.A. (1983). 'Attributions in the board room: causal reasoning in corporate annual reports', *Administrative Science Quarterly*, 28: 165.

Bhide, A (1986). 'Hustle as strategy', *Harvard Business* Review, September-October: 59–65.

Bibb, P. (1993). *It Ain't as Easy as it Looks: Ted Turner's Amazing Story*. New York: Crown.

Black, J.A. and Boal, K.B. (1994). 'Strategic resources: traits, configurations and paths to sustainable competitive advantage', *Strategic Management Journal*, Special Issue (Strategy: Search for New Paradigms) Summer, 15, 131–48.

Blumler, J.G. (ed.) (1992). *Television and the Public Interest: Vulnerable Values in West European Broadcasting*. London: Sage.

Blumler, J.G. and Nossiter, T.J. (1991). *Broadcasting Finance in Transition: A Comparative Handbook*. Oxford: Oxford University Press.

Bogner, W.C. and Barr, P.S. (2000). 'Making sense in hypercompetitive environments: a cognitive explanation of high velocity competition', *Organization Science*, (11)2: 212–26.

Boczkowski, P.B. (2004). *Digitizing the News: Innovation in Online Newspapers*, Cambridge: MIT Press.

Bolman, J.G. and Deal, T.E. (1991). *Reframing Organizations: Artistry, Choice and Leadership*. San Francisco: Jossey Bass.

Bowman, C. and Collier, N. (2006). 'A contingency approach to resource-creation processes', *International Journal of Management Reviews*, 8(4): 191–211.

Boyatzis, R. and McKee, A. (2005). *Resonant Leadership*. Boston: Harvard Business School Press.

Bradley, S.P. and Nolan, R.L. (eds) (1998). *Sense and Respond. Capturing Value in the Network Era*. Boston: Harvard Business School Press.

Bronson, P. (1999). *The Nudist on the Late Shift*. London: Secker and Warburg.

Brown, S.L. and Eisenhardt, K.M. (1997). 'The art of continuous change: linking complexity theory and time-paced evolution in relentlessly-shifting organizations', *Administrative Science Quarterly*, 42: 1–34.

Brown, S.L. and Eisenhardt, K.M. (1998). *Competing on the Edge: Strategy as Structured Chaos*. Boston: Harvard Business School Press.

Bruner, J. (1973). *Going Beyond the Information Given*. New York: Norton.

Bruner, J. (1985). Actual Minds, Possible Worlds. Cambridge, MA: Harvard University Press.

Bryman, A., Stephens, M. and Campo, C. (1996). 'The importance of context: qualitative research and the study of leadership', *The Leadership Quarterly*, 7(3): 353.

Bughin, J. and Poppe, H. (2005). 'Dwindling readership: are tabloids the answer?', *McKinsey Quarterly*, January.

Burgelman, R.A. (1983). 'Corporate entrepreneurship and strategic management: insights from a process study', *Management Science*, 29: 1349–64.

Burgelman, R.A. (1994). 'Fading memories: a process theory of strategic business exit in dynamic environments', *Administrative Science Quarterly*, 39: 24.

Burgelman, R.A. (2002). *Strategy is Destiny: How Strategy-Making Shapes a Company's Future*. New York: Free Press.

Burgelman, R.A. and Sayles, L.R. (1986). *Inside Corporate Innovation: Strategy, Structure, and Managerial Skills*. New York: Free Press.

Burns, J.M. (1978). *Leadership*. New York: Harper and Row.

Burns, T. (1977). *The BBC: Public Institution and Private World*. London: Macmillan.

Burns, T. and Stalker, G.M. (1961/1994). *The Management of Innovation*. Oxford: Oxford University Press.

Burrell, G. and Morgan, G. (1979). *Sociological Paradigms and Organizational Analysis*. London: Heinemann.

Cairncross, F. (1997). *The Death of Distance: How the Communications Revolution will Change Our Lives*. Boston: Harvard Business School Press.

Carlaw, K., Oxley, L., Walker, P., Thorns, D. and Nuth, M. (2006). 'Beyond the hype: intellectual property and the knowledge society/knowledge economy', *Journal of Economic Surveys*, 20(4): 633.

Castells, M. and Cardoso, G. (2006). *The Network Society: From Knowledge to Policy*. Washington, DC: Johns Hopkins Center for Transatlantic Relations.

Caves, R.E. (2000). *Creative Industries: Contracts between Art and Commerce*. Cambridge, MA: Harvard University Press.

Chaffee, E.E. (1985). 'Three models of strategy', *Academy of Management Review*, 10(1): 89–98.

Chakravarthy, B. (1997). 'A new strategy framework for coping with turbulence', *Sloan Management Review*, Winter, 69–82.

Chakravarthy, B. (1999). 'Shaping the new media and communications industries', keynote presentation to SMS Conference, Berlin.

Chakravarthy, B.S. and Doz, Y. (1992). 'Strategy process research – focusing on corporate self-renewal', *Strategic Management Journal*, 13: 5–14.

Chandler, A. (1969). *Strategy and Structure: Chapters in the History of American Industrial Enterprise*. Cambridge: MIT Press.

Chan-Olmsted, S.M. (2006). *Competitive Strategy for Media Firms: Strategic and Brand Management in Changing Media Markets*. New Jersey: Lawrence Erlbaum Associates.

Chan-Olmsted, S.M. and Chang, B.H. (2003). 'Diversification strategies of global media conglomerates: examining Patterns and Determinants', *Journal of Media Economics*, 16(4): 215.

Chenoweth, N. (2001). *Virtual Murdoch: Reality Wars on the Information Superhighway*. London: Secker and Warburg.

Choi, S.Y. and Winston, A.B. (2000). *The Internet Economy: Technology and Practice*. Austin TX: SmartEcon Publishing.

Christensen, C.M. (1997). *The Innovator's Dilemma: When New Technologies Cause Great Firms to Fail*. Boston: Harvard Business School Press.

Christensen, C. and Bower, J. (1996). 'Customer power, strategic investment, and the failure of leading firms', *Strategic Management Journal*, 17: 197–218.

Christensen, C.M. and Overdorf, M. (2000). 'Meeting the challenge of disruptive innovation', *Harvard Business Review*, March–April, 67–76.

Christensen, C. and Tuttle, E.G. (1999). 'Why industry leaders fail to harness disruptive technologies', *Red Herring*, May: 152–3.

Christensen, C.M., Johnson, M.W. and Rigby, D.K. (2002). 'Foundations for growth: how to identify and build disruptive new businesses', *Sloan Management Review*, Spring, 22–31.

Christopherson, S. and Storper, M. (1989). 'The effects of flexible specialization on industrial politics and the labor market: the motion picture industry', *Industrial and Labor Relations Review*, 42(3): 331–47.

Coase, R. (1937). 'The nature of the firm', *Economica*, 16(4): 386.

Cohen, W.M. and Levinthal, D.A. (1990). 'Absorbtive capacity: a new perspective on learning and innovation', *Administrative Science Quarterly*, 35: 555.

Coleridge, N. (1993). *Paper Tycoons: The Latest, Greatest Newspaper Tycoons and How they Won the World*. London: Heinemann.

Collins, R. (1990). 'Stratification, emotional energy, and the transient emotions', in T. Kemper (ed.), *Research Agendas in the Sociology of Emotions*. Albany: State University of New York Press.

Collins, R. (1998). *From Satellite to Single Market*. London: Routledge.

Collins, J., Radner, H. and Preacher Collins, A. (eds) (1993). *Film Theory goes to the Movies*. New York and London: Routledge.

Conger, J. (1989). *The Charismatic Leader: Behind the Mystique of Exceptional Leadership*. San Francisco: Jossey-Bass.

Conger, J. (1999). 'Learning the language of leadership', *Human Resource Management International Digest*, March/April 7(2): 217–28.

Conger, J.A. and Kanungo, R.N. (eds) (1988). *Charismatic Leadership: The Elusive Factor in Organizational Effectiveness*. San Francisco: Jossey-Bass.

Cottle, S. (ed.) (2003). *Media Organization and Production*. London: Sage.

Coutu, D.L. (2002). 'The anxiety of learning', *Harvard Business Review*, March: 98–106.

Croteau, D. and Hoynes, W. (2001). *The Business of Media: Corporate Media and the Public Interest*. Thousand Oaks: Pine Forge Press.

Curran, J. and Seaton, J. (1981). *Power without Responsibility: The Press and Broadcasting in Britain*. London: Fontana.

Cyert, R.M. and March, J.G. (1963). *A Behavioral Theory of the Firm*. New Jersey: Prentice Hall.

D'Aveni, R. (1994a). *Hypercompetition*. New York: Free Press.

D'Aveni, R.A. (1994b). *Managing the Dynamics of Strategic Maneuvering*. New York: Free Press.

Daft, R.L. and Weick, K.E. (1984). 'Toward a model of organisations as interpretation systems', *Academy of Management Review*, 9(2): 284–95.

Danneels, E. (2002). 'The dynamics of product innovation and firm competences', *Strategic Management Journal*. 23: 1095.

Davenport, J. (2006). 'UK film companies: project-based organizations lacking entrepreneurship and innovativeness?', *Creativity and Innovation Management*, 15(3): 250–7.

Davis, H. and Scase, R. (2000). *Managing Creativity: The Dynamics of Work and Organization*. Buckingham: Open University Press.

Deazin, R., Glynn, M.A. and Kazanjian, R.K. (1999). 'Multilevel theorizing about creativity in organizations: a sensemaking perspective', *Academy of Management Review*, 24(2): 286–92.

DeFillippi, R.J. and Arthur, M.B. (1998). 'Paradox in project-based enterprise: the case of film making', *California Management Review*, Winter, 40(2): 125–39.

Dennis, E.D., Wharley, S. and Sheridan, J. (2006). 'Doing digital: an assessment of the top 25 US media companies and their digital strategies', *Journal of Media Business Studies*, 3(1): 33, pp. 33–51.

Denzin, N.K. (1978). *The Research Act: A Theoretical Introduction to Sociological Methods*. New York: McGraw Hill.

DeVanna, M.A. and Tichy, N. (1990). 'Creating the competitive organization of the 21st century: the boundaryless corporation', *Human Resource Management*, 29: 445, pp. 445–71.

De Vany, A.S. and Walls, W.D. (1999). 'Uncertainty in the movie industry: does star power reduce the terror of the box office?', *Journal of Cultural Economics*, 23(4): 285–318.

DiMaggio, P. and Powell, W. (1983). 'The iron cage revisited: institutional isomorphism and collective rationality in organizational fields', *American Sociological Review*, 48: 147, pp. 147–60.

Dimmick, J. and McDonald, D.G. (2003). 'The conceptualization and measurement of diversity', *Communication Research*, 30(1): 60–79.

Dougherty, D. (1990). 'Understanding new markets for new products', *Strategic Management Journal*, 11: 59–78.

Downes, L. and Mui, C. (1998). *Unleashing the Killer App. Digital strategies for Market Dominance*. Boston: Harvard Business School Press.

Doyle, G. (2002a). *Media Ownership*. London: Sage.

Doyle, G. (2002b). *Understanding Media Economics*. London: Sage.

Drazin, R. and Schoonhoven, C.B. (1996). 'Community, population, and organization effects on innovation: a multilevel perspective', *Academy of Management Journal*, 39(5): 1065–83.

Drucker, P. (1985). *Innovation and Entrepreneurship*. London: Heinemann.

Drucker, P. (1994). 'The theory of the business', *Harvard Business Review*, September-October: 95–104.

Durkheim, E. (1954). *On the Division of Labor in Society*. New York: Free Press.

Dutton, J.E. and Duncan, R.B. (1987). 'Creation of momentum for strategic change through the process of strategic issue diagnosis', *Strategic Management Journal*, (8): 279–95.

Dutton, J.E., Ashford, S.J., O'Neill, R.M., Hayes, E. and Wierba, E.E. (1997). 'Reading the wind: how middle managers assess the contest for selling issues to top managers', *Strategic Management Journal*, 18(5): 407–25.

Dyke, G. (2004). *Inside Story*. London: HarperCollins.

Eisenhardt, K.M. and Brown, S.L. (1999). 'Patching: restitching business portfolios in dynamic markets', *Harvard Business Review*, May–June: 72–82.

Eisenhardt, K.M. and Martin, J.A. (2000). 'Dynamic capabilities: what are they?', *Strategic Management Journal*, Special Issue, 21(10/11): 1105–21.

Eisenmann, T.R. and Bower, J.L. (2000). 'The entrepreneurial M-Form: strategic integration in global media companies', *Organization Science*, May–June, 11(3): 348–55.

Evans, P. and Wurster, T.S. (2000). *Blown to Bits: How the New Economics of Information Transform Strategy*. Boston: Harvard Business School Press.

Fidler, R. (1997). *Mediamorphosis: Understanding New Media*. Thousand Oaks, CA: Pine Forge Press.

Fiol, C.M. and Huff, A.S. (1992). 'Maps for managers: where are we? where do we go from here?', *Journal of Management Studies*, 29: 267–85.

Fiske, S.T. and Taylor, S.E. (1984). *Social Cognition*. Reading, MA: Addison Wesley.

Florida, R. and Goodnight, J. (2005). 'Managing for creativity', *Harvard Business Review*, July: 124–34.

Ford, C.M. (1996). 'A theory of individual creative action in multiple social domains', *Academy of Management Review*, 21: 1112.

Ford, C.M. and Gioia, D.A. (eds), (1995). *Creative Action in Organizations: Ivory Tower Visions and Real World Voices*. Thousand Oaks: Sage, 1112–42.

Freeman, C. and Soete, L. (1997). *The Economics of Industrial Innovation*. Cambridge, MA: MIT Press.

Frey, B.S. and Jegen, R. (2000). 'Motivation crowding theory: a survey of empirical evidence', CESifo Working Paper Series, Munich.

Fulmer, W.E. (2000). *Shaping the Adaptive Organization: Landscape, Learning, and Leadership in Volatile Times*. New York: Amacom.

Gardner, H. (1999). *Intelligence Reframed*. New York: Basic Books.

Garnham, N. (1990). *Capitalism and Communication*. London: Sage.

Gavetti, G. and Levinthal, D. (2000). 'Looking forward and looking backward: cognitive and experiential search', *Administrative Science Quarterly*, 45: 113–37.

Georgiou, M. (1998). *Television Use in the Digital Age: A Personal Perspective on Change*. Reuter Foundation Paper No. 63.

Gergen, K.J. (1992). *Towards Transformation in Social Knowledge*. New York: Springer Verlag.

Gersick, C.J.G. (1991). 'Revolutionary change theories: a multilevel exploration of the punctuated equilibrium paradigm', *Academy of Management Review*, 16(1): 10–36.

Ghosh, S. (1998). 'Making business sense of the internet', *Harvard Business Review*, March-April: 127–33.

Gibson, J. (2007). 'Murdoch and meddling', *The Guardian*, 2 August: 25.

Gilbert, C.G. (2002). 'Can competing frames co-exist? The paradox of threatened response', working paper from the Harvard Business School Division of Research.

Gillmor, D. (2004). *We the Media: Grassroots Journalism, by the People for the People*. Sebastopol, CA: O'Reilly Media.

Gioia, D.A. and Chittipeddi, K. (1991). 'Sensemaking and sense-giving in strategic change initiation', *Strategic Management Journal*, 12: 433–48.

Gioia, D.A. and Pitre, E. (1990). 'Multiparadigm perspectives on theory building', *Academy of Management Review*, 15(4): 584–602.

Goffee, R. and Jones, G. (2000). 'Why should anyone be led by you?', *Harvard Business Review*, September-October, 78(5): 62–70.

Greco, A.N. (2004). *The Book Publishing Industry*. New Jersey: Lawrence Erlbaum.

Greenslade, R. (2003). *Press Gang: How Newspapers Make profits from Propaganda*. London: Macmillan.

Griffin, N. and Masters, K. (1996). *Hit and Run: How Jon Peters and Peter Guber Took Sony for a Ride in Hollywood*. New York: Touchstone.

Gulati, R. and Garino, J. (2000). 'Getting the right mixture of bricks and clicks', *Harvard Business Review*, May-June: 107–14.

Hall, R.I. (1984). 'The natural logic of management policy making: its implications for the survival of the organisation', *Management Science*, 30: 905–27.

Hambrick, D.C. (1983). 'Some tests of the effectiveness and functional attributes of Miles and Snow's Strategic Types', *Academy of Management Journal*, 26: 5–25.

Hamel, G. and Sampler, J. (1998). 'The e-corporation', *Fortune*, 7 December: 53–82.

Hamm, S. (1999). 'How to survive the cyber-revolution', *Business Week,* Issue 3623: 28–35.

Hampden-Turner, C.M. (1990). *Charting the Corporate Mind: From Dilemma to Strategy*. Oxford: Blackwell.

Hannan, M.T. and Freeman, J.H. (1984). 'Structural inertia and organizational change', *American Sociological Review*, 49: 149–64.

Hedberg, B. (1981). 'How organisations learn and unlearn', in P. Nystrom and W. Starbuck (eds), *Handbook of Organization Design*. New York: Oxford University Press. pp. 1–27.

Henderson, R.M. and Clark, K.B. (1990). 'Architectural innovation: the reconfiguration of existing product technologies and the failure of established firms', *Administrative Science Quarterly*, 35: 9–30.

Henten, A. and Oest, A. (2005). 'Copyright: rights-holders, users and innovators', Editorial to Special *Issue of Telematics and Informatics*, 22: 1–4, February-May: 1–9.

Henzler, H.A. (1998). 'Communications and media in the digital age', speech to mcm Forum, St Gallen.

Hesmondhalgh, D. (2002). *The Cultural Industries*. London: Sage.

Hill, C.W. and Rothaermel, F.T. (2003). 'The performance of incumbent firms in the face of technological innovation', *Academy of Management Review*, 28(2): 257.

Hirsch, P. (1972). 'Processing fads and fashions: an organization set analysis of cultural industry system', *American Journal of Sociology*, 77(4): 639–59.

Hitt, M.A. (1997). 'Current and future research methods in strategic management', synopsis of 1997 Research Methods Forum No. 2, Summer. Western Academy of Management Meetings. Available at www.aom.pace.edu/edu/rms/1997_forum_strategic_management.html, accessed 06.05.02.

Hitt, M.A., Ireland, R.D. and Hoskisson, R.E. (2001). *Strategic Management: Competitiveness and Globalization*. Cincinnati, OH: South-Western College Publishing, Thomson Learning.

Hitt, M.A., Keats, B.W. and DeMarie, S.M. (1998). 'Navigating in the new competitive landscape: building strategic flexibility and competitive advantage in the 21st century', *Academy of Management Executive*, 12(4): 22–42.

Hooper, R. (2000).'What is happening to 'convergence'?, *The Times*, 17 November.

House, R.J. (1977). 'A 1976 theory of charismatic leadership', in J.G. Hunt and L.L. Larson (eds), *Leadership: the Cutting Edge*. Carbondale: Southern Illinois University Press.

Huff, A.S. (1997). 'A current and future agenda for cognitive research in organisations', *Journal of Management Studies*, 6(34): 947–52.

Huff, J.O., Huff, A.S. and Thomas, H. (1992). 'Strategic renewal and the interaction of cumulative stress and inertia', *Strategic Management Journal*, 13: 55–75.

Hunt, J.G. and Conger, J.A. (1999). 'Charismatic and transformational leadership: taking stock of the present and future (Part II)', *Leadership Quarterly* 3(10), p. 331–334.

Hutton, W. (2007) 'Harry Potter and the secret of success', *Observer*, 22 August.

Huy, Q.N. (1999). 'Emotional capability, emotional intelligence and radical change', *Academy of Management Review*, 24(2): 325–45.

Isabella. L.A. (1990). 'Evolving interpretations as a change unfolds: how managers construe key organizational events', *Academy of Management Journal*, 33(1): 7–14.

Jago, A. (1982). 'Leadership: perspectives in theory and research', *Management Science*, 28(3): 315–36.

Janszen, F. (2000). *The Age of Innovation*. Harlow: Pearson Education.

Jelinek, M. and Schoonhoven, C.B. (1990). *The Innovation Marathon: Lessons from High Technology Firms*. Cambridge, MA: Basil Blackwell.

Johnson, G. (1987). *Strategic Change and the Management Process*. Oxford: Basil Blackwell.

Johnson, G. (1992). 'Managing strategic change – strategy, culture and action', *Long Range Planning*, 25(1): 28–36.

Johnson, G. and Scholes, K. (1989). *Exploring Corporate Strategy: Text and Cases*. Hertfordshire: Prentice Hall.

Kanter, R.M. (1983). *The Change Masters: Corporate Entrepreneurs at Work*. New York: Simon & Schuster.

Kanter, R.M. (1988). 'When a thousand flowers bloom: structural, collective, and social conditions for innovation in organization', *Research in Organizational Behavior*, 10: 169–211.

Kanter, R.M. (1992). *When Giants Learn to Dance* (new edn). London: International Thomson Business Press.

Kanter, R.M. (2004). *Confidence*. London: Random House Business Books.

Kanter, R.M. (2006). 'Innovation: the classic traps', *Harvard Business Review*, November: 73–83.

Katz, R.L. (1955). 'Skills of an effective administrator', *Harvard Business Review*, January-February: 33–42.

Katz, M.L. and Woroch, G.A. (1997). 'Introduction: convergence, regulation, and competition', *Industrial and Corporate Change*, December, 6(4): 701–18.

Kay, J. (1993). *Foundations of Corporate Success: How Business Strategies Add Value*. Oxford: Oxford University Press.

Kellerman, B. (2004). *Bad Leadership*. Boston: Harvard Business School Press.

Kelly, D. and Amburgey, T.L. (1991). 'Organizational inertia and momentum: a dynamic model of strategic change', *Academy of Management Journal*, 34(3): 591–612.

Kelly, K. (1997). 'New rules for the new economy. Twelve dependable principles for thriving in a turbulent world', *Wired*, Issue 5.09, September.

Kotter, J.P. (1988). *The Leadership Factor*. Boston: Harvard Business School Press.

Kotter, J.P. (1996). *Leading Change*. Boston: Harvard Business School Press.

Kotter, J.P. and Heskett, J.L. (1992). *Corporate Culture and Performance*. New York: Free Press.

Kuhn, R. (ed.) (1985). *The Politics of Broadcasting*. London: Croom Helm.

Kuhn, T.S. (1970). *The Structure of Scientific Revolutions*. Chicago: University of Chicago Press.

Küng, L. (2003). *When Old Dogs Learn New Tricks: The Launch of BBC News Online*. Case Study No. 303–119–1. Wharley End: European Case Clearing House.

Küng, L. (2004). 'What makes media firms tick? exploring the hidden drivers of firm performance', in P.G. Picard (ed.), *Strategic Responses to Media Market Changes*. Jönköping: Jönköping International Business School.

Küng, L. (2005). *When Innovation Fails to Disrupt. A Multi-Lens Investigation of Successful Incumbent Response to Technological Discontinuity: The Launch of BBC News Online*. Habilitationsschrift, University of St Gallen.

Küng, L. (ed.) (2006). *Leadership in the Media Industry: Changing Contexts, Emerging Challenges*. JIBS Research Reports 2006–1. Jönköping: Jönköping International Business School.

Küng, L. (2007). 'Does media management matter? Establishing the scope, rationale and future research agenda for the discipline', *Journal of Media Business Studies* (in press).

Küng-Shankleman, L. (1997). *Investigating the BBC and CNN: How Culture Drives Strategy in Broadcasting Organisations*, Doctoral Dissertation, University of St Gallen. Bamberg: Difo-Druck.

Küng-Shankleman, L. (2000). *Inside the BBC and CNN: Managing Media Organisations*. Routledge: London and New York.

Lacy, S. and Simon, T. (1993). *The Economics and Regulation of United States Newspapers*. Norwood, NJ: Ablex Publishing Corporation.

Lampel, J., Lant, T. and Shamsie, J. (2000). 'Balancing act: learning from organizing practices in cultural industries', *Organization Science*, May/June 11(3): 263–69.

Lavine, J.M. and Wackman, D.B. (1988). *Managing Media Organisations: Effective Leadership of the Media*. New York and London: Longman.

Lawrence, P.R. and Lorsch, J.W. (1967). 'Differentiation and integration in complex organisations', *Administrative Science Quarterly*, 12: 1–47.

Leonard-Barton, D. (1992). 'Core capabilities and core rigidities: a paradox in managing new product development', *Strategic Management Journal*, Summer Special Issue, 13: 111–25.

Levitt, B. and March, J.G. (1988). 'Organizational learning', *Annual Review of Sociology*, 14: 319–40.

Lieberman, M. and Montgomery, D.B. (1988). 'First-mover advantages', *Strategic Management Journal*, 9: 41–8.

Liebowitz, M. and Margolis, S. (2001). *Winners, Loser and Microsoft: Competition and Antitrust in High Technology*. Oakland, CA: The Independent Institute.

Louw, P.E. (2001). *The Media and Cultural Production*. London: Sage.

Magretta, J. (2002). 'Why business models matter', *Harvard Business Review*, 80(5): 86–92.

Makadok, R. (2001). 'Toward a synthesis of the resource-based and dynamic-capability views of rent creation', *Strategic Management Journal*, (22): 387–401.

Makridakis, S. (1990). *Forecasting, Planning, and Strategy for the 21st Century*. New York: Free Press.

Malone, T. (2004). *The Future of Work: How the New Order of Business Will Shape Your Organization, Your Management Style, and Your Life.* Boston: Harvard Business School Press.

Manning, S. (2005). 'Managing project networks as dynamic organizational forms: learning from the TV movie industry', *International Journal of Project Management*, 23: 410–14.

March, J.G. (1991). 'Exploration and exploitation in organizational learning', *Organization Science*, (2): 71–87.

March, J.G. and Simon, H. (1958). *Organizations*. New York: Wiley.

Marjoribanks, T. (2000). *News Corporation, Technology and the Workplace: Global Strategies, Local Change*. Cambridge: Cambridge University Press.

Mauzy, J. and Harriman, R. (2003). *Creativity, Inc.: Building an Inventive Organization*. Boston: Harvard Business School Press.

McChesney, R.M. (2004). *The Problem of the Media: U.S. Communication Politics in the Twentieth Century*. New York. Monthly Review Press.

McClelland, D.C. (1961). *The Achieving Society*. New Jersey: Van Nostrand.

McEachern. T. and O'Keefe, B. (1997). *Re-Wiring Business: Uniting Management and the Web*. New York: John Wiley & Sons, Inc.

McGraw, K.O. (1978). 'The detrimental effects of reward on performance: a literature review and prediction model', in M.R. Lepper and D. Green (eds), *The Hidden Costs of Reward*s. Hillsdale, NJ: Erlbaum.

McQuail, D. and the European Media Research Group (1990). 'Caging the beast: constructing a framework for the analysis of media change in Western Europe', *European Journal of Communication*, 5: 313–31.

Meyer, A.D. (1982). 'Adapting to environmental jolts', *Administrative Science Quarterly*, 27: 515–37.

Meyer, P. (2004). *The Vanishing Newspaper: Saving Journalism in the Information Age*. Missouri: University of Missouri Press.

Miles, R.E. and Snow, C.C. (1986). 'Organizations: new concepts for new forms', *California Management Review*, 28: 62–73.

Miles, R.E., Snow, C.C., Mathews, J.A., Miles, G. and Coleman, H.J. (1997). 'Organizing in the knowledge age: anticipating the cellular form', *Academy of Management Executive*, 11(4) pp. 7–20.

Miller, D. (1982). 'Evolution and revolution: A quantum view of structural change in organizations', *Journal of Management Studies*, 19: 131–51.

Miller, D. (1990). *The Icarus Paradox*. New York: Harper Collins.

Miller, D. and Shamsie, J. (1996). 'The resource-based view of the firm in two environments: the Hollywood film studios from 1936–1965', *Academy of Management Journal*, 39(3): 519–43.

Milliken, F.J. (1990). 'Perceiving and interpreting environmental change: an examination of college administrators' interpretation of changing demographics', *Academy of Management Journal*, 33: 42–63.

Mintzberg, H. (1979). 'An emerging strategy of "direct" research', *Administrative Science Quarterly*, December, 24: 582–9.

Mintzberg, H. and Westley, F. (1992). 'Cycles of organizational change', *Strategic Management Journal*, 13: 39–59.

Mintzberg, H., Ahlstrand, B. and Lampel, J. (1998). *Strategy Safari: A Guided Tour through the Wilds of Strategic Management*. New York: Free Press.

Mintzberg, H., Lampel, J., Quinn, J.B. and Ghoshal, S. (2003). *The Strategy Process: Concepts, Contexts, Cases*. Global Fourth Edition. Harlow: Prentice Hall.

Moran, A. with Malbon, J. (2006). *Understanding the Global TV Format*. Bristol: Intellect Books.

Morgan, G. (1986). *Images of Organization*. Thousand Oaks: Sage.

Mosco, V. (1996). *The Political Economy of Communication: Rethinking and Renewal*. London: Sage.

Mumford, M.D., Zaccaro, S.J., Connelly, M.S. and Marks, M.A. (2000). 'Leadership skills – conclusions and future directions', *The Leadership Quarterly*, 11(1): 155–70.

Mumford, M.D., Zaccaro, S.J., Harding, F.D., Jacobs, T.O. and Fleishman, E.A. (2000). 'Leadership skills for a changing world: solving complex social problems', *The Leadership Quarterly*, 11(1), 11–35.

Napoli, P.M. (1999). 'The marketplace of ideas metaphor in communications regulation', *Journal of Communication*, 49(4): 151–69.

Napoli, P.M. (2003). *Audience Economics: Media Institutions and the Audience Marketplace*. New York: Columbia University Press.

Neil, A. (1997). *Full Disclosure*. London: Macmillan.

Nelson, R. (1995). 'Recent evolutionary theorizing about economic change', *Journal of Economic Literature*, 33: 48–80.

Nelson, R.R. and Winter, S.G. (1982). *An Evolutionary Theory of Economic Change*. Cambridge: Belknap.

Noam, E. (1998). 'The market dynamics of convergence', speech to E-Screen '98 Conference, Monte Carlo, February.

Nohria, N. and Ghoshal, S. (1997). *The Differentiated Network: Organising Multi-National Organizations for Value Creation*. San Francisco: Jossey Bass.

Nohria, N. and Gulati, R. (1996). 'Is Slack Good or Bad for Innovation?', *Academy of Management Journal*, 39(5): 1245–64.

Northouse, P.G. (2004). *Leadership: Theory and Practice* (3rd edn). Thousand Oaks: Sage.

Obst, L. (1996). *Hello, He Lied and Other Truths from the Hollywood Trenches*. New York: Broadway Books.

OECD (1994). *The OECD Jobs Study: Facts, Analysis, Strategies*. Paris: OECD.

Oldham, G.R. and Cummings, A. (1996). 'Employee creativity: personal and contextual factors at work', *Academy of Management Journal*, 39: 607.

Pascale, R.T. and Athos, A.G. (1981). *The Art of Japanese Management*. New York: Simon and Schuster.

Pérez-Latre, F.J. and Sánchez-Tabernero, A. (2003). 'Leadership, an essential requirement for effecting change in media companies: an analysis of the Spanish market', *The International Journal on Media Management*, (3): 199–208.

Penrose, E.T. (1959). *The Theory of the Growth of the Firm*. New York: Wiley.

Peters, T. and Waterman, R.H. (1982). *In Search of Excellence: Lessons from American's Best-Run Companies*. New York: Harper and Row.

Peteraf, M.A. (1993). 'The cornerstones of competitive advantage: a resource-based view', *Strategic Management Journal*, 14, 179–90.

Pettigrew, A.M. (1992). 'The character and significance of strategy process research', *Strategic Management Journal*, 13: 5–16.

Pettigrew, A.M. (ed.) (2003). *Innovative Forms of Organizing: International Perspectives*. London: Sage.

Pettigrew, A. and Fenton, E. (eds) (2000). *The Innovating Organization*. London: Sage.

Pettigrew, A. and Whipp, R. (1991). *Managing Change for Competitive Success*. Oxford: Blackwell Publishers Ltd.

Piaget, J. (1952). *The Origins of Intelligence in Children*. New York: International Universities Press.

Picard, R.G. (1996). 'The rise and fall of communications empires', *Journal of Media Economics*, 9(4): 23–40.

Picard, R. (2002a). *The Economics and Financing of Media Companies*. New York: Fordham University Press.

Picard, R.G. (2002b). 'Changing business models of online content services. Their implications for multimedia and other content producers', *The International Journal on Media Management*, 2(2): 60–6.

Picard, R.G. (ed). (2002c). *Media Firms: Structure, Operations, and Performance*. New Jersey: Lawrence Erlbaum Associates.

Picard, R. (2003). 'Cash cows or entrecôte: publishing companies and disruptive technologies', *Trends in Communication*, 11(2): 127–36.

Picard, R.G. (2004). *Strategic Responses to Media Market Changes*. JIBS Research Reports (2). Sweden: Jönköping University.

Pooley, E. (2007). 'Exclusive: Rupert Murdoch Speaks', *Time*, accessed at www.time.com/time/printout/0,8816,1638182,00.html.

Porter, M.E. (1980). *Competitive Strategy. Techniques for Analyzing Industries and Competitors*. New York: Free Press.

Porter, M.E. (1985). *Competitive Advantage: Creating and Sustaining Superior Performance*. New York: Free Press.

Porter, M.E. (1996). 'What is a strategy?', *Harvard Business Review* (November-December): 61–78.

Powell, T.C. (2003). 'Strategy without ontology', *Strategic Management Journal*, 24: 285–91.

Prahalad, C.K. and Hamel, G. (1990). 'The core competence of the corporation', *Harvard Business Review*, 63(3): 79–91.

Prahalad, C.K. and Hamel, G. (eds) (1994). 'In search of new paradigms', *Strategic Management Journal*, Summer Special Issue, 5–16.

Price, C.L. (2006). *Rewriting the Future for Newspaper Investors*. Texas: International Newspaper Marketing Association.

Quinn, J.B. (1992). *The Intelligent Enterprise*. New York: Free Press.

Rajagopalan, N. and Spreitzer, G.M. (1996). 'Toward a theory of strategic change: a multi-lens perspective and integrative framework', *Academy of Management Review*, 22(1): 48–79.

Ravid, S.A. (1999). 'Information, blockbusters and start: a study of the film industry', *Journal of Business*, 72: 463–86.

Rayport, J.F. and Svioka, J.J. (1995). 'Exploiting the virtual value chain', *Harvard Business Review*, November-December: 75–85.

Riepl, W. (1913). *Das Nachrichtenwesen des Altertums mit besonderer Rücksicht auf die Römer*. Leipzig: Teubner.

Robins, J.A. and Wiersema, M.F. (2000). 'Strategies for unstructured competitive environments: using scarce resources to create new markets', in R.K.F. Bressler, M.A. Hitt, R.D. Nixon and D. Heuskel (eds), *Winning Strategies in a Deconstructing World*. Chichester: John Wiley and Sons Ltd.

Rogers, E.M. (2003). *Diffusion of Innovations* (5th revised edn). New York: Simon and Schuster.

Rosen, S. (1981). 'The economics of superstars', *American Economic Review*, December, 71(5): 845–58.

Rosenkopf, L. and Nerkar, A. (2001). 'Beyond local search: boundary-spanning, exploration, and impact in the optical disc industry', *Strategic Management Journal*, 22: 287–306.

Rosenstiel, T. (1994). 'The myth of CNN: why Ted Turner's revolution is bad news', *The New Republic*, 22–29 August: 27–33.

Rousseau, D. (1985). 'Issues of level in organizational research: multi-level and cross-level perspectives', in L.L. Cummings and B.M. Straw (eds), *Research in Organizational Behavior*, (7): 1–37. Greenwich, CT: JAI Press.

Rummelt, R.P., Schendel, D.E. and Teece, D.J. (eds) (1994). *Fundamental Issues in Strategy*. Boston: Harvard Business School Press.

Sackmann, S.A. (1991). *Cultural Knowledge in Organizations: Exploring the Collective Mind*. Newbury Park: Sage.

Sanchez-Runde, C.J. and Pettigrew, A.M. (2003). 'Managing dualities', in A. Pettigrew et al. (eds), *Innovative Forms of Organizing: International Perspectives*. Thousand Oaks and London: Sage.

Sanchez-Tabernero, A. and Carvajal, M. (2002). *Media Concentration in the European Market: New Trends and Challenges*. Pamplona: University of Navarra.

Savill, B. and Studley, J. (1999). 'Is content king? A value conundrum', *Telecommunication*, June: 26–35.

Saxenian, A. (1994). *Regional Advantage: Culture and Competition in Silicon Valley and Route 128*. Boston: Harvard University Press.

Scase, R. (2002). 'Create harmony, not harnesses', *Observer*, 4 August: 8.

Schatz, T. (1983). *Old Hollywood/New Hollywood: Ritual Art and Industry*. Michigan: UMI Research Press.

Schein, E. (1992). *Organizational Culture and Leadership* (2nd edn). San Francisco: Jossey Bass.

Schendel, D.E. and Hofer, C.W. (eds) (1979). *Strategic Management: A New View of Business Policy and Planning*. Boston: Little Brown.

Schön, D.A. and Rein, M. (1994). *Frame Reflection: Toward the Resolution of Intractable Policy Controversies*. New York, NY: Basic Books.

Schumann, M. and Hess, T. (eds) (1999). *Medienunternehmen im digitalen Zeitalter*, Wiesbaden: Gabler.

Schumpeter, J.A. (1934). *The Theory of Economic Development*. Cambridge, MA: Harvard University Press.

Schumpeter, J.A. (1942). *Capitalism, Socialism, and Democracy*. Harper: New York.

Schwartz, P. and Leyden, P. (1997). 'The long boom: a history of the future, 1980–2020', *Wired*, Issue 5.07 – July.

Schwartz, K.B. and Menon, K. (1985). 'Executive succession in failing firms', *The Academy of Management Journal,* 28(3): 680.

Senge, P. (1990). *The Fifth Discipline: The Art and Practice of a Learning Organisation*. Random Century: London.

Shamir, B., House, R.J. and Arthur, M.B. (1993). 'The motivational effects of charismatic leadership: a self-concept based theory', *Organization Science*, 44: 577–94.

Shamsie, J. (2003). 'HBO case', in H. Mintzberg, J. Lampel, J.B. Quinn and S. Ghoshal (eds), *The Strategy Process: Concepts, Contexts, Cases*. Harlow: Pearson.

Shapiro, C. and Varian, H.R. (1999). *Information Rules: A Strategic Guide to the Network Economy*. Boston: Harvard Business School Press.

Shaver, D. and Shaver, M.A. (1996). 'Credentials, strategy and style: the relationship between leadership characteristics and strategic direction in media companies', in L. Küng (ed.), *Leadership in the Media Industry, Changing Contexts, Emerging Challenges*. JIBS Research Reports No. 2006.

Shawcross, W. (1994). *Murdoch*. New York: Touchstone.

Shepard, S. (2000). *Telecommunication Convergence*. New York: McGraw Hill.

Sherman, H. and Schultz, R. (1998). *Open Boundaries: Creating Business Innovation Through Complexity*. Reading, MA: Perseus Books.

Shillingford, J. (1999). 'This is convergence – but not as originally envisaged', *Financial Times*, 18 March, 3.

Simon, H.A. (1955). 'A behavioural model of rational choice', *Quarterly Journal of Economics*, 69: 99–118.

Simons, R. (1995). *Levers of Control*. Boston: Harvard Business School Press.

Sjöstrand, S-E. (1997). *The Two Faces of Management. The Janus Factor*. London and Boston: International Thomson Business Press.

Sjurts, I. (2005). *Strategies in the Media Business: Fundamental Principles and Case Studies*. Wiesbaden: Gabler.

Slywotsky, A.J., Morrison, D.J. and Andelman, B. (1997). *The Profit Zone: How Strategic Business Design Will Lead You to Tomorrow's Profits*. New York: Crown.

Spar. D. (2003). *Ruling the Waves: Cycles of Discovery, Chaos, and Wealth from the Compass to the Internet*. Boston: Harvard Business School Press.

Spindler, S. and van den Brul, C. (2006–7). ' "Making it Happen", creative and audiences: a BBC case study', *NHK Broadcasting Studies*, 5: 29–55.

Starbuck, W.H. (1965). 'Organizational growth and development', in J.G. March (ed.), *Handbook of Organizations*. Rand McNally. pp. 451–583. (Reprinted in *Organizational Growth and Development*, New York: Penguin Books, 1971).

Starkey, K., Barnatt, C. and Tempest, C. (2000). 'Beyond networks and hierarchies: latent organizations in the UK television industry', *Organization Science*, 11(3): 299–305.

Staw, B.M. (1990). 'An evolutionary approach to creativity and innovation', in M.A. West and J.L. Farr (eds) *Innovation and Creativity at Work*. Chichester, UK: Wiley, 287–308.

Stewart, J.B. (2005). *Disney War: The Battle for the Magic Kingdom*. London: Simon & Schuster.

Stilson, J. (2003) 'Man with a plan', *Mediaweek*, 1 December.

Stogdill, R.M. (1974). *Handbook of Leadership*. New York: Free Press.

Storper, M. and Christopherson, S. (1987). 'Flexible specialisation and regional industrial agglomerations: the case of the US motion picture industry', *Annals of the Association of American Geographers*, 77(1).

Sundbo, J. (1996). 'The balancing empowerment: a strategic resource-based model of organizing innovation activities in service and low-tech firms'. *Technovation*, 6(8): 397–409.

Tapscott, D. (1996). *The Digital Economy: Promise and Peril in the Age of Networked Intelligence*. New York: McGraw Hill.

Teece, D.J., Pisano, G. and Shuen, A. (1997). 'Dynamic capabilities and strategic management', *Strategic Management Journal*, 18(7): 509–33.

Thomas, J., Clark, S. and Gioia, D. (1993). 'Strategic sensemaking and organizational performance: linkages among scanning, interpretation, action, and outcomes', *Academy of Management Journal*, 36: 239–70.

Thompson, J.D. (1967). *Organizations in Action: Social Science Bases of Administrative Theory*. New Brunswick: Transaction Publishers.

Thurman, N. (2007). 'The globalization of journalism online: a transatlantic study of news websites and their international readers', *Journalism*, 8(3): 285–307.

Toffler, A. (1970). *The Third Wave*. London: Collins.

Towse, R. (2000). 'Creativity, Incentive and Reward: An Economic Analysis of Copyright and Culture in the Information Age', PhD Thesis. Erasmus University Rotterdam.

Tracey, M. (1998). *The Decline and Fall of Public Service Broadcasting*. Oxford: Oxford University Press.

Tungate, M. (2004). *Media Monoliths*. London: Kogan Page.

Tunstall, J. (1971). *Journalists at Work*. London: Constable.

Tunstall, J. (1996). *Newpaper Power: The New National Press in Britain*. Oxford: Clarendon Press.

Tunstall, J. and Palmer, M. (1998). *Media Moguls*. London: Routledge.

Turner, C. (1997). 'SMEs and the evolution of the European information society: policy themes and initiatives', *European Business Journal*, 4: 47–52.

Tushman, M.L. and Anderson, P. (1986). 'Technological discontinuities and organizational environments', *Administrative Science Quarterly*, 31: 439.

Tushman, M.L. and Murmann, J. (1998). 'Dominant designs, technology cycles, and organizational outcomes', *Research in Organizational Behavior*, 20: 213.

Tushman, M.L. and Nelson, R.R. (1990). 'Introduction: technology, organizations, and innovations', *Administrative Science Quarterly*, 35: 1–8.

Tushman, M.L. and O'Reilly III, C.A. (1997). *Winning Through Innovation: A Practical Guide to Leading Organization Change and Renewal*. Boston: Harvard Business School Press.

Tushman, M.L. and Rosenkopf, L. (1992). 'Organizational determinants of technological change: toward a sociology of technological evolution', *Research in Organizational Behavior*, 14: 311–47.

Tushman, M.L. and Smith, W. (2002). 'Organizational technology', in J.C. Baum (ed.) *The Blackwell Companion to Organizations*. Oxford: Blackwell Publishers. pp. 386–414.

Tushman, M.L., Newman, W.H. and Romanelli, E. (1986). 'Convergence and upheaval: managing the unsteady pace of organizational evolution', *California Management Review*, Fall, 29: 29.

Tversky, A. and Kahneman, D. (1986). 'Rational choice and framing of decisions', *Journal of Business*, 59: 251–78.

Utterback, J.M. (1994). *Mastering the Dynamics of Innovation*. Boston: Harvard Business School Press.

Van de Ven, A.H. (1986). 'Central problems in the management of innovation', *Management Science*, 32: 590.

Van de Ven, A.H., Venkatraman, S., Polley, D. and Garud, R. (1989). 'Processes of new business creation in different organisational settings', in A.H. Van de Ven, H. Angle and M.S. Poole (eds), *Research on the Management of Innovation*. New York: Ballinger Press. pp. 221–97.

Van der Wurff, R. (2005). 'Impact of the internet on newspapers in Europe', *Gazette: The International Journal for Communication Studies*, 67(1): 107.

Van der Wurff, R. and Lauf, E. (eds) (2005). *Print and Online Newspapers in Europe: A Comparative Analysis in 16 Countries*. Amsterdam: Het Spinhuis.

Van Velsor, E. and Brittain Leslie, J. (1995). 'Why executives derail: perspectives across time and cultures', *Academy of Management Executive*, 9(4): 62–72.

Virany, B., Tushman, M.L. and Romanelli, E. (1992). 'Executive succession and organization outcomes in turbulent environments: an organisation learning approach', *Organization Science*, 3(1): 72–91.

Vogel, H.L. (1999). *Entertainment Industry Economics: A Guide for Financial Analysis* (4th edn). New York: Cambridge University Press.

Van de Ven, A.H. (1986). 'Central problems in the management of innovation', *Management Science*, 32: 590–607.

Wade, J. (1996). 'A community-level analysis of sources and rates of technological variation in the microprocessor market', *Academy of Management Journal*, 39(5): 1218–44.

Wallace, D. and Marer, M. (1991). 'Renegades 91', *Success Magazine*, 5 February, 38(1): 22–30.

Walsh, J. (1995). 'Managerial and organisational cognition: notes from a trip down memory lane', *Organisation Science*, 6: 280–321.

Wang, C.L. and Ahmed, P.K. (2007). 'Dynamic capabilities: a review and research agenda', *International Journal of Management Reviews*, 9(1): 31–51.

Wasko, J. (2003). *How Hollywood Works*. London: Sage.

Weick, K.E. (1979). *The Social Psychology of Organizing* (2nd edn). Reading, MA: Addison Wesley.

Weick, K.E. (1995). *Sensemaking in Organizations*. Thousand Oaks: Sage.

Wernerfelt, B. (1984). 'A resource-based view of the firm', *Strategic Management Journal*, 5: 171–80.

Wetlaufer, S. (2000). 'Common sense and conflict: an interview with Disney's Michael Eisner', *Harvard Business Review*, January-February: 115–24.

Whipp, R., Rosenfeld, R. and Pettigrew, A. (1989). 'Culture and Competitiveness', *Journal of Management Studies*, 26(6): 561–85.

Whittemore, H. (1990). *CNN: The Inside Story*. Boston: Little Brown.

Whittington, R. (1993). *What is Strategy and Does it Matter?* London: Routledge.

Wildman, S. (2006). 'Characteristics of Media', presentation to IMMAA Meetings, San Francisco, 3 August.

Williams, R. (1974). *Television: Technology and Cultural Form*. London: Fontana.

Williamson, O.E. (1975). *Markets and Hierarchies: Analysis and Antitrust Implications*. New York: Free Press.

Wolf, M.J. (1999). *The Entertainment Economy: How Mega-Media Forces are Transforming our Lives*. New York: Times Books.

Woodman, R.W., Sawyer, J.E. and Griffin, R.W. (1993). 'Toward a theory of organizational creativity', *Academy of Management Review,* 18(2): 293–321.

Wyatt, J. (1998). 'From roadshowing to saturation release: majors, independents, and marketing/distribution innovations', in J. Lewis (ed.), *The New American Cinema '64–86'*. Durham: Duke University Press, pp. 64–86.

Yoffie, D.B. (ed.) (1997). *Competing in the Age of Digital Convergence*. Boston: Harvard Business School Press.

Young, J.S. and Simon, W.L. (2005). *Icon Steve Jobs: The Greatest Second Act in the History of Business*. New York: John Wiley.

Yukl, G. (2002). *Leadership in Organizations* (5th International edn). New Jersey: Prentice Hall.

Index